Fodor's

BEIJING

3rd Edition

Fodor's Travel Publications   New York, Toronto, London, Sydney, Auckland

www.fodors.com

Be a Fodor's Correspondent

Share your trip with Fodor's.

Our latest guidebook to Beijing—now in full color—owes its success to travelers like you.

We are especially proud of this color edition. No other guide to Beijing is as up to date or has as much practical planning information, along with hundreds of color photographs and illustrated maps. We've also included "Word of Mouth" quotes from travelers who shared their experiences with others on our forums. If you're inspired and can plan a better trip because of this guide, we've done our job.

We invite you to join the travel conversation: Your opinion matters to us and to your fellow travelers. Come to Fodors.com to plan your trip, share an experience, ask a question, submit a photograph, post a review, or write a trip report. Tell our editors about your trip. They want to know what went well and how we can make this guide even better. Share your opinions at our feedback center at fodors.com/feedback, or email us at editors@fodors.com with the subject line "Beijing Editor." You might find your comments published in a future Fodor's guide. We look forward to hearing from you.

Happy traveling!

Tim Jarrell, Publisher

FODOR'S BEIJING

Editor: Margaret Kelly

Editorial Contributors: Helena Iveson, Eileen Wen Mooney, Paul Mooney

Production Editor: Evangelos Vasilakis
Maps & Illustrations: David Lindroth; Mark Stroud, Moon Street Cartography, *cartographers*; Bob Blake, Rebecca Baer, *map editors*; William Wu, *information graphics*
Design: Fabrizio La Rocca, *creative director*; Guido Caroti, Siobhan O'Hare, *art directors*; Tina Malaney, Nora Rosansky, Chie Ushio, Jessica Walsh, Ann McBride, *designers*; Melanie Marin, *senior picture editor*
Cover Photo: (Drawing of the Imperial Palace at Tiananmen Square, Forbidden City): Siegfried Stolzfuss/eStock Photo
Production Manager: Steve Slawsky

3rd Edition

ISBN 978-1-4000-0526-0

ISSN 1934-5518

SPECIAL SALES

This book is available at special discounts for bulk purchases for sales promotions or premiums. Special editions, including personalized covers, excerpts of existing books, and corporate imprints, can be created in large quantities for special needs. For more information, write to Special Markets/Premium Sales, 1745 Broadway, MD 6-2, New York, New York 10019, or e-mail specialmarkets@randomhouse.com.

AN IMPORTANT TIP & AN INVITATION

Although all prices, opening times, and other details in this book are based on information supplied to us at press time, changes occur all the time in the travel world, and Fodor's cannot accept responsibility for facts that become outdated or for inadvertent errors or omissions. So **always confirm information when it matters,** especially if you're making a detour to visit a specific place. Your experiences—positive and negative— matter to us. If we have missed or misstated something, **please write to us.** We follow up on all suggestions. Contact the Beijing editor at editors@fodors.com or c/o Fodor's at 1745 Broadway, New York, NY 10019.

PRINTED IN SINGAPORE

10 9 8 7 6 5 4 3 2 1

CONTENTS

Fodor's Features

ABOUT
THIS BOOK

Our Ratings

Sometimes you find terrific travel experiences and sometimes they just find you. But usually the burden is on you to select the right combination of experiences. That's where our ratings come in.

As travelers we've all discovered a place so wonderful that its worthiness is obvious. And sometimes that place is so experiential that superlatives don't do it justice: you just have to be there to know. These sights, properties, and experiences get our highest rating, **Fodor's Choice**, indicated by orange stars throughout this book.

Black stars highlight sights and properties we deem **Highly Recommended**, places that our writers, editors, and readers praise again and again for consistency and excellence.

By default, there's another category: any place we include in this book is by definition worth your time, unless we say otherwise. And we will.

Disagree with any of our choices? Care to nominate a place or suggest that we rate one more highly? Visit our feedback center at www.fodors.com/feedback.

Budget Well

Hotel and restaurant price categories from ¢ to $$$$ are defined in the opening pages of each chapter. For attractions, we always give standard adult admission fees; reductions are usually available for children, students, and senior citizens. Want to pay with plastic? **AE, D, DC, MC, V** after restaurant and hotel listings indicate if American Express, Discover, Diners Club, MasterCard, and Visa are accepted.

Restaurants

Unless we state otherwise, restaurants are open for lunch and dinner daily. We mention dress only when there's a specific requirement and reservations only when they're essential or not accepted—it's always best to book ahead.

Hotels

Hotels have private bath, phone, TV, and air-conditioning and operate on the European Plan (EP, meaning without meals), unless we specify that they use the Continental Plan (CP, with a Continental breakfast), Breakfast Plan (BP, with a full breakfast), or Modified American Plan (MAP, with breakfast and dinner) or are all-inclusive (AI, including all meals and most activities). We

always list facilities but not whether you'll be charged an extra fee to use them, so when pricing accommodations, find out what's included.

Listings	
★	Fodor's Choice
★	Highly recommended
✉	Physical address
✛	Directions or Map coordinates
🕮	Mailing address
☎	Telephone
🖷	Fax
⊕	On the Web
✎	E-mail
🎟	Admission fee
☉	Open/closed times
Ⓜ	Metro stations
▭	Credit cards
Hotels & Restaurants	
🏨	Hotel
⇥	Number of rooms
⚴	Facilities
❙❂❙	Meal plans
✕	Restaurant
⚲	Reservations
🜊	Dress code
⚐	Smoking
⚗	BYOB
Outdoors	
⚐	Golf
⚠	Camping
Other	
⚘	Family-friendly
⇨	See also
✉	Branch address
☞	Take note

Experience Beijing

THE HEART OF THE DRAGON

WHAT'S WHERE

1 Dongcheng District.
You'll only be able to truly say you've seen Beijing after wandering through Dongcheng, which is packed with the city's top must-see attractions. Tiananmen Square and the Forbidden City top anyone's list of things to do, but don't forget to explore the *hutong* (alleyway) neighborhoods surrounding the Drum and Bell towers and the Buddhist grandeur of the Lama Temple.

2 Xicheng District. Along with Dongcheng, Xicheng encompasses the historically significant areas of Beijing that once lay safe inside the city walls. Six small lakes west of the Forbidden City are at the heart of the district, which was once an imperial playground and is now home to China's top leaders. Farther west, fashionable young Beijingers spend their hard-earned cash in the side-by-side shopping malls at Xidan.

3 Chongwen and Xuanwu Districts. Situated along the road into the imperial palace, these areas once teemed with the activity of markets, gambling parlors, and less savory establishments. A historically accurate (but sanitized) re-creation of old Qianmen Street recaptures some of that lost glory. The Temple of Heaven features some of China's most impressive architecture, Panjiayuan Market (aka the Dirt Market) offers the best souvenir shopping in the country, and tea lovers won't want to miss Maliandao Tea Street.

4 Chaoyang District. This unwieldy district wraps around many of the areas forming new Beijing. With the skyline-altering Central Business District in the south, the nightlife of Sanlitun in the middle, and the 798 Art District and Olympic Park in the north, Chaoyang represents today's China: lots of flash, with very little or no connection to the country's 5,000 years of history.

5 Haidian District. The nation's brightest minds study at prestigious Tsinghua and Peking Universities in Beijing's northwestern Haidian district. China's own budding Silicon Valley, Zhongguancun, is also located here. Need to stretch your legs and get some fresh air? Head for one of the former imperial retreats at the Summer Palace, Fragrant Hills Park, or the Beijing Botanical Garden.

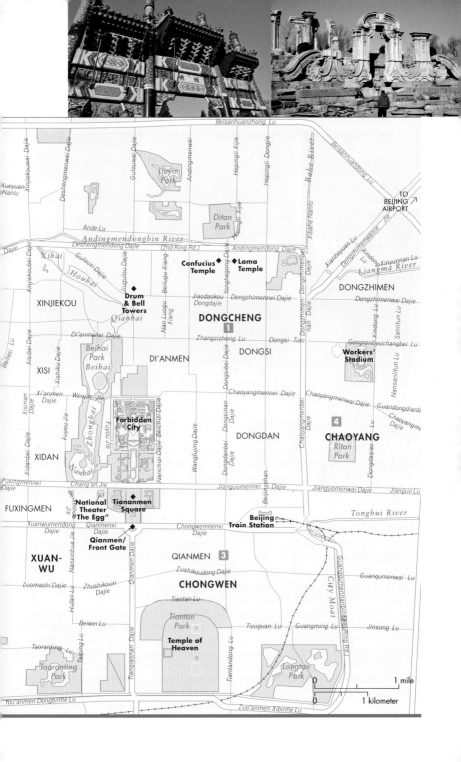

BEIJING
TOP ATTRACTIONS

Forbidden City

(A) The Forbidden City has been home to a long line of emperors, beginning with Yongle, in 1420, and ending with Puyi (made famous by Bernardo Bertolucci's film *The Last Emperor*), who was forced out of the complex by a warlord in 1924. The Forbidden City is the largest palace in the world, as well as the best preserved, and offers the most complete collection of imperial architecture in China.

Magnificent Markets

(B) It's hard to resist: so much to bargain for, so little time! Visit outdoor Panjiayuan (aka the Dirt Market), where some 3,000 vendors sell antiques, Cultural Revolution memorabilia, and handicrafts from across China. Looking for knockoffs? The Silk Alley Market is popular with tourists, but local expats prefer the Yashow Market, which has better prices.

Lama Temple

(C) The sweet smell of incense permeates one of the few functioning Buddhist temples in Beijing. When Emperor Yongzheng took the throne in 1723, his former residence was converted into this temple. During the Qianlong Period (1736–1795) it became a center of the Yellow Hat sect of Tibetan Buddhism. At its high point, 1,500 lamas lived here. The Hall of Celestial Kings houses a statue of Maitreya, and the Wanfu Pavilion has a 23-meter (75½-foot) Buddha carved from one piece of sandalwood.

Summer Palace

(D) This garden complex dates back eight centuries to when the first emperor of the Jin Dynasty built the Gold Mountain Palace on Longevity Hill. Notable sights are the Long Corridor (a covered wooden walkway) and the Hall of Benevolent Longevity. At the west end of the lake is the famous Marble Boat that Cixi built with

money intended to create a Chinese navy. The palace, which served as an imperial retreat from dripping summer heat, was ransacked by British and French soldiers in 1860 and burned in 1900 by Western soldiers seeking revenge for the Boxer Rebellion.

Confucius Temple

(E) This temple, with its towering cypress and pine trees, offers a serene escape from the crowds at nearby Lama Temple. This is the second-largest Confucian temple after that in Qufu, the master's hometown in Shandong province. First built in the 13th century, the Confucius Temple was renovated in the 18th century.

Temple of Heaven

(F) The Temple of Heaven is one of the best examples of religious architecture in China. Construction began in the early 15th century under the order of Emperor Yongle. The complex took 14 years to complete; it contains three main

buildings where the emperor, as the "Son of Heaven," offered semiannual prayers. The sprawling, tree-filled complex is a pleasant place for wandering: watch locals practicing martial arts, playing traditional instruments, and enjoying ballroom dancing on the grass.

Tiananmen Square

(G) Walking beneath the red flags of Tiananmen Square is quintessential Beijing. The political heart of modern China, the square covers 100 acres, making it the largest public square in the world. It was from the Gate of Heavenly Peace that Mao Zedong pronounced the People's Republic of China in 1949. Many Westerners think only of the massive student protests here in the 1980s, but it has been the site of protests, rallies, and marches for close to 100 years.

GREAT ITINERARIES

Be curious: Beijing rewards the explorer. Most temples and palaces have gardens and lesser courtyards that are seldom visited. Even at the height of the summer tourist rush, the Forbidden City's peripheral courtyards offer ample breathing room, even seclusion. The Temple of Heaven's vast grounds are a pleasure year-round—and enchanting after a snowfall.

The Best of Beijing in 5 Days

On Day 1, start at **Tiananmen Square**, the heart of modern China and the entry point to the spectacular **Forbidden City**. Explore the former imperial palace to your heart's content. In the afternoon, take a guided pedicab ride through a hutong to the **Drum and Bell towers**. Have Peking duck for dinner, perhaps at the **Li Qun Roast Duck Restaurant**, located in an old courtyard house a few blocks southeast of Tiananmen Square.

On Day 2, head straight for the vast grounds of the **Temple of Heaven**, one of Beijing's most important historical sights. Visit the **Lama Temple** and the nearby **Confucius Temple**, too. Save two or three hours in the afternoon for shopping at **Yangshow Market** and the **Silk Alley Market** in Chaoyang District. Have dinner or enjoy a nightcap in the Sanlitun area.

Set aside Day 3 for a tour to the **Thirteen Ming Tombs** and the **Great Wall** at Mutianyu, where a cable car offers a dramatic ride to the summit.

On Day 4, visit the rambling **Summer Palace**, and then spend a few hours at the nearby **Old Summer Palace**, an intriguing ruin. In the evening, plan to see a **Beijing opera** performance or hit the restaurants and bars in the bustling Houhai area.
⇨ *For more information about Beijing Opera, see Chapter 7.*

On Day 5, hire a car and visit the spectacular **Eastern Qing Tombs**, where a "spirit way" lined with carved stone animals and unrestored templelike grave sites rests in a beautiful rural setting. Wear walking shoes and bring a lunch. The drive takes five hours round-trip, so get an early start.

■ TIP➜ Although the Forbidden City and Tiananmen Square represent the heart of Beijing, the capital lacks a definitive downtown area in terms of shopping or business, as commercial and entertainment districts have cropped up all over.

If You Have 1 Day

Begin your day in **Tiananmen Square**— you may want to catch the flag-raising ceremony at dawn—to admire the Communist icons of modern China. Then, heading north, walk back through time into the vast **Forbidden City**. Keep in mind that in 1420, when the imperial palace was built, its structures were the tallest in Asia. You can spend the morning leisurely examining the many palaces and gardens here. Next head north into **Jingshan Park** and climb Coal Hill to get a panoramic view of the city. Then jump into a cab and head to Lotus Lane, where you can have a drink overlooking the waters of **Qianhai**.

In the afternoon, take a trip outside the city. Hire a car and driver to take you on the one-hour journey to the Badaling section of the **Great Wall**, which is the closest to Beijing. On your way back, stop at either the **Thirteen Ming Tombs** or the **Summer Palace**. The Ming Tombs are en route; the Summer Palace will add an additional half hour to your journey.

■ TIP➜ Tickets are sold until one hour before closing time at the Ming Tombs and Summer Palace.

Itinerary on Two Wheels

A great way to explore Beijing is by bicycle. A ride between Ditan Park and the Lake District includes some of the city's most famous sights and finest hutongs.

Begin at **Ditan Park**, just north of the Second Ring Road on Yonghegong Jie. Park your bike in the lot outside the south gate and take a walk around the park. Next, ride south along Yonghegong Jie until you come to the main entrance of the **Lama Temple**. Running west across the street from the temple's main gate is Guozijian Jie (Imperial Academy Street). Shops near the intersection sell Buddhist statues, incense, texts (in Chinese), and tapes of traditional Chinese Buddhist music. Browse them before riding west to the **Confucius Temple** and the neighboring **Imperial Academy**. The arches spanning Guozijian Jie are among the few of their kind remaining in Beijing.

Follow Guozijian Jie west until it empties onto Andingmennei Dajie. Enter this busy road with care (there's no traffic signal) and ride south to Gulou Dong Dajie, another major thoroughfare. Turn right (west) and ride to the **Drum Tower**. From here, detour through the alleys just north of the **Bell Tower**. A small public square crowded with city residents flying kites, playing badminton or chess, and chatting, links the two landmarks.

If you need a rest, stop in at the **Drum and Bell** (☎ 010/8403–3600), a rustic-looking bar and restaurant on the west side of the square; it has a nice rooftop terrace with views of the two towers and the square below. Retrace your route south to Di'anmenwai Dajie (the road running south from the Drum Tower), turning onto Yandai Xie Jie, the first lane on the right (next to the McDonald's). Makers of long-stem pipes once lined the lane's narrow way (one small pipe shop still does). There are a number of shops and street vendors here selling handicrafts, ethnic clothing, and folk arts. You can also sample some of Beijing's famous old street snacks such as candied haw, sweet potatoes, roast corn, and much more.

Wind southwest on Yandai Xie Jie past guesthouses, bicycle-repair shops, tiny restaurants, and crumbling traditional courtyard houses toward Houhai, or the Rear Lake. Turn left onto Xiaoqiaoli Hutong and ride to the arched **Silver Ingot Bridge**, which separates **Houhai** and **Qianhai** lakes. Before the bridge, turn right and follow the trail along Houhai's north shore, traveling toward **Soong Ching-ling's Former Residence**.

Continue around the lake until you arrive at Deshengmennei Dajie. Follow it south to the second alley, turning east (left) onto **Yangfang Hutong**, which leads back to the arched bridge. Ride along Yangfang Hutong past the stone bridge and follow Qianhai's west bank. Sip a soda, beer, or tea at one of the lakeside venues. Continue along the lane to Qianhai Xi Jie. Nearby is **Prince Gong's Palace**, 300 yards north of the China Conservatory of Music—look for the brass plaque.

■ TIP→ Love to walk? So do we! You can also do this itinerary, or parts of it, on two feet if you're so inclined.

BEIJING THEN AND NOW

Since the birth of Chinese civilization, different towns of varying size and import have stood at or near the site where Beijing is now. For example, the popular local beer, Yanjing, refers to a city-kingdom based here 3,000 years ago. With this in mind, it's not unreasonable to describe Beijing's modern history as beginning with the Jin Dynasty, approximately 800 years ago. Led by nine generations of the Jurchen tribe, the Jin Dynasty eventually fell in a war against the Mongol hordes.

Few armies had been able to withstand the wild onslaught of the armed Mongol cavalry under the command of the legendary warrior Genghis Khan. The Jurchen tribe proved no exception, and the magnificent city of the Jin was almost completely destroyed. A few decades later, in 1260, when Kublai Khan, the grandson of Genghis Khan, returned to use the city as an operational base for his conquest of southern China, reconstruction was the order of the day. By 1271 Kublai Khan had achieved his goal, declaring himself emperor of China under the Yuan Dynasty (1271–1368), with Beijing (or Dadu, as it was then known) as its capital.

The new capital was built on a scale befitting the world's then superpower. Its palaces were founded around Zhonghai and Beihai lakes. Beijing's current layout still reflects the Mongolian design.

Just as today, a limiting factor on Beijing's growth seven centuries ago was its remoteness from water. To ensure an adequate water supply, the famous hydraulic engineer Guo Shoujing (1231–1316) designed a canal that brought water from the mountains in the west. Then, to improve communications and increase trade, he designed another canal that extended to eastern China's Grand Canal.

About 100 years after the Mongolians settled Beijing they suffered a devastating attack by rebels from the south. Originally nomadic, the Mongolians had softened with the ease of city life and were easily overwhelmed by the rebel coalition, which drove out the emperor and wrecked Beijing, thus ending the Yuan Dynasty. The southern roots of the quickly unified Ming Dynasty (1368–1644) deprived Beijing of its capital status for a half century. But in 1405, the third Ming emperor, Yongle, began construction on a magnificent new palace in Beijing; 16 years later, he relocated his court there. In the interim, the emperor had mobilized 200,000 corvée laborers to build his new palace, an enormous maze of interlinking halls, gates, and courtyard homes, known as the Forbidden City.

The Ming also contributed mightily to China's grandest public works project: the Great Wall. The Ming Great Wall linked or reinforced several existing walls, especially near the capital, and traversed seemingly impassable mountains. Most of the most spectacular stretches of the wall that can be visited near Beijing were built during the Ming Dynasty. But wall building drained Ming coffers and in the end failed to prevent Manchu horsemen from taking the capital—and China—in 1644.

This foreign dynasty, the Qing, inherited the Ming palaces, built their own retreats (most notably, the Old and new Summer palaces), and perpetuated feudalism in China for another 267 years. In its decline, the Qing proved impotent to stop humiliating foreign encroachment. It lost the first Opium War to Great Britain in 1842 and was forced to cede Hong Kong "in perpetuity" as a result. In 1860 a com-

bined British and French force stormed Beijing and razed the Old Summer Palace.

After the Qing crumbled in 1911, its successor, Sun Yat-sen's Nationalist Party, struggled to consolidate power. Beijing became a cauldron of social activism. On May 4, 1919, students marched on Tiananmen Square to protest humiliations in Versailles, where Allied commanders negotiating an end to World War I gave Germany's extraterritorial holdings in China to Japan. Patriotism intensified, and in 1937 Japanese imperial armies stormed across Beijing's Marco Polo Bridge to launch a brutal eight-year occupation. Civil war followed close on the heels of Tokyo's 1945 surrender and raged until the Communist victory. Chairman Mao himself declared the founding of a new nation from the rostrum atop the Gate of Heavenly Peace on October 1, 1949.

Like Emperor Yongle, Mao built a capital that conformed to his own vision. Soviet-inspired structures rose up around Tiananmen Square. Beijing's city wall was demolished to make way for a ring road. Temples and churches were torn down, closed, or turned into factories during the 1966–76 Cultural Revolution.

In more recent years the city has suffered most, ironically, from prosperity. Many ancient neighborhoods have been bulldozed to make room for a new city of glitzy commercial developments. Preservationism has slowly begun to take hold, but *chai* (to pull down) and *qian* (to move elsewhere) remain common threats to historic neighborhoods.

Today Beijing's some 20-million official residents—including 3-million migrant workers—enjoy a fascinating mix of old and new. Early morning *taiji* (tai chi) enthusiasts, ballroom and disco dancers, old men with caged songbirds, and amateur Beijing opera crooners frequent the city's many parks. Cyclists clog the roadways, competing with cars on the city's thoroughfares. Beijing traffic has gone from nonexistent to nightmarish in less than a decade.

As the seat of China's immense national bureaucracy, Beijing carries a political charge. The Communist Party, whose self-described goal is "a dictatorship of the proletariat," has yet to relinquish its political monopoly. In 1989 student protesters in Tiananmen Square dared to challenge the party. The government's brutal response remains etched in global memory, although younger Chinese people are likely never to have heard about it. Twenty years later, secret police still mingle with tourists on the square. Mao-style propaganda persists. Slogans that preach unity among China's national minorities and patriotism still festoon the city on occasion. Yet as Beijing's robust economy is boosted even further by the massive influx of foreign investment, such campaigns appear increasingly out of touch with the cell-phone-primed generation. The result is an incongruous mixture of new prosperity and throwback politics: socialist slogans adorn shopping centers selling Gucci and Big Macs. Beijing is truly a land of opposites where the ancient and the sparkling new collide.

A CITY IN TRANSITION

The 2008 Summer Olympics changed the face of Beijing, and the changes keep on coming. Just about everywhere you look you'll find signs of the feverish development boom that is continuing where the games left off. Whole city blocks were razed to make way for state-of-the-art Olympic venues, new hotels, and modern buildings. The subway system was expanded from two to eight lines—15 lines should be open by 2015—including a link from downtown Beijing to the airport.

The new projects, many designed by top international architects, are impressive to say the least. Twelve brand-new Olympic venues were built from scratch, with another 11 existing structures renovated.

Gearing up for the Games

For the Chinese government the Olympics wasn't just about new sports venues and improved urban infrastructure. The Olympics were supposed to be the country's coming-out party, a peaceful celebration of a rising superpower. Efforts were made to reduce the serious pollution that still grips the city, and Beijing's Communist Party secretary promised to "reeducate" people used to cheering and jeering players at sporting events.

All did not go as planned from the very beginning. An international relay of the Olympic torch met with fierce anti-China protests across the globe after riots broke out in Tibet. The flame was later carried to the top of Mt. Everest, but the event was shrouded in secrecy. A huge earthquake on May 12, 2008, killed tens of thousands of people in southwest China, further dampening the festive atmosphere. Security concerns resulted in strengthened enforcement of visa policies for foreigners, giving the city the atmosphere of an armed camp. During the games, reports surfaced on the arrest and detention of Chinese citizens who had submitted applications to protest.

Growing Up: Beijing Under Construction

The skyline of Beijing was once famously flat—before a forest of pre-Olympic cranes rose above the remnants of traditional hutong neighborhoods. After winning its bid to host the 2008 Olympics, Beijing became "the world's largest construction site," a rowdy playground for international architects with little regard for traditional Chinese design. The city is now home to brash, breathtaking structures.

Beijing Capital Airport, Terminal 3

With its lantern-red roof shaped like a dragon, Beijing's airport expansion embraces traditional Chinese motifs with a 21st-century twist: its architect calls it the "world's largest and most advanced airport building." This single terminal contains more floor space than all the terminals at London's Heathrow Airport combined. Construction started in 2004 with a team of 50,000 construction workers and was completed a few months before the Olympic Games. ✉ *Beijing Capital Airport.*

Architect: Norman Foster, the preeminent British architect responsible for Hong Kong's widely respected airport.

Beijing Linked Hybrid

With 700 apartments in eight bridge-linked towers surrounding a plethora of shopping and cultural options, the Linked Hybrid has been applauded for parting from the sterility of typical Chinese housing. The elegant complex also features an impressive set of green credentials such as geothermal heating and a wastewater

recycling system. ☒ *Adjacent to the northeast corner of the Second Ring Road.*

Architects: New York–based Steven Holl, who won awards for his Museum of Contemporary Art in Helsinki, Finland, and Li Hu, who helped design China's first contemporary museum in Nanjing.

CCTV (Central Chinese Television) Tower

The most remarkable of China's new structures, the new central television headquarters twists the idea of a skyscraper quite literally into a 40-story-tall gravity-defying loop. What some have called the world's most complex building is also, with a $1.3 billion price tag, one of the world's priciest. An accompanying building that was to include a hotel, a visitor center, and a public theater was seriously destroyed after it caught on fire during the Chinese New Year fireworks display in 2009. ☒ *32 Dong San Huan Zhonglu (32 East Third Ring Middle Road).*

Architects: Rem Koolhaas (a Dutch mastermind known for his daring ideas and successful Seattle Public Library) and Ole Scheeren (Koolhaas's thirtysomething German protégé).

National Stadium ("the Bird's Nest")

Though its exterior lattice structure is said to resemble the twigs of a nest, the 42,000 tons of steel bending around its center make this 80,000-seat stadium look more like a Martian mothership. It's absolutely massive and must be seen to be believed. ☒ *Beijing Olympic Park at Bei Si Huan Lu (North Fourth Ring Road).*

Architects: Herzog and de Meuron of Switzerland, who won the prestigious Pritzker Prize for work at London's Tate Modern and the Ricola Marketing Building in Laufen, Switzerland.

National Swimming Center ("the Water Cube")

The translucent skin and hexagonal high-tech "pillows" that define this 17,000-seat indoor stadium create the impression of a building fashioned entirely out of bubbles. The structure is based on the premise that bubbles are the most effective way to divide a three-dimensional space—and they help save energy and keep the building earthquake-proof. The center has now been turned into a public aquatics center. ☒ *Beijing Olympic Park.*

Architects: PTW, the Australian firm that cut its teeth on venues for the 2000 Olympic Games in Sydney.

Grand National Theater ("the Egg")

Like the so-called Bird's Nest, "the Egg," as this bulbous glass-draped opera house is called, might cause passersby to think yet another spaceship has landed in the capital—this one near Tiananmen Square. Indeed, its close proximity to the Forbidden City and its soaring costs (more than $400 million) have earned it a hostile welcome among some Chinese architects. ☒ *Xi Chang'an Jie (just west of Tiananmen Square).*

Architect: French-born Paul Andreu, who designed the groundbreaking Terminal 1 of Paris's Charles de Gaulle airport in 1974.

BEIJING TODAY

The air is dirty, the traffic is horrendous, and almost nobody speaks more than a word or two of English—so what makes Beijing one of the world's top destinations?

Today's Beijing . . .

. . . is old and new. The flat skyline of Beijing, punctuated only by imposing ceremonial towers and the massive gates of the city wall, is lost forever. But still, standing on Coal Hill and looking south across the Forbidden City—or listening to the strange echo of your voice atop an ancient altar at the Temple of Heaven—you can't help but feel the weight of thousands of years of history. It was here that Marco Polo dined with Kublai Khan and his Mongol hordes; that Ming and Qing emperors ruled over China from the largest and richest city in the world; and that Mao Zedong proclaimed the founding of the People's Republic in 1949. Much of Beijing's charm comes from a juxtaposition of old and new. When you're riding a taxi along the Third Ring Road it may seem that the high-rise apartments and postmodern office complexes stretch on forever. They do, but tucked in among the glass and steel are elaborate temples exuding wafts of incense, and tiny alleyways where old folks still gather in their pajamas every evening to play cards and drink warm beer. Savoring these small moments is the key to appreciating Beijing.

. . . lets you eat your heart out. If you really love General Tso's chicken back at your local Chinese take-out place, you may want to skip Beijing altogether. Many a returned visitor has complained of being unable to enjoy the bland stuff back home after experiencing the myriad flavors and textures of China's varied regional cuisines. From the mouth-numbing spices of Sichuan, to the delicate presentation of an imperial banquet, or the cumin-sprinkled kebabs of China's Muslim west, Beijing has it all. If you're looking for the ultimate in authenticity, dine at a restaurant attached to one of the city's provincial representative offices, where the chefs and ingredients are imported to satisfy the taste buds of bureaucrats working far from home. The crispy skin and tender flesh of the capital's signature dish, Peking duck, is on everyone's must-eat list. Don't worry if you tire of eating Chinese food three times a day. As Beijing has grown rich in recent years, Western and fusion cuisine offerings have improved greatly, with everything from French to Middle Eastern to Texas-style barbecue now

COOL FACTS ON THE CAPITAL CITY

- With close to 20 million residents, Beijing is vying with Shanghai to become the largest city in China.

- The city has existed in various forms for 2,500 years, but *Homo erectus* fossils prove that humans have lived here for 250,000 years.

- Beijing was once surrounded by a massive city wall constructed 600 years ago during the Ming Dynasty. Of the 16 original gates, only three remain standing. The wall was demolished in 1965 to make way for the Second Ring Road.

- At 100 acres, Tiananmen Square is the largest urban square in the world. During the Cultural Revolution as many as 1 million people were able to stand on numbered spaces for huge rallies with Chairman Mao.

available. If you're looking for one special (and relatively expensive) night out, reserve a window table at the Courtyard, where east meets west, with views of the moat and walls of the Forbidden City.

. . . is part of a new world order. Beijing's transformation hasn't only been limited to Olympic venues. Prestige projects like the National Theater ("the Egg"), the new CCTV building, and a massive subway expansion are meant to show that China is ready to play with the big boys. The Chinese are fiercely patriotic, and antiforeign demonstrations occasionally break out when the country's collective pride is insulted. The official version of Chinese history taught in schools emphasizes the nation's suffering at the hands of foreign colonial powers during the 19th and 20th centuries, and the subsequent Communist liberation. Still, you'll find Beijingers infinitely polite and curious about your life back home. People here aren't quite sure what to make of their new surroundings, and they're as interested in finding out about you as you are about them. So strike up a conversation (with your hands if necessary), but go easy on the politics.

. . . is the place to make it or break it. Newcomers could be forgiven for seeing bustling Shanghai as China's go-to place. But anyone who has spent a little time in the capital city swears that it's the soul of the country. People from all over China are drawn here by the many opportunities the city offers, the cultural ferment, and the chance to reinvent themselves; there is an unusual freedom here that has made Beijing the creative center of the country, and this attracts the creative elite from all around the world. Art galleries have sprung up in hotels, courtyard houses, shut-down factories and even an ancient watchtower. This is where serious musicians must come to make it or break it. Even no-nonsense businessmen see Beijing as a mecca because they believe the challenges—and rewards—are greater here. Finally, Beijing is home to several million migrant workers who are often referred to disparagingly as outsiders. This hardworking group is often blamed for the problems that face the city. However, economists say that Beijing would not be what it is today without this army of tireless laborers, construction workers, waiters and maids, who have kept the city buzzing along, taking on the kinds of jobs most others would prefer to avoid.

■ Despite major efforts to improve Beijing's air quality, pollution levels in the city remain several times higher than World Health Organization limits. Adding to the problem, a single sandstorm can drop tens of thousands of tons of dust onto the city in mere hours.

■ Beijingers love to brew, and more than 1,000 tea shops can be found along Maliandao Tea Street in the city's southwest. Top-quality leaves can run as high as $5,000 per pound. That's U.S. dollars, not Chinese yuan!

■ The 798 Art District is the home of China's red-hot modern art scene. An example: a Yue Minjun painting inspired by the 1989 crackdown in Tiananmen Square sold for $5,000 in 1994 and resold for $6.9 million in 2008.

BEIJING
WITH KIDS

Education Without Yawns

Military Museum. A toy soldier–lover's dream come true, this museum contains endless collections of AK-47s, captured tanks, missile launchers, and other war toys. Your kids will love every minute of China's 5,000-year military history. Easy access by subway ensures they won't have to ask, "Are we there yet?"

Forbidden City. The largest surviving palace complex in the world, there are plenty of wide-open spaces here for kids to run amok. While you're appreciating the finest collection of imperial architecture in China, your little ones can imagine what it was like to have thousands of mandarins catering to their every whim. Sort of like having parents.

Blue Zoo Beijing. Not to be confused with an actual zoo, this is Asia's largest walk-through aquarium. Divers feed thousands of sea creatures, including sharks, twice a day. A visit here can be negotiated as a prize for letting you shop in peace at nearby Yashow Market.

China Science & Technology Museum. A paradise for curious kids, this museum features hands-on interactive displays with a strong focus on Chinese inventions like the compass, gunpowder, and paper. The on-site Fundazzle playground will keep your little one entertained even when the robot performance is finished.

Performances

Amazing Acrobats. Take the kids out for a night on the town to show them that hand-eye coordination doesn't only come from playing video games. To really inspire, look for a performance featuring child acrobats who dedicate every day to perfecting their awe-inspiring craft.

China Puppet Theater. Actors manipulate huge puppets through performances of Western classics like *The Nutcracker* and Chinese classics like *The Monkey King*. There's a playground, too, for kids who just won't sit still.

Activities

Go Fly a Kite. China's love affair with kites goes back nearly 3,000 years. Head for the open spaces of Tiananmen Square or the Temple of Heaven, where old folks with decades of flying experience will help send your child's kite soaring towards the heavens.

Climb the Wall. Do we really have to convince you? After climbing hundreds (or thousands) of steps, your little one will sleep soundly while dreaming of turning back the marauding Mongol hordes.

A Trip Around the World. World Park offers a bizarre collection of 100 scaled-down tourist attractions from across the globe. Kids enjoy climbing on the pyramids; parents can marvel at the outdated and politically incorrect international stereotypes.

Fun in the Sun. Ritan Park (Altar of the Sun), is an altar of fun for children of all ages. Little tykes can ride the merry-go-round, older kids can try their luck on the climbing wall, and you can stop in for a drink at the outdoor Stone Boat, perhaps the world's only kid-friendly bar.

Set Sail. Cruise the imperial lakes at Houhai in a paddleboat, and take the family for a rectangular pie at Hutong Pizza when you get back to shore. In winter the lakes freeze over, and kids in ice chairs gleefully glide across the surface.

FREE (OR ALMOST FREE)

Although Beijing isn't as inexpensive as it once was, it's still a fabulous bargain compared to travel in Europe, North America, and more developed Asian nations like Japan and South Korea. While expats have complained of rising prices—especially during the run-up to the Olympics—visitors from Western countries are often overwhelmed by a feeling that life in the city is practically free. Bottled water, snacks, subway and bus rides, or a steaming bowl of dumpling soup all cost well under the equivalent of 50 cents. Average length cab rides, a dish at a decent restaurant, or museum admission tickets will set you back only two or three dollars. And the capital is filled with acceptable hotels for about 50 bucks per night. Little is free in Beijing, but there's also very little to make much of a dent in your wallet.

ART

The modern art scene in China has exploded onto the world stage over the past decade. Beijing's 798 Art District, located northeast of the city center along the road to the airport, is the country's artistic nucleus. The complex was built under East German supervision in the 1950s to house sprawling electronics factories, but artists took over after state subsidies dried up in the late 1990s. The district is now home to at least 100 top-notch galleries, and almost all of them are free.

* 798 Space * Art Bridge Gallery * Asia Art Center * Beyond Art Space * CO2 United Creative Space * Contrasts Gallery * Mulpa Space * PaceWildenstein Beijing * Red Gate Gallery * Red T Gallery * Taikang Top Space * Ullens Center for Contemporary Art (Y20)

MUSEUMS

The city's most famous museums aren't exactly charging an arm and a leg for admission, but the smaller and quirkier museums listed here ask only for donations or charge less than Y10.

* Arthur M. Sackler Museum * Beijing Ancient Coins Exhibition Hall * Beijing Tap Water Museum * Beijing Police Museum * Cao Xueqin Former Residence * China Honey Bee Museum * Xu Beihong Museum * Song Tang Zhai Museum of Traditional Chinese Folk Carving

OFFBEAT EXPERIENCES

Beijing's urban sprawl is interrupted by a number of lovely parks designed in traditional Chinese style. Of particular historical significance are the four parks built around altars used for imperial sacrifice—the **Altar of the Sun** (Ritan), **Altar of Heaven** (Tiantan), **Altar of the Earth** (Ditan), and **Altar of the Moon** (Yuetan).

If you happen to be in Beijing for Spring Festival (Chinese New Year), you literally won't be able to avoid the party atmosphere that overtakes the city. You may have seen a display of fireworks before, but have you ever been *inside* a fireworks show? Just remember to bring earplugs, as the explosions go on at all hours for days on end.

Set aside some time for random wandering, especially through the hutong neighborhoods inside the Second Ring Road. Much of what makes Beijing special happens on a very small scale. Listen for the call of the local knife sharpener who rides by daily on his bicycle. See the old folks walking the dog in their pajamas.

FAQ

Do I need any special documents to get into the country?

Aside from a passport that's valid for at least six months after date of entry, and a valid visa, you don't need anything else to enter the country. You're required to have your passport with you at all times during your trip, but it's safer to carry a photocopy and store your passport in a safe at your hotel (if they have one).

How difficult is it to travel around the city?

It's extremely easy. Taxis are plentiful and cheap, and Beijing also has a good subway system that has expanded rapidly and now reaches more places. Stops are announced in both English and Chinese. Public buses can be a challenge because street signs are not often written in English and bus drivers are unlikely to be fluent in any foreign languages. Renting a car can be difficult and traffic and roads can be quite challenging, so driving on your own is not recommended. However, hiring a car and driver is not very expensive and is a good alternative for getting around. Beijing, with its many bike lanes, is a cycle lover's city, so consider renting some wheels for part of your stay. Riding a bicycle is also a great way to get through Beijing's increasingly common traffic snarls.

Should I consider a package tour?

If the thought of traveling unescorted to Beijing absolutely terrifies you, then sign up for a tour. But Beijing is such an easy place to get around that there's really no need. Discovery is a big part of the fun—exploring an ancient temple, walking down a narrow hutong or alleyway, stumbling upon a great craft shop or small restaurant—and that's just not going to happen on a tour. If you're more comfortable with a package tour, pick one with a specific focus, like a pedicab hutong ride or an afternoon of food shopping and cooking, so that you're less likely to get a generic package.

Do I need a local guide?

Guides are really not necessary in a city like Beijing, where it's easy to get around by taxi and public transportation, and where most of the important tourist destinations are easy to reach. An added plus is that the local people are friendly and always willing to give a hand. It's much more gratifying to tell the folks back home that you discovered that wonderful back street or interesting restaurant all by yourself.

Will I have trouble if I don't speak Chinese?

Not really. Most people in businesses catering to travelers speak at least a little English. If you encounter someone who doesn't speak English, they'll probably point you to a coworker who does. Even if you're in a far-flung destination, locals will go out of their way to find somebody who speaks your language. Or you can make use of travel services such as Bespoke Beijing, which will arm you with a mobile phone and a stylish and personalized guide to the best sites, restaurants, bars and nightlife, as well as access to a Chinese translator or English-speaking expert (⊕ *www.bespoke-beijing.com*).

Can I drink the water?

No, you can't. All drinking water must be boiled. Bottled water is easily available all over the city and in outlying areas, such as the Great Wall. Most hotels provide two free bottles of drinking water each day. To be on the safe side, you may also want to avoid ice

Are there any worries about the food?

None whatsoever. Even the humblest roadside establishment is likely to be scrupulously clean. If you have any doubts about a place, just move on to the next one. There's no problem enjoying fruit or other local products sold from the stands set up along the roads, but we strongly suggest that you thoroughly clean any fruit that you can't peel with bottled water before eating it.

Do I need to get any shots?

You probably don't have to get any vaccinations or take any special medications. The U.S. Centers for Disease Control and Prevention warn that there is some concern about malaria, especially in some of the more rural provinces south of Beijing, such as Anhui, Yunnan, and Hainan provinces. Immunizations for Hepatitis A and B are recommended for all visitors to China.

Should I bring any medications?

It can be difficult to readily find some medications in Beijing, and while the city has several international clinics, prices for even over-the-counter remedies can be quite expensive. So yes, it's advisable to make sure you have all your medications with you.

Can I use my ATM card?

Most ATMs in Beijing accept Visa and MasterCard cards, but each bank may charge a different fee for each transaction. There are Citibank ATM machines located at several places around the city. Know the exchange rate before you use an ATM for the first time so that you know about how much local currency you want to withdraw.

Do most places take credit cards?

Almost all traveler-oriented businesses accept credit cards. You may encounter smaller restaurants and hotels that don't accept them at all, but these are pretty rare. Some businesses don't like to accept credit cards because their banks charge them exorbitant fees for credit-card transactions. They will usually relent and charge you a small fee for the privilege.

What if I don't know how to use chopsticks?

Chopsticks are the utensils of choice but cutlery is available in many restaurants. That said, it's a good idea to brush up on your chopstick chops. The standard eating procedure is to hold the bowl close to your mouth and eat the food. Noisily slurping up soup and noodles is also the norm. It's considered bad manners to point or play with your chopsticks, or to place them on top of your rice bowl when you're finished eating (place the chopsticks horizontally on the table or plate). Don't leave your chopsticks standing up in a bowl of rice—they look like the two incense sticks burned at funerals.

How should I dress?

Most Chinese people dress for comfort, and you can do the same. There's little risk of offending people with your dress; Westerners tend to attract attention regardless of attire. Although miniskirts are best left at home, pretty much anything else goes.

Should I tip?

Tipping is officially forbidden by the government, and locals simply don't do it. In general, follow their lead without qualms. Nevertheless, the practice is beginning to catch on, especially among tour guides, who often expect Y10 a day. You don't need to tip in restaurants or in taxis.

GOOD WALK

Check out the West's 19th-century fingerhold in Beijing. The Old Lega-tion Quarter, a walled area where foreign businesses and government offices were once housed, was heavily vandalized during the Cultural Revolution and altered again during the '80s boom. That said, a sur-prising number of turn-of-the-century European structures can still be found here.

The Old Legation Quarter

This walk begins on Dong Jiao Min Xiang. It can easily be reached via the lobby of the Novotel Xinqiao Hotel. Exit through the back door right to the street. We'll first take you down the north side of the street and then back up on the south side. The most prominent structure that remains of the quarter is **St. Michael's Catholic Church**. Built by French Vincentian priests in 1902, this Gothic church is still crowded during Sunday masses.

Foreign Emissaries

The red building opposite the church started out as the **Belgian Embassy** and later became the **Burmese Embassy** follow-ing Burma's liberation. Today it's part of the Ruijin Hotel.

On the north side of the street at No. 15 is the former location of the **French Legation**. Former Cambodian leader Prince Siha-nouk stayed here during his many visits to China. The old **French Post Office** is now a Sichuan restaurant. **Hongdu Tailors** (No. 28) was once tailor to the top Commu-nist officials who came here to have their revolutionary Mao jackets custom made.

At the northeast corner of Zhengyi Lu, known in those days as Rue Meiji, in honor of the Japanese emperor who ruled during those days, is a grand looking building that was formerly the **Yokohama Species Bank** (now the China Huacheng Finance Corp); peek in for a look at the turn-of-the-century interior and ceilings. The pleasant patch of greenery you see running down the center of Zhengyi Road was created in 1925, when the old rice-transport canal was filled in with earth. Continue west on Dong Jiao Min Xiang. In the middle of the next block on your right is the gleaming new headquarters of **China's Supreme People's Court** (27 Dongjiao Minxiang), which sits on the site of the former Russian Legation. A gate remains here from the original Russian complex.

Financial Street

Walking up the south side of the street, you'll see a building with thick Roman columns; this was first the **Russia Asiatic Bank,** and afterwards the **National City Bank of New York**—the fading letters NCB can still be seen in a concrete shield at the top of the building. This is now the **Beijing Police Museum.** Down a bit further on the north side of the street, just before Tiananmen Square, is the old **French Hos-pital.** Opposite the hospital is the former **American Legation** (this is the last complex just before the steps leading to Tiananmen Square). It was rebuilt in 1901 after being destroyed by the Boxers.

1

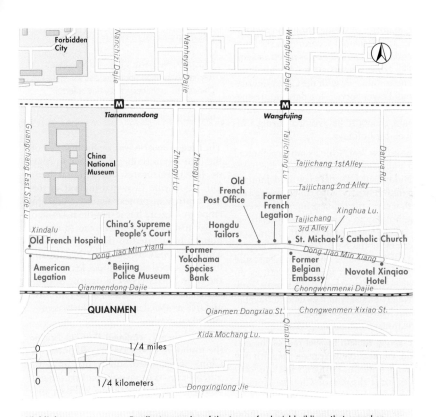

Highlights:	Excellent examples of the types of colonial buildings that served as western legations, shops, and financial institutions around the turn of the century.
Where to Start:	Dong Jiao Min Xiang.
Length:	One hour if you're walking at a leisurely pace (just over a mile).
Where to Stop:	Right back where you started. This walk takes you up and down one street.
Best Time to Go:	Early morning or late afternoon when the weather is better.
Worst Time to Go:	In the afternoon during the heat of the day.
Good in the Hood:	Masion Boulud.

FABULOUS FESTIVALS

The majority of China's holidays and festivals are calculated according to the lunar calendar and can vary by as much as a few weeks from year to year. Check a lunar calendar online or with the China International Travel Service for dates more specific than those here. Tourism and travel should generally be avoided during China's major holidays.

Chinese New Year, China's most celebrated and important holiday, follows the lunar calendar and falls between mid-January and mid-February. Also called Spring Festival, it gives the Chinese an official weeklong holiday to visit family and relatives, eat special meals, and set off firecrackers to celebrate the New Year and its respective Chinese zodiac animal. Students and teachers get up to four weeks off, as do some factory workers. △ It's a particularly crowded—and very noisy—time to travel in China. Many offices and services reduce their hours or close altogether.

The **Spring Lantern Festival** marks the end of the Chinese New Year on the 15th day of the first moon. Residents flock to local parks for a display of Chinese lanterns and fireworks.

Not so much a holiday as a day of worship, **Qing Ming** (literally, "clean and bright"), or Tomb Sweeping Festival, gathers relatives at the graves of the deceased on April 5th to clean the surfaces and leave fresh flowers. As the dead are now required by law to be cremated in China, this festival has lost much of its original meaning.

Labor Day falls on May 1, and is another busy travel time. In 2008 the government reduced the length of this holiday from five days to two, but the length of the holiday now changes from year to year.

The **Dragon Boat Festival,** on the fifth day of the fifth moon (falling sometime in May or June), celebrates the national hero Qu Yuan, who drowned himself in the 3rd century in protest against a corrupt emperor. Legend has it that the fishermen who unsuccessfully attempted to rescue him by boat, tried to distract fish from eating his body by throwing rice dumplings wrapped in bamboo leaves into the river. Today crews in narrow dragon boats race to the beat of heavy drums, and rice wrapped in bamboo leaves is consumed en masse.

On October 1, **National Day** celebrates the founding of the People's Republic of China. Tiananmen Square fills up with a hefty crowd of visitors on this official holiday. This is a weeklong holiday, and the city fills with domestic tourists from around the country.

Mid-Autumn Festival is celebrated on the 15th day of the eighth moon, which generally falls between mid-September and mid-October. The Chinese spend this time gazing at the full moon and exchanging tasty moon cakes (so named because they resemble the full moon) filled with meat, red-bean paste, lotus paste, salted egg, date paste, and other delectable surprises.

Terracotta soldiers

THE AGE OF EMPIRES

When asked his opinion on the historical impact of the French Revolution, Chairman Mao quipped, "It's too early to tell." Though a bit tongue in cheek, China does measure its history in millennia, and in its grand timeline, interactions with the West have been mere blips.

According to historical records, Chinese civilization stretches back to the 15th century BC—markings found on turtle shells carbon dated to around 1500BC bear some similarity to modern Chinese script. China then resembled city-states rather than a unified nation. Iconic figures such as Lao Tzu (the father of Taoism), Sun Tzu (author of the Art of War), and Confucius lived during this period. Generally, 221BC is accepted as the beginning of Imperial China, when the city-states united under various banners.

Over the next 2,200 years (give or take a few), China alternated between periods of harmony and political upheaval. Its armies conquered new territory and were in turn conquered by external invaders (most of whom wound up themselves being assimilated).

By the early 18th century, the long, slow decline of the Qing—the last of China's Imperial dynasties—was already in progress, making the ancient nation ripe for exploitation by rising European powers. The Imperial era ended with the forced abdication of child Emperor Puyi (whose life is chronicled in Bernardo Bertolucci's The Last Emperor), and it's here that the history of modern China, first with the founding of the republic under Sun Yat-sen and then with the establishment of the People's Republic under Mao Zedong, truly begins.

Writing Appears

1500BC   1200BC   900BC

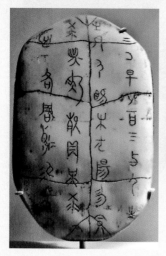

(left) Oracle shell with early Chinese characters. (top, right) The Great Wall stretches 4,163 miles from east to west. (bottom, right) Confucius, Lao-tzu, and a Buddhist Arhat.

Writing Appears

circa 1500 BC

The earliest accounts of Chinese history are still shrouded in myth and legend, and it wasn't until 1959 that stories were verified by archaeological findings. For millennia, people formed communities in the fertile lands of what is now central China. The first recorded Chinese characters are said to have been developed 3,500 years ago. Though sometimes referred to as the Shang Dynasty, this period was more of a precursor to modern Chinese dynasties than a truly unified kingdom.

The Warring States Period

722-475 BC

China was so far from unified that these centuries are collectively remembered as the Warring States Period. As befitting such a contentious time, military science progressed, iron replaced bronze, and weapons material improved. Some of China's greatest luminaries lived during this period, including the father of Taoism, Lao-tzu, Confucius, and Sun-Tzu, one of the greatest military tacticians and the author of the infamous *Art of War*, which is still studied in military academies around the world.

The First Dynasty

221-207 BC

The Qin Dynasty eventually defeated all of the other warring factions thanks to their cutting-edge military technology, namely the cavalry. The Qin were also called Ch'in, which may be where the word China first originated. The first Emperor, Qin Shi Huang, unified much of the lands and established a legal code and vast bureaucracy to hold it together. The Qin dynasty also standardized the written and spoken language and introduced a common currency.

(left) Terracotta warrior.
(top right) Temple of Xichan in Fuzhou

In order to protect his newly unified country, Qin Shi Huang ordered the creation of the massive Great Wall of China, which was built and rebuilt over the next 1,000 years. He was also a sculpture enthusiast and commissioned a massive army of stone soldiers to follow him into the afterlife. Buried with him, these terracotta warriors would remain hidden from the eyes of the world for two thousand years, until they were found by a farmer digging in a field just outside of Xian. These warriors are among the most important archaeological finds of the 20th century.

Buddhism Arrives

220-265 BC

Emperor Qin's dreams of a unified China fell apart, and eventually the kingdom split into three warring factions. But what was bad for stability turned out to be good for literature. The Three Kingdoms Period is still remembered in song and story. *The Romance of the Three Kingdoms* is as popular among Asian book worms as the *Legend of King Arthur* is among Western readers. It's still widely read and has been translated into almost every language. Variations of the story have been adapted for manga, television series, and video games.

The Three Kingdoms period was filled with court intrigue, murder, and massive battles that, while exciting to read about centuries later, weren't much fun at the time. Armies ravaged the countryside, and most people lived and died in misery. Perhaps it was the carnage and disunity of the time that turned the country into a magnet for forces of harmony; it was during this period that Buddhism was first introduced into China, traveling over the Himalayas from India, via the Silk Road.

(left) Statue of Genghis Khan. (top right) Donguan Mosque in Xining, Qinghai. (bottom right) Empress Shengshen

Religion Diversifies

618-845

Chinese spiritual life continued to diversify. Nestorian Monks from Asia Minor arrived bearing news of Christianity, and Saad ibn Abi Waqqas (a companion of the Prophet Muhammad) supposedly visited the Middle Kingdom to spread the word of Islam. During this era, Wu Zetian, onetime concubine, seized power from the Tang Dynasty and became the first (and only) woman to assume the title of emperor. She ruled for 25 years through puppet emperors and finally, for 15 years as Emperor Shengshen.

Ghengis Invades

1271-1368

In Xanadu did Kublai Khan a stately pleasure dome decree . . .

Or so goes the famed Coleridge poem. But Kublai's grandfather Temujin (better known as Ghengis Khan) had bigger things in mind. One of the greatest war tacticians in history, he united the restive nomads of Mongolia's grassy plains and eventually sacked, looted, and pillaged much of the known west and most of the Chinese landmass.

By the time Ghengis died in 1227, his grandson was well-tutored and ready to take on the rest of China.

By 1271, Kublai had established a capital in a land-locked city that would only much later become known as Beijing. This marks the beginning of the first (but not last) non-Han dynasty. Kublai Khan kept fighting southward and by 1279, Guangzhou fell to the Mongols, and Khan became the ultimate monarch of China. Though barbarians at heart, the Mongols must be credited for encouraging the arts and a number of early public works projects, including extending the highways and grand canals.

(left) Emperor Chengzu of the Ming Dynasty. (top right) Forbidden City in Beijing (bottom right) Child emperor Puyi.

Ming Dynasty

1368-1644

Many scholars believe that the Mongols' inability to relate with the Han is what ultimately pushed the Han to rise up and overthrow them. The reign of the Ming Dynasty was the last ethnically Han Dynasty to rule over a unified China. At its apex, the Bright Empire encompassed a landmass easily recognized as China, even by today's mapmakers. The Ming Emperors built a huge army and navy, refurbished the agricultural system, and printed many books using movable type long before Gutenberg. In the 13th century, Emperor Yongle began construction of the famous Forbidden City in Beijing, a veritable icon of China.

Also during the Ming Dynasty, China's best known explorer, Zheng He, plied the seven seas in massive treasure fleets that dwarfed in size and range the ships of Christopher Columbus. A giant both in stature and persona, Admiral Zheng (who was also a eunuch) spent two decades expanding China's knowledge of the world outside of its already impressive borders. He traveled as far as India, Africa, and (some say) even the coast of the New World.

Qing Dynasty

1644-1911

The final dynasty represented a serious case of minority rule. They were Manchus from the northeast. The early Qing dynasty was a brutal period as forces loyal to the new emperor crushed those loyal to the old. The Qing Dynasty peaked in the mid-to-late 18th century but soon after, its military powers began to wane. In the 19th century, Qing control weakened and prosperity diminished. By 1910 China was fractured, a baby sat on the Imperial throne, and the Qing Dynasty was on its deathbed.

(top left) A depiction of the Second Opium War. (bottom left) Chiang Kai-shek (top, right) Mao Zedong on December 6, 1944. (bottom, right) Sun Yat Sen.

The Opium Wars

1834–1860

European powers were hungry to open new territories up for trade, but the Qing weren't buying. The British East India Company, strapped for cash, realized they could sell opium in China at huge profits. The Chinese government quickly banned the nefarious trade and in response, a technologically superior Britain declared war. After a humiliating defeat in the first Opium War, China was forced to cede Hong Kong. Other foreign powers soon followed with territorial demands of their own.

Republican Era

1912–1949

China's Republican period was chaotic and unstable. The revolutionary Dr. Sun Yat-sen —revered by most Chinese as the father of modern China—was unable to build a cohesive government without the aid of regional warlords and urban gangsters. When he died of cancer in 1925, power passed to Chiang Kai-shek, who set about unifying China under the Kuomintang. What began as a unified group of both left- and right-wingers quickly deteriorated, and by the mid-1920s, civil war between the Communists and Nationalists was brewing.

The '30s and '40s were bleak decades for the Chinese people, caught between a vicious war with Japan and periodic clashes between Kuomintang and Communist forces. After Japan's defeat in 1945, China's civil war kicked into high gear. Though the Kuomintang were armed with superior weapons and backed by American money, the majority of Chinese people rallied behind the Communists. Within four years, the Kuomintang were driven off the mainland to Taiwan, where the Republic of China exists to the present day,

(top left) 1950s Chinese stamp with Mao and Stalin.
(top right) Shenzhen
(bottom left) Poster of Mao's slogans.

1949-Present

The People's Republic

On October 1, 1949, Mao Zedong declared from atop Beijing's Gate of Heavenly Peace that "The Chinese People have stood up." And so the People's Republic of China was born. The Communist party set out to overhaul China's ancient feudal system, emphasizing class struggle, redistribution of wealth, and elimination of foreign dominance. The next three decades would see a massive, often painful transformation of Chinese society from feudalism into the modern age.

The Great Leap Forward was a disaster—Chinese peasants were encouraged to cram 100 years of industrial development into as many weeks. Untenable decisions led to industrial and agricultural ruin, widespread famine, and an estimated 30 million deaths. The trauma of this period, however, pales in comparison to The Great Proletarian Cultural Revolution. From 1966–1976, fear and zealotry gripped the nation as young revolutionaries heeded Chairman Mao's call to root out class enemies. During this decade, millions died, millions were imprisoned, and much of China's accumulated religious,

historical, and cultural heritage literally went up in smoke.

Like a phoenix rising from its own ashes, China rose from its own self-inflicted destruction. In the early 1980s, Deng Xiao-ping took the first steps in reforming China's stagnant economy. With the maxim "To Get Rich is Glorious," Deng loosened central control on the economy and declared Special Economic Zones where the seeds of capitalism could be incubated. Three decades later, the nation is one of the world's most vibrant economic engines. Though China's history is measured in millennia, her brightest years may well have only just begun.

ENGLISH	PINYIN	CHINESE CHARACTERS
Beihai Park	Běihǎi gōngyuán	北海公园
Beijing Ancient Architecture Museum	Běijīng gǔdài jiànzhú bówùguǎn	北京古代建筑博物馆
Beijing Urban Planning Museum	Běijīng shì guīhuà zhǎnlǎnguǎn	北京市规划展览馆
Confucius Temple	Kǒngmiào	孔庙
Cultural Palace of Minorities	Mínzú wénhuàgōng	民族文化宫
Ditan Park (Altar of the Earth)	Dìtán gōngyuán	地坛公园
Forbidden City	Gùgōng	故宫
Great Hall of the People	Rénmín dàhuìtáng	人民大会堂
Houhai (Back Lake)	Hòuhǎi	后海
Jingshan Park (Coal Hill)	Jǐngshān gōngyuán	景山公园
Lama Temple	Yōnghégōng	雍和宫
Lu Xun House and Museum	Lǔxùn guǎn	鲁迅馆
Mao Zedong Memorial Hall	Máozhǔxí jìniàntáng	毛主席纪念堂
Museum of Antique Currency	Gǔdàiqiánbì bówùguǎn	古代钱币博物馆
Nanluoguxiang	Nánluógǔ xiàng	南锣鼓巷
Poly Art Museum	Bǎolì yìshù bówùguǎn	保利艺术博物馆
Qianhai (Front Lake)	Qiánhǎi	前海
Ritan Park (Altar of the Sun)	Rìtán gōngyuán	日坛公园
Silver Ingot Bridge	Yíndìng qiáo	银锭桥
Summer Palace	Yíhéyuán	颐和园
Taxi	chū zū chē	出租车
Temple of Heaven	Tiāntán	天坛
Tiananmen Square	Tiānānmén guǎngchǎng	天安门广场
Xiangshan Park (Fragrant Hills)	Xiāngshān gōngyuán	香山公园

Exploring

WORD OF MOUTH

"If you want to see Mao's body at Chairman Mao's Mausoleum, go first thing in the morning. We made the mistake of coming out of the subway at Gate of Heavenly Peace, and by the time we saw that and walked over to the Mausoleum, the line was huge!"
—luv2globetrot

Updated by
Paul Mooney

Beijing is a vibrant jumble of neighborhoods and districts. It's a city that was transformed almost overnight in preparation for the 2008 Olympics, often leveling lively old *hutongs* (alleyway neighborhoods) to make way for the glittering towers that are fast dwarfing their surroundings. Still, day-to-day life seems to pulse the lifeblood of a Beijing that once was.

Hidden behind Beijing's pressing search for modernity is an intriguing historic core. Many of the city's ancient sites were built under the Mongols during the Yuan Dynasty (1271–1368). A number of the capital's imperial palaces, halls of power, mansions, and temples were rebuilt and refurbished during the Ming and Qing dynasties. Despite the ravages of time and the Cultural Revolution, most sites are in good shape, from the Niujie Mosque, with Koranic verse curled around its arches, to Tiananmen Square, the bold brainchild of Mao Zedong.

GETTING ORIENTED

Laid out like a target with ring roads revolving around a bull's-eye, with **Chang'an Jie** (Eternal Peace Avenue) cutting across the middle, Beijing is a bustling metropolis sprawling outward from the central point of the **Forbidden City.** The ring roads are its main arteries and, along with Chang'an Jie, you will find yourself traveling them just about anytime you go from one place to another aboveground. As you explore Beijing, you'll find that taxis are often the best way to get around. However, if the recently expanded subway system goes where you're headed, it's often a faster option than dealing with traffic, which has become increasingly congested in recent years with the rise of private automobiles.

The city is divided into 18 municipal and suburban districts (*qu*). Only six of these districts are the central stomping grounds for most visitors; this chapter focuses on those districts. **Dongcheng** ("east district") encompasses the Forbidden City, Tiananmen Square, Wangfujing (a major shopping street), the Lama Temple, and many other historical sites dating back to imperial times. **Xicheng** ("west district"), directly west of Dongcheng, is a lovely lake district that includes Beihai Park, former playground of the imperial family, and a series of connected lakes bordered by willow trees, courtyard-lined hutongs, and lively bars. The southern districts include **Chongwen** in the southeast and **Xuanwu** in the southwest. These areas have some of the oldest neighborhoods in the city, and a long history of traditional folk arts, with opera theaters and acrobatic shows still staged here. The Chongwen District is also home to some of the city's most famous restaurants, some more than 100 years old. **Chaoyang** is the biggest and busiest district, occupying the areas north, east, and south of the eastern Second Ring Road. As it lies outside the second ring road, which marked the eastern demarcation of the old city wall, there is little of historical interest here. The district is home to foreign embassies, multinational companies, the Central Business District, and the Olympic Park. **Haidian**, the technology and university district, is northwest of the Third Ring Road; it's packed with shops selling electronics and students cramming for the next exam.

STREET VOCABULARY

Here are some terms you'll see over and over again. These words will appear on maps and street signs, and they are part of the name of just about every place you go:

Dong is east, **xi** is west, **nan** is south, **bei** is north, and **zhong** means middle. **Jie** and **lu** mean street and road respectively, and **da** means big.

Gongyuan means park. Jingshan Park is also called Jingshan Gongyuan.

Nei means inside and **wai** means outside. You will often come across these terms on streets that used to pass through a gate of the old city wall. Andingmen Nei Dajie, for example, is the section of the street located inside the Second Ring Road (where the gate used to be), whereas Andingmen Wai Dajie is the section outside the gate.

Qiao, or bridge, is part of the place name at just about every entrance and exit on the ring roads.

Men, meaning door or gate, indicates a street that once passed through an entrance in the old wall that surrounded the city until it was mostly torn down in the 1960s. The entrances to parks and some other places are also referred to as *men*.

PLANNING

WHEN TO GO

The best time to visit Beijing is spring or early fall, when the weather is pleasant and crowds are a bit smaller. Book at least one month in advance for travel during these two times of year. In winter Beijing's Forbidden City and Summer Palace can look fantastical and majestic, when the traditional tiled roofs are covered with a light dusting of snow and the venues are devoid of tourists.

Avoid the two long national holidays: Chinese New Year, which ranges from mid-January to mid-February; and National Day holiday, the first week of October, when Chinese normally get a lengthy holiday. Millions of Chinese travel during these weeks, making it difficult to book hotels, tours, and transportation.

The weather in Beijing is at its best in September and October, with a good chance of sunny days and mild temperatures. Winters are cold, but it seldom snows. Although hotels are usually well heated, some restaurants may be poorly heated, so be prepared with a warm sweater when dining out. Late April through June is lovely, but come July the days are hot and excruciatingly humid with a greater chance of rain. Spring is also the time of year for Beijing's famous dust storms.

GETTING AROUND

On Foot: Though traffic and modernization have put a bit of a cramp in Beijing's walking style, meandering remains one of the best ways to experience the capital—especially the old hutongs that are rich with culture and sights.

By Bike: The proliferation of cars (some 1,000 new automobiles take to the streets of the capital every day bringing the total to more than 4 million vehicles) has made biking less pleasant and more dangerous here. Fortunately, most streets have wide, well-defined bike lanes often separated from other traffic by an island. If a flat tire or sudden brake failure strikes, seek out the nearest street-side mechanic, easily identified by the bike parts and pumps. Bikes can be rented at many hotels and next to some subway stations.

By Subway: The subway is the best way to avoid Beijing's frequent traffic jams. With the opening of new lines, Beijing's subway service is becoming increasingly convenient. Beijing now has eight lines, and an express line to the airport. Most tourist spots are located close to Line 1, which runs east–west through Tiananmen Square, and Line 2, which runs in a loop tracing Beijing's ancient city walls (and the Second Ring Road). Transfers between these lines can be made at the Fuxingmen and Jianguomen stations. The subway runs from about 5 AM to midnight daily, depending on the station. Fares are Y2 per ride for any distance and transfers are free. Stations are marked in both Chinese and English, and stops are also announced in both languages.

By Taxi: The taxi experience in Beijing has improved significantly as the city's taxi companies gradually shift to cleaner, more comfortable new cars. In the daytime, flag-fall for taxis is Y10 for the first 3 km (2 mi) and Y2 per km thereafter. The rate rises to Y3 per km on trips over 15 km and after 11 PM, when the flag-fall also increases to Y11. At present, there is also a Y1 gas surcharge for any rides exceeding 3 km. ■**TIP→ Be sure to check that the meter has been engaged to avoid fare negotiations at your destination.** Taxis are easy to hail during the day, but can be difficult during evening rush hour, especially when it's raining. If you're having difficulty, go to the closest hotel and wait in line there. Few taxi drivers speak English, so ask your hotel concierge to write down your

Shoppers enjoy a sunny day in the Xidan neighborhood.

destination in Chinese. ■ **TIP→** You can also use the translations through-out this book; simply point at the Chinese character and your cabbie will know where to go. Be sure to take a hotel card with you for the return trip.

GOOD TOURS

Taking a tour will make it easier to sightsee without the hassle. How-ever, if you're adventurous, you can easily explore the city on your own, even if you don't speak Chinese. You can't rely on taxi drivers to know the English names of the major tourist sites, but armed with the names in Chinese in this guide, you should have few or no problems getting around. If you do opt for an organized tour, keep in mind that a little research pays off.

GENERAL TOURS

China Culture Center. With a reputation for well-informed English-speaking guides, CCC is popular with both visitors and expats look-ing for more than just the standard tour highlights. ⊠ *Kent Center, 29 Anjialou, Liangmaqiao Road, Chaoyang District* ☎ *010/6432–9341; 010/6432–1041 weekends* ⊕ *www.chinaculturecenter.org.*

China International Travel Service. CITS is China's official travel agency, dating to 1954. In Beijing the company offers everything from custom-ized tours to group tours and business trips. ⊠ *28 Jianguomenwai Dajie, Chaoyang District* ✛ *Across from the Friendship Store* ☎ *010/6515–8565* ⊕ *www.cits.net.*

WildChina. This foreign-managed travel company is probably the best in China. WildChina has excellent guides who know the city well and who don't waste your time taking you to souvenir shops. The company offers a three-day tour of Beijing that includes major historic sites, a

hike on a wild part of the Great Wall, a visit to the hutongs, and an introduction to the cuisines of the capital city. It's pricey but worth it. ⊠ *Room 801, Oriental Place, 9 East Dongfang Lu, North Dongsanhuan Lu, Chaoyang District* ☎ *010/6465–6602* ⊕ *www.wildchina.com.*

BIKE TOURS

Many of Beijing's pleasures are best sampled off the subway and out of taxis. In other words, pedal! Rent bikes (available at many hotels and near some subway exits) and take an impromptu sightseeing tour. Beijing is flat, and there are bike lanes on most main roads. Pedaling among the city's cyclists isn't as challenging as it looks: copy the locals—keep it slow and ring your bell often. And, of course, be very careful. Punctured tire? Not to worry: curbside repairmen line most streets. Remember to park your bike (and lock it to something stationary, as bike theft is common) only in designated areas. There are designated bike-parking lots throughout the city with attendants charging a nominal fee, usually about 3 mao.

CycleChina. If a guided three-hour afternoon bicycle tour of a hutong, or a trip through Beijing sitting in a motorbike sidecar sounds like fun, call CycleChina. They also offer bike tours of the Great Wall. ⊠ *12 Jingshan East Street, Dongcheng District* ✛ *Across from the east gate of Jingshan Park* ☎ *010/6402–5653 or 139/1188–6524* ⊕ *www.cyclechina.com.*

Bicycle Kingdom. Offering bicycle rentals and suggested itineraries covering some of Beijing's lesser known historical sites, Kingdom is a great resource. A variety of bikes are available for rent here from Y100 for the first day and Y50 for each additional day (or Y300 per week). Helmets are available for Y20 per day or Y100 a week. ⊠ *34 Dong Huangchenggen Nanjie, Wangfujing, Dongcheng District* ☎ *133/8140–0738 (English); 010/6526–5857* ⊕ *www.bicyclekingdom.com.*

PEDICAB TOURS

Pedicabs (basically large tricycles with room for passengers behind a pedaling driver) were once the vehicles of choice for Beijingers laden with a week's worth of groceries or tourists eager for a street's-eye city tour. Today many residents are wealthy enough to bundle their purchases into taxis or their own cars, and the tourist trade has moved on to the tight schedules of air-conditioned buses. But pedicabs have made a big comeback in Beijing in recent years and can now be hired near major tourist sites. A ride through the hutongs near Houhai is the most popular pedicab journey. ■TIP➡ Be absolutely sure to negotiate the fare in advance, clarifying which currency will be used (yuan or dollars), whether the fare is considered a one-way or round-trip (some drivers will demand payment for a round-trip whether or not you use the pedicab for the return journey), and whether it is for one person or two. Beginning in 2008, government-approved pedicab tours were supposed to be fixed at Y35 per hour, though the actual price is often higher. Feel free to tip your driver for good service on longer tours. Independent pedicabs for hutong tours can be found in the small plaza between the Drum Tower and the Bell Tower.

Beijing Hutong Tourist Agency. This agency was one of the first to offer guided pedicab tours of Beijing's back alleys, with glimpses of old courtyard houses and daily Beijing life. This half-day trip winds its way

BEIJING'S SUBWAY

The subway in Beijing is faster and cheaper than a taxi, and the city plans to expand the system by 2015. Although Beijing's subway system has been expanded to eight lines, most first-time visitors to Beijing stick to the original two lines, which provide access to the most popular areas of the capital, and the airport extension. Line 1 runs east and west along Chang'an Jie past the China World Trade Center, Jianguomen (one of the embassy districts), the Wangfujing shopping area, Tiananmen Square and the Forbidden City, Xidan (another major shopping location), and the Military Museum before heading out to the far western suburbs. Line 2 (the loop line) runs along a sort of circular route around the center of the city shadowing the Second Ring Road. Important destinations include the Drum and Bell towers, Lama Temple, Dongzhimen (with a connection to the airport express), Dongsishitiao (near Sanlitun and the Worker's Stadium), Beijing Train Station, and Qianmen (Front Gate) south of Tiananmen Square. Free transfers between Line 1 and 2 can be made at either Fuxingmen or Jianguomen stations. ■TIP→ Need a visual? Flip to the inside back cover of this book for a helpful subway map.

If both you and your final destination are near the Second Ring Road or on Chang'an Jie, the best way to get there is probably by subway. It stops just about every half mile, and you'll easily spot the entrances (with blue subway logos) dotting the streets. Each stop is announced in both English and Chinese, and there are clearly marked signs in English or pinyin at each station. Transferring between lines is easy and free, with the standard Y2 ticket including travel between any two destinations. ■TIP→ When planning a trip on Line 13, make sure you are transferring from the correct station. If your destination is on the west side of the line, leave from Xizhimen; if it's on the east side of the line, leave from Dongzhimen.

Subway tickets can be purchased from electronic kiosks and ticket windows in every station. Start off by finding the button that says "English," insert your money, and press another button to print. Single-ride tickets cost Y2, and unless you want a pocketful of coins you'll need to pay with exact change; the machines don't accept Y1 bills, only Y1 coins. It's also possible to buy a stored value subway card with a Y20 deposit and a purchase of Y10–Y100.

In the middle of each subway platform, you'll find a map of the Beijing subway system along with a local map showing the position of exits. Subway cars also have a simplified diagram of the line you're riding above the doors.

Trains can be very crowded, especially during rush hour, and it's not uncommon for people to push onto the train before exiting passengers can get off. Prepare to get off by making your way to the door before you arrive at your station. Be especially wary of pickpockets.

⚠ Unfortunately, the subway system is not convenient for disabled people. In some stations there are no escalators, and sometimes the only entrance or exit is via steep steps.

through what was once Beijing's most prestigious neighborhood (Hou-hai), stops at the Drum and Bell towers, and finishes with tea at Prince Gong's Palace. It's also possible to arrange to visit the home of a local family. Advance reservations are recommended. Tours, which begin at the entrance to Qianhai (Lotus Lane) directly opposite the north entrance of Beihai Park, start at 9 and 2 daily, and cost Y180 per person, or Y360 if you're riding solo. ⊠ *26 Di'anmen Xidajie, Dongcheng District* ☎ *010/6615–9097.*

HIKING TOURS

Beijing Hikers. This outfitter offers guided group and private hiking trips aimed at expat hikers and tourists. The trips are rated from 1 to 5 in terms of difficulty, and they take you into the hills around Beijing. You might visit a rural village, historic temple, or the Great Wall. Group tours depart from the Starbucks in the Lido Hotel and start at Y250 per person. Book in advance. ⊠ *26 Xinhualian, Ligang Building No. 2, Suite 601, Chaoyang District* ☎ *010/6432–2786 or 139/1002–5516* ⊕ *www.beijinghikers.com.*

VISITOR CENTERS

Beijing Travel Hotline (☎ *12301* ⊕ *www.bjta.gov.cn*)

Beijing International Travel and Tours Company (⊠ *28 Jianguomenwai Dajie, Chaoyang District* ✢ *Behind Gloria Plaza Hotel* ☎ *010/6515–8565* ⊕ *www.btgtravel.com.cn.*

THE FORBIDDEN CITY

Undeniably sumptuous, the Forbidden City, once home to a long line of emperors, is Beijing's most enduring emblem. Magnificent halls, winding lanes, and stately courtyards await you—welcome to the world's largest palace complex.

As you gaze up at roofs of glazed-yellow tiles—a symbol of royalty—try to imagine a time when only the emperor ("the son of God") was permitted to enter this palace, accompanied by select family members, concubines, and eunuch-servants. Now, with its doors flung open, the Forbidden City's mysteries beckon.

The sheer grandeur of the site—with 800 buildings and more than 8,000 rooms—conveys the pomp and circumstance of Imperial China. The shady palaces, musty with age, recall life at court, where corrupt eunuchs and palace officials schemed and bored concubines gossiped.

BUILDING TO GLORY
Under the third Ming emperor, Yongle, 200,000 laborers built this complex over the course of 14 years, finishing in 1420. Yongle relocated the Ming capital to Beijing (from Nanjing in the south) to strengthen China's northern frontier. After Yongle, the palace was home to 23 Ming and Qing emperors, until the dynastic system crumbled in 1911.

In imperial times, no buildings were allowed to exceed the height of the palace. Moats and massive timber doors protected the emperor. Gleaming yellow roof tiles marked the vast complex as the royal court's exclusive dominion. Ornate interiors displayed China's most exquisite artisanship, including ceilings covered with turquoise-and-blue dragons, walls draped with priceless scrolls, intricate cloisonné screens, sandalwood thrones padded in delicate silks, and floors of golden-hued bricks. Miraculously, the palace survived fire, war, and imperial China's collapse.

MORE THAN FENG SHUI
The Forbidden City embodies Feng Shui, architectural principles used for thousands of years throughout China. Each main hall faces south, opening to a courtyard flanked by lesser buildings. This symmetry repeats itself along a north–south axis that bisects the imperial palace, with a broad walkway paved in marble. This path was reserved exclusively for the emperor's sedan chair.

The entire complex follows the principles of Feng Shui.

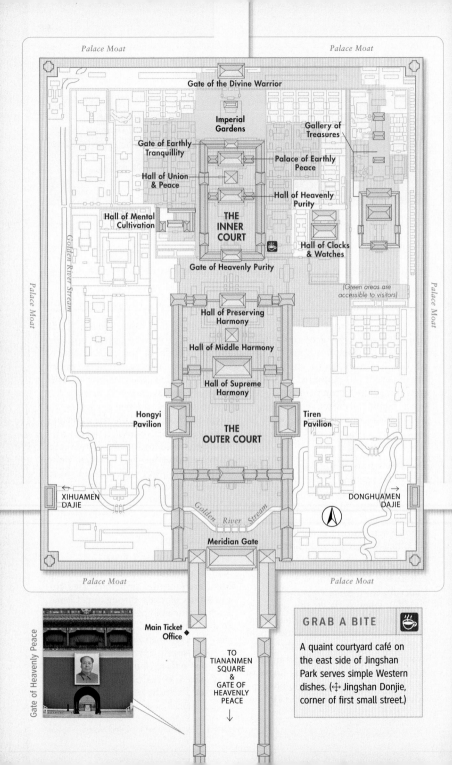

Palace Moat   Palace Moat

Gate of the Divine Warrior

Imperial
Gardens

Gallery of
Treasures

Gate of Earthly
Tranquillity

Palace of Earthly
Peace

Hall of Union
& Peace

Hall of Heavenly
Purity

Hall of Mental
Cultivation

THE
INNER
COURT

Hall of Clocks
& Watches

Gate of Heavenly Purity

*(Green areas are
accessible to visitors)*

Hall of Preserving
Harmony

Hall of Middle Harmony

Hall of Supreme
Harmony

Hongyi
Pavilion

Tiren
Pavilion

THE
OUTER
COURT

← XIHUAMEN
DAJIE

DONGHUAMEN →
DAJIE

Golden   River   Stream

Meridian Gate

Palace Moat   Palace Moat

Golden River Stream

Palace Moat   *Palace Moat*

Main Ticket
Office ◆

TO
TIANANMEN
SQUARE
&
GATE OF
HEAVENLY
PEACE
↓

Gate of Heavenly Peace

GRAB A BITE

A quaint courtyard café on
the east side of Jingshan
Park serves simple Western
dishes. (⚓ Jingshan Donjie,
corner of first small street.)

WHAT TO SEE

The most impressive way to reach the Forbidden City is through the **Gate of Heavenly Peace** (Tiananmen), connected to Tiananmen Square. The Great Helmsman himself stood here to establish the People's Republic of China on October 1, 1949.

The **Meridian Gate** (Wumen), sometimes called Five Phoenix Tower, is the main southern entrance to the palace. Here, the emperor announced yearly planting schedules according to the lunar calendar; it's also where errant officials were flogged. The main ticket office and audio-guide rentals are just west of this gate.

The central entrance of the Meridian was reserved for the emperor. The one day the empress was allowed to walk through it was her wedding day.

THE OUTER COURT

The **Hall of Supreme Harmony** (Taihedian) was used for coronations, royal birthdays, and weddings. Bronze vats, once kept brimming with water to fight fires, ring this vast expanse. The hall sits atop three stone tiers with an elaborate drainage system with 1,000 carved dragons. On the top tier, bronze cranes symbolize longevity. Inside, cloisonné cranes flank the imperial throne, above which hangs a heavy bronze ball—placed there to crush any pretender to the throne.

Take a close look at the bronze vats and you'll see the telltale scratch marks of greedy foreign soldiers who scraped the gold with their bayonets.

Emperors greeted audiences in the **Hall of Middle Harmony** (Zhonghedian). It also housed the royal plow, with which the emperor would turn a furrow to commence spring planting.

The highest civil service examinations, which were personally conducted by the emperor, were once administered in the **Hall of Preserving Harmony** (Baohedian). Behind the hall, a 200-ton marble relief of dragons, the palace's most treasured stone carving, adorns the staircase.

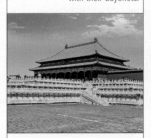

The Hall of Supreme Harmony was the site of many imperial weddings.

A short jaunt to the right is **Hall of Clocks and Watches** (Zhongbiaoguan), where you'll find a collection of early timepieces. It's pure opulence: there's a plethora of jeweled, enameled, and lacquered timepieces (some astride elephants, others implanted in ceramic trees). Our favorites? Those crafted from red sandalwood. *(Admission: Y10)*

You'll see that lions in the palace live in pairs. A female lion playing with a cub symbolizes imperial fertility. A male lion, sitting majestically with a sphere beneath his paw, represents power.

Marble dragons will greet you behind the Hall of Preserving Harmony.

Emperors Throne in the Palace of Heavenly Purity

THE INNER COURT

Now you're approaching the very core of the palace. Several emperors chose to live in the Inner Palace with their families. The **Hall of Heavenly Purity** (Qianqinggong) holds another imperial throne; the **Hall of Union and Peace** (Jiaotaidian) was the venue for the empress's annual birthday party; and the **Palace of Earthly Peace** (Kunninggong) was where royal couples consummated their marriages. The banner above the throne bizarrely reads DOING NOTHING.

On either side of the Inner Palace are six western and six eastern palaces—the former living quarters of concubines, eunuchs, and servants. The last building on the western side, the **Hall of Mental Cultivation** (Yangxindian), is the most important of these; starting with Emperor Yongzheng, all Qing Dynasty emperors attended to daily state business in this hall.

AN EMPEROR CHEAT SHEET

JIAJING (1507–1567)

Ming Emperor Jiajing was obsessed with Taoism, which he hoped would give him longevity, but which also led him to ignore state affairs for 25 years. His other fixation was the pursuit of girls: his 18 concubines conspired to strangle him in his sleep, but their plot was uncovered. Nearly all of the girls, and their families, were killed.

YONGZHENG (1678–1735)

The third emperor of the Qing Dynasty, Yongzheng was tyrannical but efficient. He became emperor amid rumors that he had forged his father's will. He appeased his brothers by promoting them, but then proceeded to murder and imprison anyone who posed a challenge, including his own brothers, two of whom died in prison.

Pagoda in the Imperial Garden

Address: The main entrance is just north of the Gate of Heavenly Peace, which faces Tiananmen Square on Chang'an Jie.

Phone: 010/8513-2255

Web site: www.dpm.org.cn

Admission: Y60

Hours: Oct. 16–Apr. 15, daily 8:30–4:30; Apr. 16–Oct. 15, daily 8:30–5

UNESCO Status: Declared a World Heritage Site in 1987. You must check your bags prior to entry and also pass through a metal detector.

The Gallery of Treasures (Zhenbaoguan), actually a series of halls, has breathtaking examples of imperial ornamentation. The first room displays candleholders, wine vessels, tea sets, and a golden pagoda commissioned by Qing emperor Qian Long in honor of his mother. A cabinet on one wall contains the 25 imperial seals. Jade bracelets, golden hair pins, and coral fill the second hall; carved jade landscapes a third. *(Admission: Y10)*

HEAD FOR THE GREEN
North of the Forbidden City's private palaces, beyond the **Gate of Earthly Tranquillity**, lie the most pleasant parts of the Forbidden City: the **Imperial Gardens** (Yuhuayuan), composed of ancient cypress trees and stone mosaic pathways. During festivals, palace inhabitants climbed the Hill of Accumulated Elegance. You can exit the palace at the back of the gardens through the park's **Gate of the Divine Warrior** (Shenwumen).

■ The palace is always packed with visitors, but it's impossibly crowded on national holidays.

■ Allow 2–4 hours to explore the palace. There are souvenir shops and restaurants inside.

■ You can hire automated audio guides at the Meridian Gate for Y40 and a Y100 returnable deposit.

CIXI (1835–1908)

The Empress Dowager served as de facto ruler of China from 1861 until 1908. She was a concubine at 16 and soon became Emperor Xianfeng's favorite. She gave birth to his only son to survive: the heir apparent. Ruthless and ambitious, she learned the workings of the imperial court and used every means to gain power.

PUYI (1906–1967)

Puyi, whose life was depicted in Bertolucci's classic *The Last Emperor*, took the throne at age two. The Qing dynasty's last emperor, he was forced to abdicate after the dynasty fell. During an attempted restoration in 1917, he held the throne for 12 days. Puyi was forced out of the Imperial City in 1924 by a warlord.

DONGCHENG DISTRICT 东城区

Sightseeing
★★★★☆

Dining
★★★☆☆

Lodging
★★★★☆

Shopping
★★★☆☆

Nightlife
★★★☆☆

Dongcheng District, with its idyllic hutongs and plethora of historical sites, is one of Beijing's most pleasant areas. It's also one of the smaller districts in the city, which makes it easy to get around. A day exploring Dongcheng will leave you feeling as if you've been introduced to the character of the capital. From the old men playing chess in the hutongs to the sleek, chauffeured Audis driving down Chang'an Jie, to the colorful shopping on Wangfujing, Dongcheng offers visitors a thousand little tastes of what makes Beijing a fascinating city. ■TIP→ Note that indoor photography in many temples and sites like the Forbidden City is not permitted.

EXPLORING

TOP ATTRACTIONS

Fodor's Choice
★

Confucius Temple 孔庙. This tranquil temple to China's great sage has endured close to eight centuries of additions and restorations. The Hall of Great Accomplishment in the temple houses Confucius's funeral tablet and shrine, flanked by copper-colored statues depicting China's wisest Confucian scholars. As in Buddhist and Taoist temples, worshippers can offer sacrifices (in this case to a mortal, not a deity). The 198 tablets lining the courtyard outside the Hall of Great Accomplishment contain 51,624 names belonging to advanced Confucian scholars from the Yuan, Ming, and Qing dynasties. Flanking the Gate of Great Accomplishment are two carved stone drums dating to the Qianlong period (1735–96). In the Hall of Great Perfection you'll find the central shrine to Confucius. Check out the huge collection of ancient musical instruments.

In the front and main courtyards of the Templem you'll find a cemetery of stone tablets. These tablets, or stelae, stand like rows of creepy crypts. On the front stelae you can barely make out the names of thousands of scholars who passed imperial exams. Another batch of stelae, carved in the mid-1700s to record the *Thirteen Classics*, philosophical works attributed to Confucius, line the west side of the grounds.

■TIP→ We recommend combining a tour of the Confucius Temple with the nearby Lama Temple. Access to both is convenient from the Yonghegong subway stop at the intersection of Line 2 and Line 5. You can also easily get to the Temple of Heaven by taking Line 5 south to Tiantandongmen.

Though many sights were damaged during the Cultural Revolution, Confucian temples can still be seen.

The complex is now combined with the Imperial Academy next door, once the highest educational institution in the country. Established in 1306 as a rigorous training ground for high-level government officials, the academy was notorious, especially during the early Ming Dynasty era, for the harsh discipline imposed on scholars perfecting their knowledge of the Confucian classics. ⊠ *Guozijian Lu off Yonghegong Lu near Lama Temple, Dongcheng District* ☎ *010/8401–1977* ✉ *Y30* ⊙ *Daily 8:30–5* Ⓜ *Yonghegong.*

★ **Drum Tower 鼓楼**. Until the late 1920s, the 24 drums once housed in this tower were Beijing's timepiece. Sadly, all but one of these huge drums have been destroyed. Kublai Khan built the first drum tower on this site in 1272. You can climb to the top of the present tower, which dates from the Ming Dynasty. The nearby **Bell Tower,** renovated after a fire in 1747, offers fabulous views of the hutongs. ⊠ *North end of Dianmen Dajie, Dongcheng District* ☎ *010/6404–1710* ✉ *Y20 for Drum Tower, Y15 for Bell Tower* ⊙ *Daily 9–5:15* Ⓜ *Guloudajie.*

Forbidden City. ⇨ *See the feature earlier in this chapter.*

Jingshan Park (Coal Hill Park) 景山公园. This park was built around a small peak formed from earth excavated for the Forbidden City's moats. Ming rulers ordered the hill's construction to improve the feng shui of their new palace to the south. Climb a winding stone staircase past peach and apple trees to Wanchun Pavilion, the park's highest point. ⊠ *Jingshanqian Dajie, opposite the north gate of the Forbidden City, Xicheng and Dongcheng districts* ☎ *010/6404–4071* ✉ *Y2* ⊙ *Daily 6 AM–10 PM.*

GETTING ORIENTED

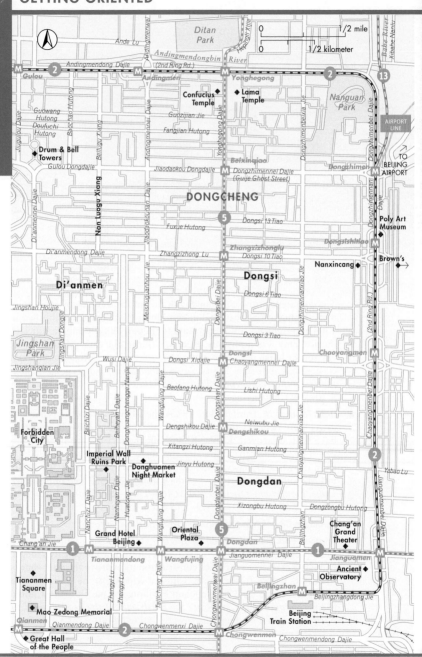

Ditan Park

Ande Lu

Andingmendongbin (2nd Ring Rd.) River

Heping Xijie

0   1/2 mile

0   1/2 kilometer

M Gulou ② Andingmendong Dajie

M Andingmen

Andingmenwai

M Yonghegong ②

⑬

AIRPORT LINE

TO BEIJING AIRPORT

Guowang Hutong
Doufuchi Hutong

Baochao Hutong

◆ Confucius Temple

◆ Lama Temple

Nanguan Park

Dongzhimenbeixiao Jie

Jingulou Dajie

Guozijian Jie

Dongzhimenwai Dajie

Fangjian Hutong

Yonghegong Dajie

◆ Drum & Bell Towers

Gulou Dongdajie

Beiluo Xiang

Jiaodaokou Dongdajie

M Beixinqiao
Dongzhimennei Dajie
(Guije Ghost Street)

Dongzhimen

M

Dongzhimennei Dajie

Nan Luogu Xiang

Jiaodaokouan Dajie

DONGCHENG

⑤ M

Dongsi 13 Tiao

Poly Art Museum

Dongzhimennan Dajie

Fuxue Hutong

Dongsishitiao

Di'anmennei Dajie

Di'anmendong Dajie

Zhangzizhong Lu

Zhangzizhonglu
M Dongsi 10 Tiao

Brown's ◆→

Di'anmen

Meishuguanhou Jie

Dongsibei Dajie

Dongsi

Nanxincang ◆

Dongsi 6 Tiao

Dongzhimennanxiao Jie

Jingshan Houjie

Dongsi 3 Tiao

Jingshan Park

Jingshanqian Jie

Jingshan Dongjie

Wusi Dajie

Dongsi Xidajie

Dongsi
M Chaoyangmennei Dajie

Chaoyangmen M

Wangfujing Dajie

Baofang Hutong

Lishi Hutong

Chaoyangmenbei Dajie

Forbidden City

Beichizi Dajie

Beiheyan Dajie

Dengshikou Dajie

Dengshikou
M Neiwubu Jie

Imperial Wall Ruins Park ◆

Nanheyan Dajie

Dongdan

Huangcheng Genye Nanjie

◆ Donghuamen Night Market

Jinyu Hutong

Xitangzi Hutong

Ganmian Hutong

Dongdan

Chaoyangmennanxiao Jie

Nanchizi Dajie

Wangfujing Dajie

Dongdanbei Dajie

Xizongbu Hutong

Dongzongbu Hutong

Yabao Lu

②

Jianguomennei Dajie

◆ Grand Hotel Beijing

Zhengyi Lu

Zhengyi Lu

Taijichang Dajie

◆ Oriental Plaza

⑤ Dongdan
M

M Tiananmendong

Wangfujing

Jianguomennei Dajie

① Jianguomen M

Tiananmen Square ◆

Chang'an Jie ①

Chang'an Grand Theater ◆

Ancient ◆ Observatory

Beijingzhan

Beijingzhan
M

Beijingzhangdong Jie

◆ Mao Zedong Memorial

Beijing Train Station

M Qianmen ②

Qianmendong Dajie

Chongwenmenxi Dajie

M Chongwenmen

Chongwenmennei Dajie

Chongwenmenwai Dajie

◆ Great Hall of the People

Bahe River
Xibahe Nanlu

QUICK BITES

Have a cup of fresh yogurt at **Wenyu Nailao** (✉ *49 Nan Luogu Xiang* ☎ *010/6405–7621*), which makes its yogurt the traditional Chinese way. The **Pass By Bar** (✉ *108 Nan Luogu Xiang* ☎ *010/8403—8004*) offers good drinks, food, and wireless Internet access.

For a nighttime-munchies cure, head to **Guijie** *(Ghost Street)*, which is full of restaurants serving up every Chinese specialty, from noodles to hotpot to fried delights. One of the most popular dishes here is *malaxia,* or spicy crawfish.

In Wangfujing and looking for something good and quick to eat? Check out the food court in **Oriental Plaza** (**M** *Wangfujing*), with a wide selection of China's various regional cuisines.

NEIGHBORHOOD TOP 5

1. Explore the wonders of the **Forbidden City** and **Tiananmen Square**. Then climb the hill in **Jingshan Park** for a view of the golden rooftops of the Forbidden City.

2. Visit the **Lama Temple**, Beijing's most famous Tibetan Buddhist temple, then the **Confucius Temple**; finally, cross the street for a stroll through **Ditan Park**.

3. Have dinner in the renovated courtyard of **The Source** (⇨ *Chapter 6)*, then walk to **Nan Luogu Xiang**, the city's hippest hutong area.

4. Walk up **Wangfujing**, Beijing's premier shopping spot, and check out the shops at **Oriental Plaza**.

5. Walk along the well-landscaped **Imperial Wall Ruins Park**, which begins one block north of Chang'an Jie on Nan Heyan Dajie.

GETTING HERE

Dongcheng is easily accessible by subway, with stops along most of its perimeter: Tiananmen East station to Jianguomen on Line 1 forms the south side of this district; Jianguomen to Gulou Dajie on Line 2 forms the district's north and east sides. Line 2 stops at the Lama Temple, the Ancient Observatory, Wangfujing, and Tiananmen Square. Taxi travel during peak hours (7 to 9 AM and 5 to 8 PM) is difficult. At other times traveling by taxi is affordable, convenient, and the fastest option (especially at noon, when much of the city is at lunch, and after 10 PM). Renting a bike to see the sites is also a good option. ⚠ If you do rent a bike, be extremely cautious of traffic. Think about renting a helmet as well. Bus travel within the city, especially during rush hours, is laborious and should be avoided unless you speak or read Chinese.

MAKING THE MOST OF YOUR TIME

Most of Dongcheng can be seen in a day, but it's best to set aside two, because the **Forbidden City** and **Tiananmen Square** will likely take the better part of one day. The climb up Coal Hill (also called Prospect Hill) in **Jingshan Park** will take about 30 minutes for an average walker. From there, hop a taxi to the **Lama Temple**, which is worth a good two hours, then visit the nearby **Confucius Temple**.

DID YOU KNOW?

The Lama Temple (Yonghe Temple) is one of the largest and most important Tibetan Buddhist monasteries in the world. The building originally served as an official residence for court eunuchs but was later turned into a lamasery. In addition to many other works of art, in the center of the hall you'll find the Temple's 55-feet-high golden statue of Maitreya Buddha. The temple is rumored to have survived the Cultural Revolution thanks to the intervention of Prime Minister Zhou Enlai.

2

★ **Lama Temple 雍和宫**. Beijing's most-visited religious site and one of the most important functioning Buddhist temples in Beijing, this Tibetan Buddhist masterpiece has five main halls and numerous galleries hung with finely detailed *thangkhas* (Tibetan religious scroll paintings). The entire temple is decorated with Buddha images—all guarded by somber lamas dressed in brown robes. Originally a palace for Prince Yong-zheng, it was transformed into a temple once he became the Qing's third emperor in 1723. The temple flourished under Emperor Qianlong, housing some 500 resident monks. This was once the official "embassy" of Tibetan Buddhism in Beijing but today only about two-dozen monks live in this complex.

DID YOU KNOW?

Unlike most "feudal" sites in Beijing, the Lama Temple survived the 1966–1976 Cultural Revolution unscathed on the direct orders of Premier Zhou Enlai.

Don't miss the **The Hall of Heavenly Kings**, with statues of Maitreya, the future Buddha, and Weitou, China's guardian of Buddhism, this hall is worth a slow stroll. In the courtyard beyond, a pond with a bronze mandala represents paradise. The Statues of Buddhas of the Past, Present, and Future hold court in **The Hall of Harmony**. Look on the west wall where an exquisite silk thangkha of White Tara—the embodiment of compassion—hangs. Images of the Medicine and Longevity Buddhas line **The Hall of Eternal Blessing**. In **The Pavilion of Ten Thousand Fortunes** you see the breathtaking 26-meter (85-foot) Maitreya Buddha carved from a single sandalwood block. ■TIP→ Combine a visit to the Lama Temple with the Confucius Temple and the Imperial Academy, which are a five-minute walk away, within the hutong neighborhood opposite the main entrance. ☒ *12 Yonghegong Dajie, Beixingqiao, Dongcheng District* ☎ *010/6404–4499* ☐ *Y25* ☼ *Daily 9–4:30* Ⓜ *Yonghegong, Line 2.*

Fodor's Choice

★ **Tiananmen Square 天安门广场**. The world's largest public square, and the very heart of modern China, Tiananmen Square owes little to grand imperial designs and everything to Mao Zedong. At the height of the Cultural Revolution, hundreds of thousands of Red Guards crowded the square; in June 1989 the square was the scene of tragedy when student demonstrators were killed.

Today the square is packed with sightseers, families, and undercover policemen. Although formidable, the square is a little bleak, with no shade, benches, or trees. Come here at night for an eerie experience—it's a little like being on a film set. Beijing's ancient central axis runs right through the center of Mao Zedong's mausoleum, the Forbidden City, the Drum and Bell towers, and the Olympic Green. The square is sandwiched between two grand gates: the Gate of Heavenly Peace (Tiananmen) to the north and the Front Gate (Qianmen) in the south. Along the western edge is the Great Hall of the People. The National Museum of China lies along the eastern side. The 125-foot granite obelisk you see is the Monument to the People's Heroes; it commemorates those who died for the revolutionary cause of the Chinese people. ☒ *Bounded by Chang'an Jie to the north and Qianmen Dajie to the south, Dongcheng District* ☐ *Free* ☼ *24-hrs year-round* Ⓜ *Tiananmen East.*

A network of tunnels lies beneath Tiananmen Square. Mao Zedong is said to have ordered them dug in the late 1960s after Sino-Soviet relations soured. They extend across Beijing.

Wangfujing 王府井. Wangfujing, one of the city's oldest and busiest shopping districts, is still lined with a handful of *laozihao*, or old brand name shops, some dating back a century. This short walking street is a pleasant place for window-shopping. Also on Wangfujing is the gleaming Oriental Plaza, with it's expensive high-end shops (think Tiffany's, KENZO, Paul Smith, Burberry, Ermenegildo Zegna, and Audi), interspersed with Levi Jeans, Esprit, Starbucks, Pizza Hut, KFC, Häagen-Dazs and a modern cinema multicomplex. ⊠ *Wangfujing, Dongcheng District.*

IF YOU HAVE TIME

Ditan Park *(Temple of Earth Park)* 地坛公园. In this 16th-century park are the square altar where emperors once made sacrifices to the earth god and the Hall of Deities. This is a lovely place for a stroll, especially if you're already near the Drum Tower or Lama Temple. ⊠ *Yonghegong Jie, just north of Second Ring Rd., Dongcheng District* 🕾 *010/6421–4657* 🎫 *Y2* 🕙 *Daily 6 AM–9 PM.*

Guijie *(Ghost Street)* 簋街. This 1442-meter stretch is lined with more than 100 restaurants, many open 24 hours a day, so it attracts the spill off from nightclubs. Although the restaurants here are generally just average, at night the street is crawling with diners, more likely attracted by shiny red lanterns and lights than the food. There are a wide number of cuisines and restaurants serve a diversity of dishes, including Sichuan, Beijing, Cantonese, Xinjiang, and much more. ⊠ *Guijie, Dongcheng District.*

Mao Zedong Memorial Hall 毛主席纪念堂. Sentries here will assure that your communion with the Great Helmsman is brief. After waiting in a long winding line, you'll be guided into a spacious lobby dominated by a marble Mao statue and then to the Hall of Reverence, where his embalmed body lies in state, wrapped in the red flag of the Communist Party of China inside a crystal coffin that is lowered each night into a subterranean freezer. In a bid to limit Mao's deification, a second-story museum was added in 1983; it's dedicated to the former Premier Zhou Enlai, former general Zhu De, and China's president before the Cultural Revolution, Liu Shaoqi (who was persecuted to death during the Cultural Revolution). The hall's builders willfully ignored Tiananmen Square's geomancy: the mausoleum faces north, boldly contradicting centuries of imperial ritual. ⊠ *Tiananmen Sq., Dongcheng District* 🕾 *010/6513–2277* 🎫 *Free* 🕙 *Tues.–Sun. 8 AM–11:30 AM.*

Nanxincang 南新仓. China's oldest existing granary, dating back to the Yongle period (1403–24), is now Beijing's newest entertainment venue. It's home to three art galleries, a teahouse, and several bars and restaurants. The structures at Nanxincang—just 10 years younger than those of the Forbidden City—were among the more than 300 granaries that existed in this area during imperial days. Have a glass of wine on the second floor of Yuefu, an audio and book shop, where you can admire

Tiananmen square

the old interior, then have dinner at one of the excellent restaurants in the compound. ⊠ *Dongsi Shitiao, one block west of the Second Ring Road, Dongcheng District.*

The Poly Art Museum 保利艺术博物馆. This very impressive museum, located in the New Poly Plaza, a gleaming new glass office tower, was established in 1998 to promote traditional art and to protect Chinese art from being lost to foreign countries. The museum has focused on the overseas acquisition of ancient bronzes, sculpture, and painting. The museum is divided into two galleries, one for the display of early Chinese bronzes, and the other for Buddhist scriptures carved in stone. ⊠ *Poly Plaza, 9 New Poly Plaza Tower, 1 Chaoyangmen Bei Dajie, Dongcheng District* ♁ *Located next to the Dongshisitiao subway stop on Line 2.* ☎ *010/6500–8117* ☞ *Y20* ⊙ *Daily 9:30–4:30.*

NEED A BREAK? **Crunchy deep-fried scorpions and other critters are sold at the Donghua-men Night Market, at the northern end of Wangfujing's wide walking boulevard.**

Nan Luogu Xiang 南锣鼓巷. The narrow Nan Luogu Xiang, or South Gong and Bell Alley, which goes back some 700 years, got a new lease on life a few years ago when it was discovered by young entrepreneurs who raced in to open blocks and blocks of souvenir shops, boutiques, cafes, bars, and restaurants in the aging but rustic structures that line the sidewalks. The narrow street is flanked by eight historic hutongs to the east and west that are worth exploring. ⊠ *Nan Luogu Xiang, Dongcheng District.*

XICHENG DISTRICT 西城区

Sightseeing
★★★☆☆

Dining
★★☆☆☆

Lodging
★☆☆☆☆

Shopping
★★☆☆☆

Nightlife
★★★☆☆

Xicheng District is home to an eclectic mix of a few of Beijing's favorite things: delicious food, venerable hutongs and old courtyard houses, charming lakes, and engaging nightlife. The lakes at Shichahai are fun for all ages, both day and night. Take a boat ride on the lake in the warmer months, or ice-skate here in the cold winter months when the lakes are crowded with parents taking their children out for a day of fun.

Our top experience? Taking a walk or bicycle tour of the surrounding hutongs: there is no better way to scratch the surface of this sprawling city (before it disappears!) than by exploring the hutongs lined by courtyard houses. Wander in and out of historic sites in the area, such as Prince Gong's palace, the courtyard house of famed opera legend Mei Lanfang and the Drum and Bell towers (which fall right between Dongcheng and Xicheng). In the evening, find a restaurant or bar with a view of the lake.

SNAPSHOT

Time seems to be standing still in the Yangfang Hutong. A street stand sells steamed meat buns beside a parked cart piled high with watermelons. Peddlers shout out while, at the corner, boys crowd around a hawker with dozens of small woven baskets the size of plums. Inside are crickets. A gaggle of grandmothers sit on short stools nearby, some holding grandchildren, others snoozing in the sun. One woman hangs her thick cotton blanket to air out. Pedicabs glide by, on constant prowl for passengers. Along the lake elderly men are absorbed in the same pastimes that their ancestors enjoyed a century ago. One group, sitting beneath a willow tree, is playing Chinese chess, another mah-jongg—the sound of clicking tiles can be heard long before you reach the spot.

Beihai Park.

A GOOD WALK

Start just north of the Forbidden City at **Jingshan Park.** From here you can walk several blocks west to the south gate of **Beihai Park,** which is beautiful in August's lotus season. Exit at the north gate; after crossing Di'anmen Xi Dajie, you'll arrive at **Qianhai,** or "front lake."

Walk on the right, or east, side of the lake for about 10 minutes until you reach the famous Ming Dynasty **Silver Ingot Bridge.** Take a side trip to the **Bell Tower,** which is a short walk northeast of the bridge. (To get there, head down Yandai Xiejie, turn left at the end and you'll see the tower. Directly behind it is the Drum Tower.) Return to the Silver Ingot Bridge and follow the lake's northern shore until you arrive at **Soong Ching-ling's Former Residence.** Next, take a short cab ride to **Prince Gong's Palace** behind the opposite side of the lake, to see how imperial relatives once lived. An alternative to those lavish interiors is the **Museum of Antique Currency,** where you can feast your eyes on rare Chinese coins.

EXPLORING

TOP ATTRACTIONS

★ **Beihai Park 北海.** A white stupa is perched on a small island just north of the south gate. Also at the south entrance is the **Round City,** which contains a white-jade Buddha and an enormous jade bowl given to Kublai Khan. Nearby, the well-restored **Temple of Eternal Peace** houses a variety of Buddhas. Climb to the stupa from Yongan Temple. Once there, you can pay an extra Y1 to ascend the Buddha-bedecked **Shanyin Hall.**

GETTING ORIENTED

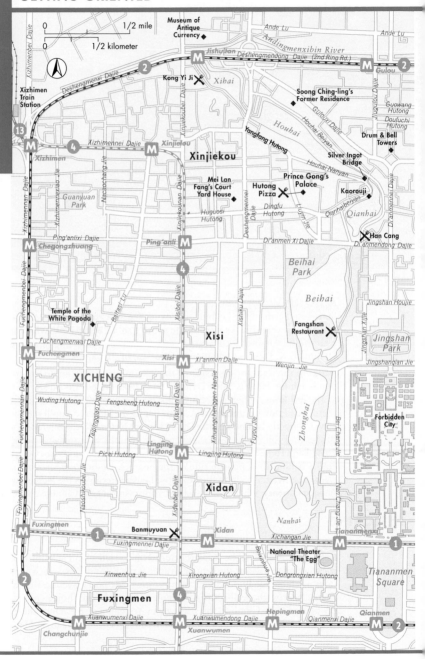

MAKING THE MOST OF YOUR TIME

Xicheng's must-see sites are few in number but all special. Walk around **Beihai Park** in the early afternoon. When you get tired, either retire to one of Houhai's many cafés or take a pedicab hutong tour. If you come to Beijing in the winter, **Qianhai** will be frozen and you can rent skates, runner-equipped bicycles to pedal across the ice or, the local favorite, a chair with runners welded to the bottom and a pair of metal sticks with which to propel yourself—quite a tiring sport. Dinner along the shores of **Houhai** is a great option—stick around into the evening to enjoy the booming bar scene. Plan to spend a few hours shopping at **Xidan** on your last day in Beijing; this is great place to pick up funky, cheap gifts.

QUICK BITES

The shores of Houhai and Qianhai are lined with great restaurants. Try **Kong Yi Ji** (☎ 010/6618–4915) on the western edge of Houhai. It's named after a story by famous writer Lu Xun and serves some of the dishes mentioned in the story.

Rustic **Han Cang** (☎ 010/6404–2259) specializes in the hearty dishes of the Hakkas, or China's Guest People. It's located at the southeast corner of Qianhai, on the east side of the lake just two minutes north of Di'anmen Xi Dajie, with a great view of the lake from the second floor.

Hutong Pizza (⊠ 9 Yindingqiao Hutong ☎ 010/8322–8916) is a great choice for their fantastic thin-crust square pies. It's located in a renovated courtyard house in a hutong just west of the Silver Ingot Bridge.

For a simple meal in the Xidan area, try **Banmuyuan** (⊠ 45 Fuxingmen Nei Dajie ☎ 010/5851–8208 Ⓜ Xidan), a Taiwanese-owned restaurant that serves chewy zhajiang noodles, beef dishes, and vegetarian pies. It's located directly behind the Bank of China headquarters (which was designed by I. M. Pei).

GETTING HERE

The Line 1 subway stops include Tiananmen West, Xidan, and Fuxingmen, while Line 2 makes stops from Fuxingmen to the Drum Tower (Gulou), following Xicheng's perimeter. Xizhimen is a major terminus with access to the northwest via subway. ■TIP➔ Houhai and Beihai Park are more conveniently reached by taxi.

NEIGHBORHOOD TOP 5

1. Sipping coffee or an evening cocktail lakeside at **Houhai** or on one of the rooftop restaurants or bars overlooking the lake.

2. Exploring Houhai's well-preserved hutongs and historical sites by pedicab or bicycle.

3. Skating on **Houhai Lake** in winter or, in the warmer months, taking an evening boat tour of the lake. Dine onboard on barbecued lamb provided by **Kaorouji** (⊠ 14 Qianhai Dongyan, just southeast of the Silver Ingot Bridge ☎ 010/6404–2554), an old lakeside restaurant. Romantics, take note: you'll be serenaded by your own personal pipa (four-stringed lute) musician.

4. Wandering the hills and temples of historic Beihai Park. In the evening, eat the way the emperors did with an imperial banquet at **Fangshan Restaurant** (⇨ Chapter 3) in the park.

5. Shopping for great gifts and snazzy clothes on the cheap at **Xidan**.

DID YOU KNOW?

This white porcelain Avalokiteśvara statue can be found in the Capital Museum in Beijing. It was made by the porcelain master He Chaozong during the Ming Dynasty. Avalokiteśvara is a bodhisattva who embodies the compassion of all Buddhas. He (or she) is one of the more widely revered bodhisattvas in mainstream Mahayana Buddhism.

The lake is Beijing's largest and most beautiful public waterway. On summer weekends the lake teems with paddleboats. The **Five Dragon Pavilion,** on Beihai's northwest shore, was built in 1602 by a Ming Dynasty emperor who liked to fish under the moon. ⊠ *Beihai Nan Men, Weijin Lu, Xicheng District* ☎ *010/6404–0610* 🎫 *Y10; extra fees for some sites* ☉ *Daily 6* AM*–8:30* PM.

Capital Museum 首都博物馆. Moved to its architecturally striking new home west of Tiananmen Square in 2005, this is hands down China's finest cultural museum. Artifacts are housed in the unique multistoried bronze cylinder that dominates the building's facade, while paintings, calligraphy, and photographs of historic Beijing fill the remaining exhibition halls. The museum gets extra points for clear English descriptions and modern, informative displays. ⊠ *16 Fuxingmenwai Dajie, Xicheng District* ☎ *010/6337–0491* 🎫 *Y30* ☉ *Tues.–Sun. 9–5.*

Qianhai and Houhai 前海 and 后海. Most people come to these lakes, along with Xihai to the northwest, to stroll and enjoy the shoreside bars and restaurants. In summer you can boat or fish. In winter, sections of the frozen lakes are fenced off for skating. Easily combined with a trip to Beihai Park or the Bell and Drum towers. ⊠ *North of Beihai Lake, Xicheng District.*

Xidan 西单. This is an area full of shopping malls and small shops selling clothing and accessories. There is also Tushu Dasha, aka Beijing Books Building, said to be the biggest bookstore in China, which has a small selection of English books in the basement. Ⓜ *Xidan.*

IF YOU HAVE TIME

Beijing Ancient Architecture Museum 北京古代建筑博物馆. This little-known museum, located inside a Ming Dynasty temple, exhibits photos, objects, and elaborate models of ancient Chinese architecture from ancient huts and mud homes to Ming and Qing Dynasty palaces. The sand-table model of old Beijing is fascinating. ⊠ *21 Dongjing Lu, Xuanwu District* ☎ *010/6301–7620* 🎫 *Y15* ☉ *Daily 9–4.*

Cultural Palace of Nationalities 民族文化宫. Dedicated to the 56 official ethnic groups that make up China's modern population, this museum houses traditional clothing and artifacts from the country's remote border regions. Exhibits on topics like the "peaceful liberation of Tibet" are as interesting for the official government line as for what's left out. Entrance is free, but you'll need to show your passport to get in. ⊠ *49 Fuxingmennei Dajie, next to the Minzu Hotel, Xicheng District* ☎ *010/6602–4433* 🎫 *Free* ☉ *Daily 9–4.*

Great Hall of the People 人民大会堂. This solid edifice owes its Stalinist weight to the last years of the Sino-Soviet pact. Its gargantuan dimensions (205,712 square yards of floor space) exceed that of the Forbidden City. It was built by 14,000 laborers who worked around the clock for eight months. China's legislature meets in the aptly named Ten Thousand People Assembly Hall, beneath a panoply of 500 star lights revolving around a giant red star. Thirty-one reception rooms are distinguished by the arts and crafts of the provinces they represent. Have someone who speaks Chinese call a day ahead to confirm that it's open, as the hall often closes for political events and concerts—call

010/8308–4776. ⊠ *West side of Tiananmen Sq., Xicheng District* ☎ *010/6309–6156* 💳 *Y30* ⊙ *Daily 8:30–3.*

Museum of Antique Currency 北京古代钱币博物馆. This museum in a tiny courtyard house within the Deshengmen tower complex, showcases a small but impressive selection of rare Chinese coins. Explanations are in Chinese only. Also in the courtyard are coin and curio dealers. ⊠ *Deshengmen Jianlou, Bei'erhuan Zhonglu, Xicheng District* ☎ *010/6201–8073* 💳 *Y20* ⊙ *Tues.–Sun. 9–4.*

Prince Gong's Palace 恭王府. This grand compound sits in a neighborhood once reserved for imperial relatives. Built in 1777 during the Qing Dynasty, it fell to Prince Gong—brother of Qing emperor Xianfeng and later an adviser to Empress Dowager Cixi—after the original inhabitant was executed for corruption. With nine courtyards joined by covered walkways, it was once one of Beijing's most lavish residences. The largest hall offers summertime Beijing opera and afternoon tea to guests on guided hutong tours. Some literary scholars believe this was the setting for *Dream of the Red Chamber,* one of China's best-known classical novels. ⊠ *17 Qianhai Xijie, Xicheng District* ☎ *010/8328–8149* 💳 *Y40* ⊙ *Daily 7:30–4:30.*

Soong Ching-ling's Former Residence 宋庆龄故居. Soong Ching-ling (1893–1981) was the youngest daughter of the wealthy, American-educated bible publisher, Charles Soong. At the age of 18, disregarding her family's strong opposition, she eloped to marry the much older Sun Yat-sen. When her husband founded the Republic of China in 1911, Soong Ching-ling became a significant political figure. In 1924 she headed the Women's Department of the Nationalist Party. Then in 1949 she became the vice president of the People's Republic of China. Throughout her career she campaigned tirelessly for the emancipation of women, and she helped lay the foundations for many of the rights that modern-day Chinese women enjoy today. This former palace was her residence and workplace and now houses a small museum, which documents her life and work. ⊠ *46 Houhai Beiyan, Xicheng District* ☎ *010/6407–3653* 💳 *Y20* ⊙ *Daily 9–5.*

Temple of the White Pagoda 白塔. This 13th-century Tibetan stupa, the largest of its kind in China, dates from Kublai Khan's reign and owes its beauty to an unnamed Nepalese architect who built it to honor Shakyamuni Buddha. It stands bright and white against the Beijing skyline. Once hidden within the structure were Buddha statues, sacred texts, and other holy relics. Many of the statues are now on display in glass cases in the **Miaoying** temple, at the foot of the stupa. There is also a great English-language display on the temple's history and renovation. ⊠ *Fuchenmennei Dajie near Zhaodengyu Lu, Xicheng District* ☎ *010/6616–0211* 💳 *Y20* ⊙ *Tues.–Sun. 9–4.*

SOUTHERN DISTRICTS: CHONGWEN AND XUANWU 崇文区 AND 宣武区

Sightseeing
★★★☆☆
Dining
★★☆☆☆
Lodging
★☆☆☆☆
Shopping
★★★☆☆
Nightlife
★☆☆☆☆

Life in the southern part of Beijing has a completely different rhythm. The sites in this part of town are ancient reminders of the Beijing that once was—a more religious and artistically inspired Beijing, a Beijing as rich in culture and history as it was in resources and political power. This area is crowded with small shops, European architecture, opera and acrobatic theaters, and street performers and magicians. A lazy stroll through Source of Law Temple or Antiques Street (Liulichang) on a quiet afternoon is sure to remind you of the city's past.

SNAPSHOT

Dazhalan, a street and neighborhood in Xuanwu, immediately southwest of the Forbidden City, is packed with people, cars, and bicycles—each competing for the limited space on its narrow streets, already crowded with hawkers' stands and overflowing restaurants. Dive into the hutong and you are immediately rubbing elbows with the masses. Many *laozihao*, or old brand-name shops, continue to do a booming business here.

The **Ruifuxiang Silk Shop** 瑞蚨祥绸布店 (⊠ *5 Dazhalan Dajie* ☎ *010/6303–5313*), established in 1893, has thick bolts of silk, cotton, cashmere, and wool piled high, in more colors than you'll find in a box of crayons: chartreuse, candy-pink, chocolate-brown, fresh-cut-grass-green—you name it. Clerks deftly cut yards of cloth while tailors take measurements for colorful *qipaos* (traditional gowns). In this corner of Beijing, life seems to continue much as it did a century ago.

GETTING ORIENTED

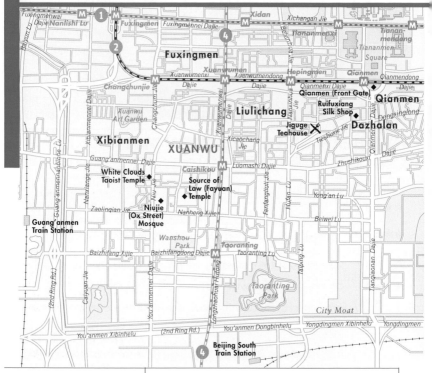

GETTING HERE

The southern portion of the Line 2 subway runs across the northern fringe of these districts, making stops at Beijing Train Station, Chongwenmen, Qianmen, Hepingmen, Xuanwumen, and Changchun Jie. Line 5 stops at the Temple of Heaven and runs north–south with transfers to Line 1 at Dongdan, and transfers to Line 2 at Chongwenmen and the Lama Temple.

For destinations in the south of Chongwen and Xuanwu, it's advisable to take a taxi, as things are a bit more spread out, and it may be hard to find your way on foot.

MAKING THE MOST OF YOUR TIME

The southern districts of Beijing have some great attractions beyond the major players, like the **Temple of Heaven.**

Liulichang is renowned for paintings and Chinese art supplies; it's worth spending a few hours browsing here. The **Source of Law Temple** and the **Niujie Mosque** are laid-back, interesting temples; a trip to one makes visiting the other quite easy, as they are very close together. Visiting the reconstructed **Ming Dynasty City Wall Ruins** makes for a pleasant stroll before dinner.

WORD OF MOUTH

"In Beijing, both Liulichang and Wangfujing have some interesting shopping. However, more and more of the old buildings are being torn down. Of the two, Liulichang is probably more charming. I assume you will be doing a tour of the old hutongs and Bell/Drum towers. That is one of the best ways to see the old Beijing." –Cicerone

2

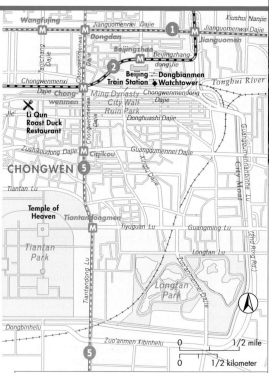

QUICK BITES

Old shops line the sides of Liulichang, where high-rises are juxtaposed with ancient courtyards and teahouses.

You can get a bowl of noodles and a cup of tea upstairs at the **Jiguge Teahouse** (⊠ *136 Liulichang Dong Jie 136* ☏ *010/ 6301–7846*), next to the stone pedestrian bridge.

Every nonvegetarian visitor to the city should sample Beijing duck at least once.

Though it's not the best-known spot, **Li Qun Roast Duck Restaurant** (⇨ *Chapter 3*) has the most succulent, tasty duck around; it's located in an old courtyard house and has interesting 1950s decor.

NEIGHBORHOOD TOP 5

1. Exploring the sprawling grounds of the **Temple of Heaven**.

2. Checking out the old art-supply shops and galleries at **Liulichang**.

3. Walking down Ox Street with a visit to the **Niujie Mosque** and the **Source of Law Temple**.

4. A walk along the rebuilt section of the **Ming Dynasty City Wall Ruins** along Chongwenmen Dajie and a visit to the **Red Gate Gallery** in the Dongbianmen Watch Tower.

5. Eating Beijing duck and other toothsome treats at one of the many restaurants around **Qianmen**.

EXPLORING

TOP ATTRACTIONS

Dongbianmen Watch Tower 东便门角楼. This is Beijing's last remaining Ming watchtower. Be sure to check out the Red Gate Gallery located inside, which shows works by well-known contemporary Chinese artists. The gallery was set up in 1991 by Brian Wallace, an Australian who studied art history at China's Central Academy of Fine Arts. The second and third floors are devoted to the history of the Chongwen District. ⊠ *Dongbianmen Watchtower, Chongwen District* ☎ *010/6525–1005* ⊕ *www.redgategallery.com* ✉ *Free* ☽ *Daily 9–5.*

★ **Liulichang** (*Antiques Street*) **琉璃厂**. This quaint old street is best known for its antiques, books, and paintings. The street has been completely restored and a multitude of small shops, many privately owned, make it a fun place to explore, even if you're just window-shopping. Liulichang was built more than 500 years ago during the Ming Dynasty. It was the site of a large factory that made glazed tiles for the Imperial Palace. Gradually other smaller tradesmen began to cluster around and at the beginning of the Qing Dynasty, many booksellers moved there. The area became a meeting place for intellectuals and a prime shopping district for art objects, books, handicrafts, and antiques. In 1949, Liulichang still had over 170 shops, but many were taken over by the state; the street was badly ransacked during the Cultural Revolution. Following large-scale renovation of the traditional architecture, the street reopened in 1984 under the policy that shops could only sell arts, crafts, and cultural objects. Today the street is a mixture of state-run and privately owned stores. ⊠ *Liulichang, Xuanwu District.*

Ming Dynasty City Wall Ruins Park 明城墙遗址公园. The new Ming Dynasty City Wall Ruins Park is a renovated section of Beijing's old inner-city wall. The structure was rebuilt using original bricks that had been snatched decades earlier after the city wall had been torn down. This rebuilt section of the wall is a nicely landscaped area with paths full of Chinese walking their dogs, flying kites, practicing martial arts, and playing with their children. At the eastern end of the park is the grand Dongbianmen Watch Tower, home to the popular Red Gate Gallery. ⊠ *Dongbianmen, Dongdajie Street Chongwen District* ✉ *Free* ☽ *Daily 8–5:30.*

★ **Niujie (Ox Street) Mosque 牛街清真寺**. Originally built during the Liao Dynasty in 996, Nuijie is Beijing's oldest and largest mosque. It sits at the center of the Muslim quarter and mimics a Chinese temple from the outside, with its hexagonal wooden structure. When the mosque was built, only traditional Chinese architecture was allowed in the capital. An exception was made for the Arabic calligraphy that decorates many of the mosque's walls and inner sanctums. The interior arches and posts are inscribed with Koranic verse, and a special moon tower helps with determining the lunar calendar. The Spirit Wall stands opposite the main entrance and prevents ghosts from entering the mosque, this wall covered with carved murals works on the premise that ghosts can't turn sharp corners. Two dark tombs with Chinese and Arabic inscriptions are kept in one of the small courtyards. They belong to two Persian

Liulichang (Antiques Street) in the Xuanwu District.

imams who came to preach at the mosque in the 13th and 14th centuries. Because Muslims must pray in the direction of Mecca, which is westward, the main prayer hall opens onto the east. At the rear of the complex is a minaret from which a muezzin calls the faithful to prayer. From this very tower, imams (the prayer leaders of a mosque) measure the beginning and end of Ramadan, Islam's month of fasting and prayer. Ramadan begins when the imam sights the new moon, which appears as a slight crescent.

The hall is open only to Muslims and can fit up to 1,000 worshippers. All visitors must wear long trousers or skirts and keep their shoulders covered. Women are not permitted to enter some areas. It's most convenient to get to the mosque by taxi. If you want to take the subway, it's a 20-minute walk from Line 2's Changchunjie station, though Line 4 will get you closer when it opens. ⊠ *88 Niu Jie, Xuanwu District* 🖃 *Y10* ⊘ *Daily 6* AM–8 PM.

Fodor's Choice **Temple of Heaven** 天坛. A prime example of Chinese religious architec-
★   ture, this is where emperors once performed important rites. It was a site for imperial sacrifices, meant to please the gods so they would generate bumper harvests. Set in a huge, serene, mushroom-shaped park southeast of the Forbidden City, the Temple of Heaven is surrounded by splendid examples of Ming Dynasty architecture, including curved cobalt blue roofs layered with yellow and green tiles. Construction began in the early 15th century under Yongle, whom many call the "architect of Beijing." Shaped like a semicircle on the northern rim to represent heaven and square on the south for the earth, the grounds were once believed to be the meeting point of the two. The area is

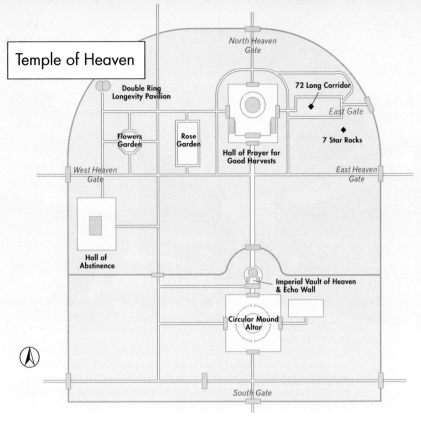

North Heaven Gate

Double Ring Longevity Pavilion

72 Long Corridor

East Gate

Flowers Garden

Rose Garden

7 Star Rocks

West Heaven Gate

Hall of Prayer for Good Harvests

East Heaven Gate

Hall of Abstinence

Imperial Vault of Heaven & Echo Wall

Circular Mound Altar

South Gate

double the size of the Forbidden City and is still laid out to divine rule: buildings and paths are positioned to represent the right directions for heaven and earth. This means, for example, that the northern part is higher than the south.

The temple's hallmark structure is a magnificent **blue-roofed wooden tower** built in 1420. It burned to the ground in 1889 and was immediately rebuilt using Ming architectural methods (and timber imported from Oregon). The building's design is based on the calendar: 4 center pillars represent the seasons, the next 12 pillars represent months, and 12 outer pillars signify the parts of a day. Together these 28 poles, which also correspond to the 28 constellations of heaven, support the structure without nails. A carved dragon swirling down from the ceiling represents the emperor.

Across the Danbi Bridge, you'll find the **Hall of Prayer for Good Harvests**. The middle section was once reserved for the Emperor of Heaven, who was the only one allowed to set foot on the eastern side, while aristocrats and high-ranking officials walked on the western strip. ■ **TIP→** If you're coming by taxi, enter the park through the southern entrance (Tiantan Nanmen). This way you approach the beautiful Hall of Prayer for Good Harvests via the Danbi Bridge—the same route the emperor favored.

MAO ZEDONG (1893–1976)

Some three decades after his passing, Mao Zedong continues to evoke radically different feelings. Was he the romantic poet-hero who helped the Chinese stand up against foreign aggression? Or was he a monster whose policies caused the deaths of tens of millions of people? Born into a relatively affluent farming family in Hunan, Mao became active in politics at a young age; he was one of the founding members of the Chinese Communist Party in 1921. When the People's Republic of China was established in 1949, Mao served as chairman. After a good start in improving the economy, he launched radical programs in the mid-1950s. The party's official assessment is that Mao was 70% correct and 30% incorrect. His critics reverse this ratio.

Directly east of this hall is a long, twisting platform, which once enclosed the animal-killing pavilion, the Long Corridor was traditionally hung with lanterns on the eve of sacrifices. Today it plays host to scores of Beijingers singing opera, playing cards and chess, and fan dancing.

Be sure to whisper into the echo wall encircling the **Imperial Vault of Heaven**. This structure allows anyone to eavesdrop. It takes a minute to get the hang of it, but with a friend on one side and you on the other it's possible to hold a conversation by speaking into the wall. Tilt your head in the direction you want your voice to travel for best results. Just inside the south gate is the **Round Altar**, a three-tiered, white-marble structure where the emperor worshipped the winter solstice; it is based around the divine number nine. Nine was regarded as a symbol of the power of the emperor, as it is the biggest single-digit odd number, and odd numbers are considered masculine and therefore more powerful.

The Hall of Abstinence, on the western edge of the grounds, this is where the emperor would retreat three days before the ritual sacrifice. To understand the significance of the harvest sacrifice at the Temple of Heaven, it is important to keep in mind that the legitimacy of a Chinese emperor's rule depended on what is known as the *tian ming*, or the mandate of heaven, essentially the emperor's relationship with the gods.

A succession of bad harvests, for example, could be interpreted as the emperor losing the favor of heaven and could be used to justify a change in emperor or even in dynasty. When the emperor came to the Temple of Heaven to pray for good harvests and to pay homage to his ancestors, there may have been a good measure of self-interest to his fervor.

The sacrifices consisted mainly of animals and fruit placed on altars surrounded by candles. Many Chinese still offer sacrifices of fruit and incense on special occasions, such as births, deaths, and weddings.

■TIP➡ **We recommend buying an all-inclusive ticket. If you only buy a ticket into the park, you will need to pay an additional Y20 to get into each building.**

Beijing's new subway Line 5 (purple line) makes getting to the Temple of Heaven easier than ever. Get off at the Tiantan Dongmen (Temple

祈年殿

DID YOU KNOW?

The Temple of Heaven's overall layout symbolizes the relationship between Heaven and Earth. Earth is represented by a square and Heaven by a circle. The temple complex is surrounded by two cordons of walls; the taller outer wall is semi-circular at the northern end (Heaven) and shorter and rectangular at the southern end (Earth). Both the Hall of Prayer for Good Harvests and the Circular Mound Altar are round structures on a square yard.

TIPS FOR TOURING WITH KIDS

Although incense-filled temples and ancient buildings do not, at first glance, seem child-friendly, Beijing's historic sites do offer some unique and special activities for under-agers. The Summer Palace is a great place for kids to run around and go splashing in paddle-boats; the old Summer Palace has a fun maze; Tiananmen Square is a popular spot to fly kites; the Drum Tower holds percussion performances; and the Temple of Heaven's Echo Wall offers up some unusual acoustical fun.

Budding astronomers might also be intrigued by the Ancient Observatory with its Ming Dynasty star map and early heaven-gazing devices built by early Jesuit missionaries who worked for the imperial court. Wherever you go, remember this: Chinese kids are generally allowed to run around and act like children, so don't worry that your own tyke's behavior will be viewed as inappropriate.

of Heaven East Gate) stop. The line also runs to the Lama Temple (Yonghegong), so combining the two sites in a day makes perfect sense.

Automatic audio guides (Y40) are available at stalls inside all four entrances. ⊠ *Yongdingmen Dajie (South Gate), Xuanwu District* ☎ *010/6702–8866* 🎫 *All-inclusive ticket Y35; entrance to park only Y15* ⊙ *Daily 6*AM*–10*PM*; ticket booth closes 4:30* PM.

IF YOU HAVE TIME

Qianmen (Front Gate) 前门大街. From its top looking south, you can see that the Qianmen is actually two gates: Sun-Facing Gate (Zhengyangmen) and Arrow Tower (Jian Lou), which was, until 1915, connected to Zhengyangmen by a defensive half-moon wall. The central gates of both structures opened only for the emperor's biannual ceremonial trips to the Temple of Heaven. The gate now defines the southern edge of Tiananmen Square. ⊠ *Xuanwumen Jie, Xuanwu District* Ⓜ *Qianmen.*

Source of Law Temple 法源寺. This temple is also a school for monks—the Chinese Buddhist Theoretical Institute houses and trains them here. Of course, the temple functions within the boundaries of current regime policy. You can observe both elderly practitioners chanting mantras in the main prayer halls, as well as robed students kicking soccer balls in a side courtyard. Before lunch the smells of a vegetarian stir-fry tease the nose. The dining hall has simple wooden tables set with cloth-wrapped bowls and chopsticks. Dating from the 7th century but last rebuilt in 1442, the temple holds a fine collection of Ming and Qing statues, including a sleeping Buddha and an unusual grouping of copper-cast Buddhas seated on a 1,000-petal lotus. ⊠ *7 Fayuan Si Qianjie, Xuanwu District* ☎ *010/6353–4171* 🎫 *Y5* ⊙ *Daily 8:30–3:30.*

White Clouds Taoist Temple 白云观. This lively Taoist temple founded in the 8th century serves as a center for China's only indigenous religion. Monks wearing blue-cotton coats and black-satin hats roam the grounds in silence. Thirty of them now live at the monastery, which also houses the official All-China Taoist Association. Visitors bow and burn incense to their favorite deities, wander the back gardens in search of a master of *qigong* (a series of exercises that involve slow movements and meditative breathing techniques), and rub the bellies of the temple's three monkey statues for good fortune.

In the first courtyard, under the span of an arched bridge, hang two large brass bells. Ringing them with a well-tossed coin is said to bring wealth. In the main courtyards, the **Shrine Hall for Seven Perfect Beings** is lined with meditation cushions and low desks. Nearby is a museum of Taoist history (explanations in Chinese). In the western courtyard, the temple's oldest structure is a shrine housing the **60-Year Protector.** Here the faithful locate the deity that corresponds to their birth year, bow to it, light incense, then scribble their names, or even a poem, on the wooden statue's red-cloth cloak as a reminder of their dedication. A trinket stall in the front courtyard sells pictures of each protector deity. Also in the west courtyard is a shrine to Taoist sage Wen Ceng, depicted in a 3-meter- (10-foot-) tall bronze statue just outside the shrine's main entrance. Students flock here to rub Wen Ceng's belly for good luck on their college entrance exams. The area around the temple is packed with fortune-tellers. ⊠ *Lianhuachidong Lu near Xibianmen Bridge, Xuanwu District* ☎ *010/6346–3531* ☜ *Y10* ☉ *Daily 8:30–4:30.*

MUSLIM QUARTER

Recent urban renewal has wiped out much of Beijing's old Muslim Quarter, one of the oldest areas in the city dating back to the tenth century. The main survivor is the **Niujie (Ox Street) Mosque**, which was built in 996; it is often crowded with members of Beijing's Muslim community. Like other mosques in China, the Niujie Mosque looks like a traditional Buddhist temple with the addition of inscriptions in Arabic. The Tower for Observing the Moon and the main hall have restricted entry, and women can only visit certain areas. A few Muslim shops—mainly halal restaurants and butchers—remain in the neighborhood, which is now dominated by high-rise apartment buildings.

CHAOYANG DISTRICT 朝阳区

Sightseeing
★☆☆☆☆
Dining
★★★★☆
Lodging
★★★★☆
Shopping
★★★★☆
Nightlife
★★★★☆

Chaoyang is where you'll find a lot of the action in Beijing: the nightlife in this district is positively sizzling. The bars and clubs are vibrant and full of Chinese office workers and university students as well as foreigners including expats, English teachers, and embassy staff. During the day, all these people work in this area, as it's home to the CBD (Central Business District), as well as the embassies and the residences of the people who run Beijing's portion of the global economy.

SNAPSHOT

A steady stream of Beijing's beautiful people passes through the north gate of the **Workers' Stadium,** drawn toward the hip-hop music that throbs from several of the bars that have displaced spaces once devoted to basketball and Ping-Pong. The crowd runs the gamut from Chinese college kids to well-heeled Beijing tycoons to Mongolian prostitutes, plus expats and foreign diplomats. Downstairs in Vics it's wall-to-wall people who are drinking, dancing, or lost in conversation. A young woman, French beret pulled down over her eyes, leans against her boyfriend; an older woman straight from the society pages of Hong Kong's newspapers sips wine. There's even a Chinese Elvis, his hair defying physics to remain aloft inches into the air. Welcome to the new China.

BY THE LAKE

If you're near Ritan Park and need a nighttime (or afternoon) pick-me-up, check out the **Stone Boat Café,** located on the west side of the park alongside the lake. (Use Ritan Park's West Gate entrance if arriving after 9 PM.)

GETTING ORIENTED

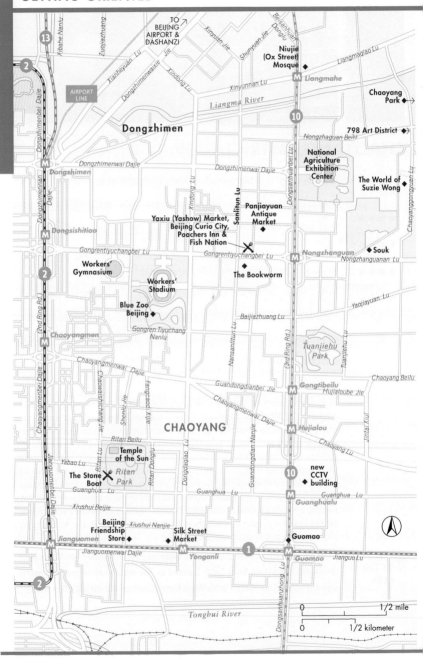

QUICK BITES

If you're looking for Western food, check out the restaurants surrounding **Poachers Inn** (✉ *43 Bei Sanlitun Lu* ☎ *010/ 6417–2632 Ext. 8506*), which is behind the Yashow Market. **Fish Nation** (✉ *On the north side of the Poachers Inn* ☎ *010/6415–0119*) has inexpensive fantastic fish-and-chips.

The Serbian-owned **Kiosk** (✉ *On Nali St., a lane off Sanlitun*), serves excellent chicken and sausage gyros on crisp baguettes.

Annie's Café (✉ *Chaoyang Park West Gate* ☎ *010/6951– 1931* ✉ *88 Jianguo Lu, west side of SOHO New Town*) has two locations serving up great pizza and Italian-American style specialties in a family-friendly atmosphere.

NEIGHBORHOOD TOP 5

1. Grab dinner in Sanlitun and if you're up for a long walk (40 minutes at least), head down to the **Stone Boat Café** (Ritan Park) for a well-mixed drink in an idyllic setting.

2. Check out what's really going on in Chinese art today in the **798 Art District.** After strolling through the galleries, grab something to eat or a drink at one of the many hip bars or cafés within the factory complex.

3. Do some shopping at the **Yashow Market,** where you can buy anything from knockoff jeans to a custom-tailored suit. Then take a half-hour walk north on **Sanlitun North Street** and pick a place to grab an espresso or some top-quality Western grub.

4. Enjoy a drink or meal, along with some great books, at **The Bookworm** in the first alley to the left on Sanlitun South Street. Readings and musical events take place throughout the week, usually in the evening.

5. Go for an early-morning stroll in **Chaoyang Park** and watch the traditional Chinese exercises.

GETTING HERE

The heart of Chaoyang District is accessible via Lines 1 and 2 on the subway, but the district is huge and the sites are broadly distributed. Taking taxis between sites is usually the easiest way to get around. The 798 Art District is especially far away from central Beijing, and so a taxi is also the best bet (about Y30 from the center of town). Buses go everywhere, but they are slow and amazingly crowded.

MAKING THE MOST OF YOUR TIME

You can spend years lost in the Chaoyang District and never get bored. There's plenty to do, but very few historical sights. Spend a morning shopping at the **Silk Alley Market** or **Panjiayuan Antiques Market** and the afternoon cooling off at **Ritan Park** or Chaoyang Park, the latter a large and pleasant park with a lot of activities for kids. Next, head to one of the numerous bar streets for refreshment. If you like contemporary art, browse the galleries at **798 Art District.** There are a number of nice cafés here as well. **Vincent Café & Creperie** (☎ *010/8456–4823*) serves a variety of crepes and fondues. **Cafe Pause** has great coffee, a modest but good wine selection, and great atmosphere.

EXPLORING

TOP ATTRACTIONS

★ **798 Art District** 798艺术区. The Art District, to northeast of Beijing, is the site of several state-owned factories, including Factory 798, which originally produced electronics. Beginning in 2002, artists and cultural organizations began to move into the area, gradually developing the old buildings into galleries, art centers, artists' studios, design companies, restaurants, and bars. There are regularly scheduled art exhibits. ⊠ *Chaoyang District.*

Ancient Observatory 北京古观象台. This squat tower of primitive stargazing equipment peeks out next to the elevated highways of the Second Ring Road. It dates to the time of Genghis Khan, who believed that his fortunes could be read in the stars. Many of the bronze devices on display were gifts from Jesuit missionaries who arrived in Beijing and shortly thereafter ensconced themselves as the Ming court's resident stargazers. To China's imperial rulers, interpreting the heavens was key to holding onto power; a ruler knew when, say, an eclipse would occur, or he could predict the best time to plant crops. Celestial phenomena like eclipses and comets were believed to portend change; if left unheeded they might cost an emperor his legitimacy—or mandate of heaven. Records of celestial observations at or near this site go back more than 500 years, making this the longest documented astronomical viewing site in the world.

The main astronomical devices are arranged on the roof. **Writhing bronze dragon** sculptures adorn some of the astronomy pieces at Jianguo Tower, the main building that houses the observatory. Among the sculptures are an armillary sphere to pinpoint the position of heavenly bodies and a sextant to measure angular distances between stars, along with a celestial globe. Inside, the dusty exhibition rooms shelter ancient star maps with information dating back to the Tang Dynasty. A Ming Dynasty star map and ancient charts are also on display. Most of the ancient instruments were looted by the Allied Forces in 1900, only to be returned to China at the end of World War I. ⊠ *2 Dongbiaobei Hutong, Jianguomenwai Dajie, Chaoyang District* ☎ *010/6524–2202* 🚇 *Y10* 🕐 *Daily 9–4* Ⓜ *Jianguomen.*

Central Business District (CBD) 商业中心区. The fast-rising CBD encompasses the **China World Trade Center** (the recently completed third tower is the tallest building in Beijing) and a slew of new and impressive skyscrapers, some designed by internationally known architects. One example is the new CCTV Tower. The multimillion-dollar complex employs a continuous loop of horizontal and vertical sections, and locals have taken to calling it the "boxer shorts" or "bird's legs" building. Opposite the China World Trade Center is Jianwai Soho, a collection of gleaming white high-rises in a nicely laid-out complex with dozens of restaurants and shops and the Park Hyatt Hotel, one of Beijing's most stylish hotels. ⊠ *Chaoyang District.*

Ritan Park *(Temple of the Sun Park)* 日坛公园. A cool oasis of water and trees just west of the Central Business District, Ritan Park is highly popular. Locals go to stretch their legs, but the embassy crowd is drawn

798 Art District Dashanzi in the Chaoyang district

in by the mojitos served at the Stone Boat. ⊠ *Ritan Lu, northeast of Jianguomen, Dongcheng District* ☎ *010/8561–4261* ⊠ *Free* ⊙ *Daily* 6AM–9PM.

Sanlitun 三里屯. The famous Sanlitun Bar Street, several blocks east of the Workers' Stadium, is known for great bars catering to foreigners, expats, and young Chinese. The hottest clubs are always changing, but Vics and Mix at the north gate of the Workers' Stadium are popular places. The Village, Beijing's hottest shopping complex, has changed the face of Sanlitun. The Japanese-designed open-air walking complex includes a number of international shops as well as a movie theater and some of Beijing's best new restaurants and cafes, and has become *the* hangout for the city's in crowd, local and foreign alike. ⊠ *Dongcheng District.*

IF YOU HAVE TIME

Chaoyang Park 朝阳公园. The sprawling Chaoyang Park lacks the imperial aura that marks other Beijing parks, but offers quite a bit in terms of recreation. About one-fourth of the park is water, and so boating of various kinds is available here, primarily pedal-powered paddleboats. There's a very nice (and not too crowded) swimming pool, beach volleyball grounds, tennis courts, a gymnasium, and a small amusement park. You can hire a slow-going electromobile (Y30 for 30 minutes) for easy mobility around this sprawling park on your own. There are many snack stands serving simple dishes, but if you're looking for something more substantive, walk around to the west gate of the park where you'll find a street lined with popular Western and Chinese eateries. The west gate of the park is famous for its bustling bar scene. ⊠ *Nongzhanguan*

Ritan park in the morning.

Road South, Chaoyang District ✉ *Y5* ☉ *Mid-Mar.–mid-Nov., daily 6–9; mid-Nov.–mid-Mar., daily 6–8.*

Jianguomen 建国门. The embassy area has some good foreign restaurants, but is mostly quiet blocks of gated embassy compounds; in the center there is lovely Ritan Park with its winding paths, lotus-flower ponds, climbing wall, and even a few upmarket restaurants. The area is also the heart of Beijing's new Central Business District, aka CBD, and it's home to some of the city's most impressive new architecture, including the new CCTV Tower, the Park Hyatt Hotel and the China Summit Wing, the latter towering two providing magnificent views of the city. ⊠ *Chaoyang District.*

Workers' Stadium 工人体育场. North of Ritan Park is the Workers' Stadium complex, where many of the biggest visiting acts (including Britney Spears and Celine Dion) perform. The famous Sanlitun Bar Street is several blocks east of Workers' Stadium and runs north–south; this is the area that's known for great bars catering to foreigners, expats, and young Chinese. ⊠ *Gongti Rd, Chaoyang District* ✉ *Varies according to event* ☉ *Varies according to event* Ⓜ *Dongsishitiao.*

HAIDIAN DISTRICT 海淀区

Sightseeing
★★★☆☆
Dining
★☆☆☆☆
Lodging
★★☆☆☆
Shopping
★☆☆☆☆
Nightlife
★★☆☆☆

In the last decade or so, with the Chinese Internet and tech booms, the rise of the middle class, and, with it, university education, Haidian has become an educational and techno mecca. The major IT players are all located here (including offices of Microsoft, Siemens, NEC, and Sun).

SNAPSHOT

It's just after lunch and almost every table at the **Bridge Café**—a popular student hangout in Wudaokou—is full. Some Korean students are carefully writing Chinese in their practice books; a group laughs as they watch a rerun of *Friends*. American-language students sit with their exchange partners; beside them people chat happily while surfing wireless Internet. Among all these, young waitresses wearing aprons glide around the room with cappuccinos, sandwiches, and pizzas, shouting above the loud music to deliver their orders to the kitchen.

A GOOD TOUR

Haidian may be Beijing's technology and university district, but there's a lot of Old Beijing left here. Before you leave your hotel, ask for a boxed lunch (or grab some food at a nearby supermarket). Jump in a cab and head for the **Summer Palace.** Saunter around the lakes and ancient pavilions, and finally settle down somewhere secluded to enjoy a picnic.

When you're done with lunch and sightseeing, hop a cab to **Hailong Shopping Mall.** Go in and explore—the five-story shopping mall has every kind of computer or electronic device you could possibly want, often at deep discounts. ■TIP→ Be careful when buying software, though, as most of it is pirated and illegal to bring back to the United States.

After you've shopped and you're ready to drop, head over to the **Wudaokou Binguan** for a selection of wonderful "snacks" that usually add up to a great dinner, and don't miss the *zhapi*, or mugs of fresh-from-the-tap beer. Taxi it on home in the wee hours.

GETTING ORIENTED

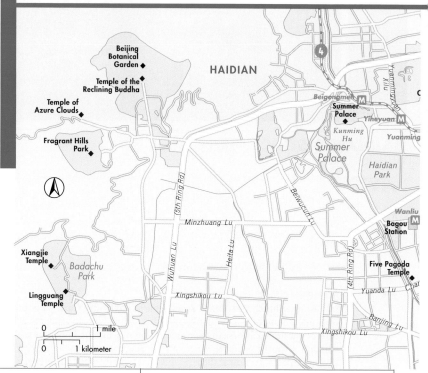

GETTING HERE

Subway Line 13 stops at Wuda-okou, the heart of Haidian. Line 4 stops at both the Beijing Zoo and the Old Summer Palace. Otherwise, the Summer Palace, Old Summer Palace, Fragrant Hills Park, and the Beijing Botanical Garden are all rather far away in the northwest of the city and are best reached by taxi. To save money, take the train to the Xizhimen (or Wuda-okou) subway station and take a taxi from there.

MAKING THE MOST OF YOUR TIME

Because the **Summer Palace** is so large, with its lovely lakes and ancient pavilions, it makes for an entire morning of great exploring. The **Old Summer Palace** is close by, so visiting the two sites together is ideal if you've got the energy.

Fragrant Hills Park makes for a charming outing, but keep in mind that it takes at least an hour and a half to get there from the city center. The **Botanical Garden,** with some 2,000 types of orchids, bonsai, and peach and pear blossoms, along with the **Temple of the Reclining Buddha,** is also fun, especially for green thumbs. Plan to spend most of a day if you go to either of these sites.

If you want to shop for electronics, spend an afternoon wandering the five floors of the **Hailong Shopping Mall** (⊠ *1 Zhongguancun Dajie*).

Evenings in Wudaokou are a pleasure. After dinner, take advantage of the hopping beer gardens. A mug of Tsingtao is a great way to start a summer night off right.

2

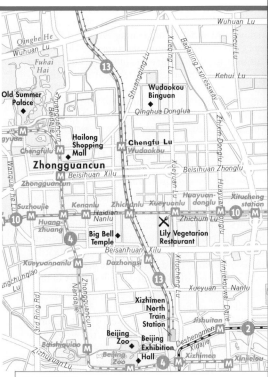

NEIGHBORHOOD TOP 5

1. Spending a low-key day at the vast **Summer Palace** and **Old Summer Palace**. Don't miss getting out onto the water at either the Kunming Lake or the Fuhai Lake.

2. Eating and chatting all evening at the **Wudaokou Binguan** beer garden.

3. Browsing the biggest selection of electronics and computer goods (both legitimate and pirated) this side of the Pacific at **Hailong Shopping Mall.**

4. Listening to China's biggest bell toll at the **Big Bell Temple**. Here you'll find bells, both big and small, from the Ming, Song, and Yuan dynasties.

5. Getting out of town with a day trip to the **Fragrant Hills Park** or the **Beijing Botanical Garden.**

QUICK BITES

There are plenty of restaurants on campus and around Zhongguancun, but the coolest places to eat in Haidian are in Wudaokou.

Try excellent and innovative Korean barbecue at **Hanguokeli** (✉ *35 Chengfu Lu* ☎ *010/6256–3749* Ⓜ *Wudaokou*).

Another hopping eatery is **Youle** (✉ *On Shuangqing Lu, just off Chengfu Lu* ☎ *010/5872–2028*), a Japanese noodle house on the first floor of Weixin Guoji Dasha, or the Weixin International Mansion.

The **Bridge Café** (☎ *010/8286–7026*), also on Chenfu Lu one block west of the subway station, serves up great sandwiches, salads, and desserts popular with the student crowd.

EXPLORING

TOP ATTRACTIONS

Beijing Botanical Garden 北京植物园. Sitting at the feet of the Western Hills in Beijing's northwestern suburbs, the Beijing Botanical Garden, opened in 1955, hosts China's largest plant collection: 6,000 different plant species from all over northern China, including 2,000 types of trees and bushes, more than 1,600 species of tropical and subtropical plants, 1,900 kinds of fruit trees and 500 flower species. With its state-of-the-art greenhouse and a variety of different gardens, this is a pleasant place to explore, especially in spring, when the peach trees burst with pretty blooms. An added feature is the wonderful Temple of the Reclining Buddha, which has an enormous statue that, it's said, took 7,000 slaves to build. ⊠ *Xiangshan Wofosi, Haidian District* ☎ *010/6259–1283* ⊕ *www.beijingbg.com/English/index.asp* ⊠ *Y5 for the outdoor garden* ⊙ *7–5 for the outdoor garden.*

★ **Big Bell Temple** 大钟寺. This 18th-century temple shields China's biggest bell and more than 400 smaller bells and gongs from the Ming, Song, and Yuan dynasties. The Buddhist temple—originally used for rain prayers—has been restored after major damage inflicted during the Cultural Revolution. Before it opened as a museum in 1985, the buildings were used as Beijing No. 2 Food Factory. The bells here range from a giant 7 meters (23 feet) high to hand-sized chimes, many of them corroded to a pale green by time.

The giant, two-story bell, cast with the texts of more than 100 Buddhist scriptures (230,000 Chinese characters), is also said to be China's loudest. Believed to cast during Emperor Yongle's reign, the 46-ton relic can carry more than 15 km (10 mi) when struck forcibly. The bell rings 108 times on special occasions like Spring Festival, one strike for each of the 108 personal worries defined in Buddhism. People used to throw coins into a hole in the top of the bell for luck. The money was swept up by the monks and used to buy food. Enough money was collected in a month to buy provisions that would last for a year. ■ TIP➜ You can ride the subway to the temple: transfer from Dongzhimen on Line 2 to the aboveground Line 13, and go one stop north to Dazhong Si station. ⊠ *1A Beisanhuanxi Lu, Haidian District* ☎ *010/6255–0843* ⊠ *Y10* ⊙ *Daily 8:30–4:30* Ⓜ *Dazhong Si.*

Fodor's Choice **Old Summer Palace** 圆明园. About the size of New York's Central Park,
★ this ruin was once a grand collection of palaces—the emperor's summer retreat from the 15th century to 1860, when it was looted and blown up by British and French soldiers. More than 90% of the original structures were Chinese-style wooden buildings, but only the European-style stone architecture (designed after Versailles by Jesuits and added during the Qing Dynasty) survived the fires. Many of the priceless relics that were looted are still on display in European museums, and China's efforts to recover them have been mostly unsuccessful. Beijing has chosen to preserve the vast ruin as a "monument to China's national humiliation," though the patriotic slogans that were once scrawled on the rubble have now been cleaned off.

The ruins of the Old Summer Palace

The palace is made up of three idyllic parks: Yuanmingyuan (Garden of Perfection and Light) in the west, Wanchunyuan (Garden of 10,000 Springs) in the south, and Changchunyuan (Garden of Everlasting Spring) where the ruins are like a surreal graveyard to European architecture. Here you'll find ornately carved columns, squat lion statues, and crumbling stone blocks that lie like fallen dominoes. An engraved concrete wall maze, known as Huanghuazhen (Yellow Flower), twists and turns around a European-style pavilion. Recently restored and located just to the left of the west gate of Changchunyuan, it was once the site of lantern parties during midautumn festivals. Palace maids would race each other to the pavilion carrying lotus lanterns. The park costs an extra Y15 to enter, but it's well worth it. The park and ruins take on a ghostly beauty if you come after a fresh snowfall. There's also skating on the lake when it's frozen over. ■ TIP → It's a long trek to the European ruins from the main gate. Electric carts buzz around the park; hop on one heading to Changchunyuan if you feel tired. Tickets are Y5.

If you want to save money, take subway Line 13 to Wudaokou and then catch a cab to Yuanmingyuan. The recently opened Line 4 stops at the Old Summer Palace. ⊠ *Qinghuan Xilu (just northeast of the Summer Palace), Haidian District* ☎ *010/6265–8207* ⊠ *Park Y10; extra Y15 fee for sites* ⊙ *Daily 7–7.*

Fodor's Choice **Summer Palace** 颐和园. Emperor Qianlong commissioned this giant
★ royal retreat for his mother's 60th birthday in 1750. Anglo–French forces plundered, then burned, many of the palaces in 1860, and funds were diverted from China's naval budget for the renovations. Empress Dowager Cixi retired here in 1889. Nine years later it was here that she

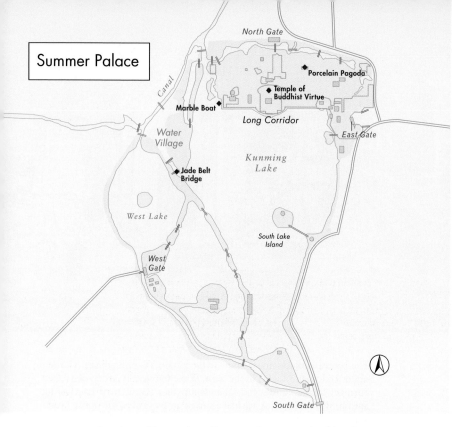

Summer Palace

imprisoned her nephew, Emperor Guangxu, after his reform movement failed. In 1903, she moved the seat of government from the Forbidden City to the Summer Palace, from where she controlled China until her death in 1908.

Nowadays the place is undoubtedly romantic. Pagodas and temples perch on hillsides; rowboats dip under arched stone bridges; and willow branches brush the water. The greenery provides a welcome relief from the loud, bustling city. It also teaches a fabulous history lesson. You can see firsthand the results of corruption: the opulence here was bought with siphoned money as China crumbled, while suffering repeated humiliations at the hands of colonialist powers. The entire gardens were for the Empress Dowager's exclusive use. UNESCO placed the Summer Palace on its World Heritage list in 1998.

The **Hall of Benevolent Longevity** is where Cixi held court and received foreign dignitaries. It is said that the first electric lights in China shone here. Just behind the hall and next to the lake is the **Hall of Jade Ripples**, where Cixi kept the hapless Guangxu under guard while she ran China in his name. Strung with pagodas and temples, including the impressive Tower of the Fragrance of Buddha, Glazed Tile Pagoda, and the Hall that Dispels Clouds, **Longevity Hill** is the place where you can escape the hordes of visitors—take your time exploring the lovely northern side of the hill.

Most of this 700-acre park is underwater. **Kunming Lake** makes up around three-fourths of the complex, and is largely man-made. The excavated dirt was used to build Longevity Hill. This giant body of water extends southward for 3 km (2 mi); it's ringed by tree-lined dikes, arched stone bridges, and numerous gazebos. In winter, you can skate on the ice. The less-traveled southern shore near Humpbacked Bridge is an ideal picnic spot. ■TIP➔ Arrive like Cixi did: come to the park by boat. In summer, craft leave every hour from near the Millennium Monument in Xizhimen (on Fuxing Lu), or from near Beijing Zoo. The journey takes about an hour and Y158 gets you onto the boat and into the Summer Palace.

At the west end of the lake you'll find the **Marble Boat**, which doesn't actually float and was built by the Dowager Empress Cixi with money meant for the navy. The **Long Corridor** is a wooden walkway that skirts the northern shoreline of Kunming Lake for about half a mile until it reaches the marble boat. The ceiling and wooden rafters of the Long Corridor are richly painted with thousands of scenes from legends and nature—be on the lookout for Sun Wukong (the Monkey King). Cixi's home, in the Hall of Joyful Longevity, is near the beginning of the Long Corridor. The residence is furnished and decorated as Cixi left it. Her private theater, called the Grand Theater Building, just east of the hall, was constructed for her 60th birthday and cost 700,000 taels of silver.

Subway Line 10 will get you pretty close if you take it all the way to Bagou, and then catch a taxi for Y10. Line 4 may be open by the time you read this and will have a Summer Palace stop. Otherwise, you'll have to take a taxi. It's best to come early in the morning to get a head start before the busloads of visitors arrive. You'll need the better part of a day to explore the grounds. Automatic audio guides can be rented for Y40 at stalls near the ticket booth. ✉ *Yiheyuan Lu and Kunminghu Lu, 12 km (7½ mi) northwest of downtown Beijing, Haidian District* ☎ *010/6288–1144; for information on arrival by boat: 010/6858–9215* ✆ *Y60 summer all-inclusive, Y50 winter* ☉ *Daily 6:30–8 (ticket office closes at 6 PM).*

Xiangshan Park *(Fragrant Hills Park)* 香山公园. This hillside park northwest of Beijing was once an imperial retreat. From the eastern gate you can hike to the summit on a trail dotted with small temples. If you're short on time, ride a cable car to the top. ✉ *Haidian District* ☎ *010/6259–1155* ✆ *Y10; one-way cable car, Y60* ☉ *Daily 6–6.*

IF YOU HAVE TIME

Beijing Zoo 北京动物园. Though visitors usually go straight to see the giant pandas, don't miss the other interesting animals, like tigers from the northeast, yaks from Tibet, enormous sea turtles from China's seas, and red pandas from Sichuan. The zoo started out as a garden belonging to one of the sons of Shunzhi, the first emperor of the Qing dynasty. In 1747, the Qianlong emperor had it refurbished (along with other imperial properties, including the summer palaces) and turned it into a park in honor of his mother's 60th birthday. In 1901, the Empress Dowager gave it another extensive facelift and used it to house a collection of

The Summer Palace.

animals given to her as a gift by a Chinese minister who had bought them during a trip to Germany. By the 1930s, most of the animals had died and were stuffed and put on display in a museum on the grounds. ✉ *137 Xiwai Dajie, Haidian District* 🖼 *Apr.–Oct., Y15; Nov.–Mar., Y10 plus Y5 for the panda site* 🕙 *Apr.–Oct., 7:30–6; Nov.–Mar., 7:30–5.*

Five-Pagoda Temple 五塔寺. Hidden among trees just behind the zoo and set amid carved stones, the temple's five pagodas reveal obvious Indian influences. It was built during the Yongle years of the Ming Dynasty (1403–1424), in honor of an Indian Buddhist who came to China and presented a temple blueprint to the emperor. Elaborate carvings of curvaceous figures, floral patterns, birds, and hundreds of Buddhas decorate the pagodas. Also on the grounds is the **Beijing Art Museum of Stone Carvings,** with its collection of some 1,000 stelae and stone figures. ✉ *24 Wuta Si, Baishiqiao, Haidian District* 🕾 *010/6217–3836* 🖼 *Y15* 🕙 *Daily 9–4:30.*

Military Museum of the Chinese People's Revolutions 中国人民革命军事博物馆. Stuffed with everything from AK-47s to captured tanks to missile launchers, this is a must-see for military buffs. Five thousand years of Chinese military history are on display, and kids especially love every minute of it. Easily accessible by taking a 10-minute subway ride west from Tiananmen Square. ✉ *9 Fuxing Road, Haidian District* 🕾 *010/6696–6244* 🖼 *Y20* 🕙 *Daily 8–5:30.*

Temple of Azure Clouds 碧云寺. Once the home of a Yuan Dynasty official, the site was converted into a Buddhist temple in 1366 and enlarged during the 16th and 17th centuries by imperial eunuchs who hoped to be buried here. The temple's five main courtyards ascend a slope in

Fragrant Hills Park. Although severely damaged during the Cultural Revolution, the complex has been beautifully restored.

The main attraction is the Indian-influenced **Vajra Throne Pagoda.** Lining its walls and five pagodas are gracefully carved stone-relief Buddhas and bodhisattvas. The pagoda once housed the remains of Nationalist China's founding father, Dr. Sun Yat-sen, who lay in state here between March and May 1925, while his mausoleum was being constructed in Nanjing. A hall in one of the temple's western courtyards houses about 500 life-size wood and gilt arhats (Buddhists who have reached Enlightenment)—each displayed in a glass case. ⊠ *Xiangshan Park, Haidian District* ☎ *010/6259–1155* ⊴ *Park Y10; temple Y10* ☯ *Daily 8–4:30, park closes at 6.*

Temple of Longevity 万寿寺. A Ming empress built this temple to honor her son in 1578. Qing emperor Qianlong later restored it as a birthday present to his mother. From then until the fall of the Qing, it served as a rest stop for imperial processions traveling by boat to the Summer Palace and Western Hills. The site also served as a Japanese military command center during occupation. Today the temple is managed by the Beijing Art Museum and houses a small but exquisite collection of Buddha images. The Buddhas in the main halls include Shakyamuni sitting on a 1,000-petal, 1,000-Buddha bronze throne and dusty Ming-period Buddhas. ⊠ *Xisanhuan Lu, on the north side of Zizhu Bridge, Haidian District* ☎ *010/6841–3380* ⊴ *Y20* ☯ *Tues.–Sun. 9:30–4:30*

Temple of the Reclining Buddha 卧佛寺. Although the temple was damaged during the Cultural Revolution and poorly renovated afterward, the Sleeping Buddha remains. Built in 627–629, during the Tang Dynasty, the temple was named after the reclining Buddha that was brought in during the Yuan Dynasty (1271–1368). An English-language description explains that the casting of the beautiful bronze, in 1321, enslaved 7,000 people. The temple is inside the **Beijing Botanical Garden;** stroll north from the entrance through the neatly manicured grounds. ⊠ *Xiangshan Lu, 2 km (1 mi) northeast of Xiangshan Park, Haidian District* ☎ *010/6259–1209* ⊴ *Temple Y5; gardens Y10* ☯ *Daily 8:30–4:30.*

ENGLISH	PINYIN	CHINESE
798 Art District	Qījiǔbā yìshù qū	798艺术区
Ancient Observatory	Běijīng gǔguānxiàng tái	北京古观象台
Liulichang (Antiques Street)	Liúlíchǎng	琉璃厂
Beihai Park (North Lake)	Běihǎi	北海
Beijing Ancient Architecture Museum	Běijīng gǔdài jiànzhù bówùguǎn	北京古代建筑博物馆
Beijing Botanical Garden	Běijīng zhíwù yuán	北京植物园
Beijing Zoo	Běijīng dòngwù yuán	北京动物园
Bell Tower	Zhōng lóu	钟楼
Big Bell Temple	Dàzhōngsì	大钟寺
Capital Museum	Shǒdū bówùguǎn	首都博物馆
Central Business District	Shāng yè zhōng xīn qū	商业中心区
Chang'an Avenue	Chángānjiē	长安街
Chang'an Grand Theater	Chángān dàxì yuàn	长安大戏院
Chaoyang District	Cháoyáng qū	朝阳区
Chaoyang Park	Cháoyáng gōngyuán	朝阳公园
China World Trade Center	Zhōngguó shìjièmàoyì zhōngxīn	中国世界贸易中心
Chongwen District	Chóngwén qū	崇文区
Confucius Temple	Kǒngmiào	孔庙
Cultural Palace of Nationalities	Mínzú wénhuà gōng	民族文化宫
Ditan Park (Temple of the Earth)	Dìtán gōngyuán	地坛公园
Dongbianmen Watch Tower	Dōngbiànmén jiǎolóu	东便门角楼
Dongcheng District	Dōngchéng qū	东城区
Donghuamen Night Market	Dōnghuāmén yèshì	东华门夜市
Drum Tower	Gǔlóu	鼓楼
Five-Pagoda Temple	Wǔ Tǎ Sì	五塔寺
Forbidden City	Gùgōng	故宫
Great Hall of the People	rénmín dàhuìtáng	人民大会堂
Guijie (Ghost Street)	Guǐjiē	簋街
Haidian District	Hǎidiàn qū	海淀区
Hall of Prayer for Good Harvests	Qínián diàn	祈年殿
Houhai (Back Lake)	Hòuhǎi	后海
Imperial Academy	Guózǐjiān	国子监
Jianguomen	Jiànguómén	建国门
Jingshan Park (Coal Hill)	Jīngshān gōngyuán	景山公园
Kunming Lake	Kūnmínghú	昆明湖

2

ENGLISH	PINYIN	CHINESE
Lama Temple	Yōnghégōng	雍和宫
Liulichang	Liúlíchǎng	琉璃厂
Mao Zedong Memorial Hall	Máozhǔxí jìniàntáng	毛主席纪念堂
Military Museum of the Chinese People's Revolution	zhōngguó rénmín gémìng jūnshì bówùguǎn	中国人民革命军事博物馆
Ming Dynasty City Wall Ruins Park	Míng chéngqiáng yízhǐ gōngyuán	明城墙遗址公园
Monument to the People's Heroes	Rénmínīngxióng ǐnìanbēi	人民英雄纪念碑
Museum of Antique Currency	Běijīng gǔdài qiánbì bówùguǎn	北京古代钱币博物馆
Nan Luogu Xiang	Nánluógǔxiàng	南锣鼓巷
Nanhai (south lake)	Nánhǎi	南海
Nanxincang	Nánxīncāng	南新仓
Niujie (Ox Street) Mosque	Niújiē qīngzhēnsì	牛街清真寺
Old Summer Palace	uánmíngyuán	圆明园
Oriental Plaza	Dōngfāng guǎngchǎng	东方广场
Ox Street	Niújiē	牛街
Panjiayuan Antiques Market	Pānjiāyuán shìchǎng	潘家园市场
Peking University	Běijīng dàxué	北京大学
The Poly Art Museum	Bǎolì yìshù bówùguǎn	保利艺术博物馆
Prince Gong's Palace	Gōngwángfǔ	恭王府
Qianhai (Front Lake)	Qiánhǎi	前海
Qianmen Dajie	Qiánmén dàjiē	前门大街
Ruifuxiang Silk Shop	ruìfúxiáng chóubù diàn	瑞蚨祥绸布店
Ritan Park (Temple of the Sun)	Rìtán gōngyuán	日坛公园
Sanlitun	Sānlǐtún	三里屯
Second Ring Road	èrhuán lù	二环路
Shichachai	Shíchàhài	什刹海
Silk Alley Market	Xiùshuǐ jiē	秀水街
Soong Ching-ling's Former Residence	Sòng Qìnglíng gùjū	宋庆龄故居
Source of Law Temple	Fǎyuánsì	法源寺
Summer Palace	Yíhéyuán	颐和园
Temple of Azure Clouds	Bìyún sì	碧云寺
Temple of Heaven	Tiāntán gōngyuán	天坛公园
Temple of Longevity	Wànshòu sì	万寿寺
Temple of the Reclining Buddha	Wòfó sì	卧佛寺

ENGLISH	PINYIN	CHINESE
Temple of the White Pagoda	Báitǎ	白塔
Tiananmen Square	Tiānānmén guǎngchǎng	天安门广场
Tsinghua University	Qīnghuá dàxué	清华大学
Tushu Dasha (Beijing Books Building)	Túshū dàshà	图书大厦
Wangfujing	Wángfǔjǐng	王府井
White Clouds Taoist Temple	Báiyúnguān	白云观
Workers' Stadium	Gōngrén tǐyùcháng	工人体育场
Wudaokou	Wǔdàokǒu	五道口
Xiangshan Park (Fragrant Hills)	Xiāngshān gōngyuán	香山公园
Xicheng District	Xīchéng qū	西城区
Xidan (Shopping Area)	Xīdān	西单
Xuanwu District	Xuānwǔ qū	宣武区
Yashow Market	Yǎxiù shìchǎng	雅秀市场
Yin Ding Qiao (Silver Ingot Bridge)	yíndìngqiáo	银锭桥
Zhongguancun	Zhōngguāncūn	中关村
Zhonghai (Middle Lake)	Zhōnghǎi	中海

Where to Eat

WORD OF MOUTH

"Houhai (Back Lake) is an excellent recommendation. Lots of places to dine, especially along the lake—avoid the overly priced ones and you'll be fine."

—easytraveler

Updated by Eileen Wen Mooney

China's economic boom has fueled a culinary revolution in Beijing, with just about every kind of food now available in the capital. Today you can eat a wide variety of regional cuisines, including unusual specialties from Yunnan, earthy Hakka cooking from southern China, Tibetan yak and *tsampa* (barley flour), numbingly spicy Sichuan cuisine, and chewy noodles from Shaanxi.

The capital also offers plenty of international cuisines, including French, German, Thai, Japanese, Brazilian, Malaysian, and Italian, among others.

You can spend as little as $5 per person for a decent meal or $100 and up on a lavish banquet. The venues are part of the fun, ranging from swanky restaurants to holes-in-the-wall and refurbished courtyard houses. Reservations are always a good idea so book as far ahead as you can, and reconfirm as soon as you arrive.

People tend to eat around 6 PM and even though the last order is usually taken around 9 PM, some places remain open until the wee morning hours. Tipping can be tricky. Though it isn't required, some of the larger, fancier restaurants will add a 15% service charge to the bill. Be aware before you go out that small and medium venues only take cash payment; more established restaurants usually accept credit cards.

Great local beers and some international brands are available everywhere in Beijing, and many Chinese restaurants now have extensive wine menus.

WHAT IT COSTS IN YUAN				
	¢	$	$$	$$$	$$$$
Restaurants	under Y40	Y40–Y80	Y81–Y120	Y121–Y180	over Y180

Prices are for a main course. Note: the term "main course" may not be appropriate for some restaurants, as Chinese dishes are normally shared.

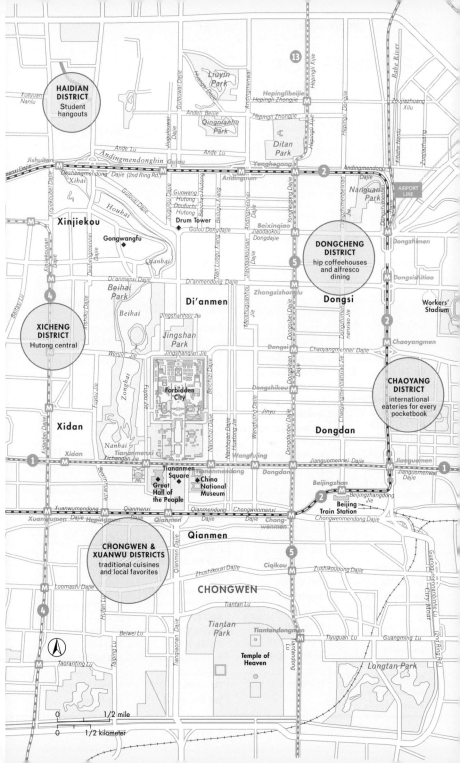

BEST BETS FOR BEIJING DINING

With thousands of restaurants to choose from, how will you decide where to eat? Fodor's writers and editors have selected their favorite restaurants by price, cuisine, and experience in the Best Bets lists here. In the first column, Fodor's Choice properties represent the "best of the best" in every price category. You can also search by neighborhood for excellent eats—just peruse our reviews on the following pages.

Fodor's Choice ★

- Alameda, p. 119
- Capital M, p. 117
- Din Tai Fung, p. 121
- Huang Ting, p. 103
- Li Qun Roast Duck Restaurant, p. 117
- Mei Fu, p. 115
- Red Capital Club, p. 113
- The Source, p. 113
- Shin Yeh, p. 127
- Yotsuba, p. 128
- Yuxiang Renjia, p. 129

Best By Price

¢

- Paomo Guan, p. 111
- Qin Tangfu, p. 111
- Yue Bin, p. 113

$

- Bellagio, p. 120
- Bookworm, The, p. 120
- Ju'er Renjia, p. 104
- Mosto, p. 125
- Still Thoughts, p. 113
- Yuxiang Renjia, p. 129

$$

- 1/5 Taverna, p. 118
- Argana, p. 119
- La Dolce Vita, p. 124
- Lei Garden, p. 104
- Li Qun Roast Duck Restaurant, p. 117
- Madam Zhu's Kitchen, p. 124
- Xiheyaju, p. 128

$$$

- Alameda, p. 119
- Din Tai Fung, p. 121
- Morio J-Cuisine, p. 125

$$$$

- Aria, p. 119
- Bei, p. 120
- Capital M, p. 117
- Cepe, p. 114
- Fangshan, p. 114
- Fennel, p. 122
- Huang Ting, p. 103
- Jing, p. 104
- The Source, p. 113

Best By Experience

BUSINESS DINING

- Barolo, p. 120
- Maison Boulud, p. 104

GREAT VIEW

- Assaggi, p. 119
- Capital M, p. 117

HUTONG EATERIES

- Café Sambal, p. 99
- Dali Courtyard, p. 99
- Dezhe Xiaoguan, p. 103
- Guo Yao Xiao Ju, p. 103
- Huang Ting, p. 103
- Li Qun Roast Duck Restaurant, p. 117
- Mei Fu, p. 115
- Private Kitchen No. 44, p. 111
- Red Capital Club, p. 113
- The Source, p. 113
- Yue Bin, p. 113

Best By Cuisine

GUIZHOU

- Jia No. 21, p. 122

HUNAN

- Karaiya Spice House, p. 124

BEIJING

- Dong Lai Shun, p. 103
- Duck de Chine, p. 121
- Old Beijing Noodle King, p. 118
- Shaguo Ju, p. 115
- Yue Bin, p. 113

SHANGHAINESE AND JIANGZHE

- Din Tai Fung, p. 121
- Kong Yi Ji, p. 115

SICHUAN

- The Source, p. 113
- Yuxiang Renjia, p. 129

TAIWANESE

- Bellagio, p. 120
- Shin Yeh, p. 127

YUNNAN

- Dali Courtyard, p. 99

NORTHERN CHINESE

- Ding Ding Xiang, p. 129
- Jinyang Fanzhuang, p. 117
- Old Beijing Noodle King, p. 118
- Paomo Guan, p. 111
- Qin Tangfu, p. 111

RESTAURANT REVIEWS

Listed alphabetically within neighborhoods

Use the coordinate (✛A1) at the end of each listing to locate a site on the corresponding map.

DONGCHENG DISTRICT 东城区

Dongcheng runs from the eastern flank of the Forbidden City to the Second Ring Road. There are plenty of good restaurants here, along with an impressive wealth of historical sights. Try one of Beijing's growing number of traditional courtyard eateries, where you can dine alfresco in the warmer months. Or walk down Nan Luogu Xiang, an old alleyway, where you pick from more than a dozen Western and Chinese restaurants, coffeehouses, and bars. Good places here are the Cambulac for aperitif, or Italian dessert wine, Ju'er Renjia for simple rice with savory minced meat toppings, and The Source for mouth-numbing Sichuan specialties.

$$
FRENCH
✗**Café de la Poste** 云游驿. In almost every French village, town, or city there is a Café de la Poste, where people go for a cup of coffee, a beer, or a simple family meal. This haunt lives up to its name: It's a steak-lover's paradise, with such favorites as finely sliced marinated beefsteak served with lemon-herb vinaigrette and steak tartare. If the next table orders banana flambé, we promise the warm scent of its rum will soon have you smitten enough to order it yourself. ✉ *58 Yonghegong Dajie, Dongcheng District* ☎ *010/6402–7047* ▭ *No credit cards* Ⓜ *Yonghegong* ✛ *E1.*

$$
MALAYSIAN
✗**Café Sambal.** This cozy traditional courtyard house has been transformed into one of the city's most popular eateries. A snug alfresco dining area, well-worn antique furnishings, and a chilled-out vibe make this a great place to relax over a Malaysian meal. The curried crab and braised lobster must be ordered in advance, but these dishes are a bit unreliable. Best stick to the piquant home cooking the restaurant is most known for, such as the fiery beef rendang or the seductive buttery prawns. ✉ *43 Doufuchi Hutong, Jiugulou Dajie, Dongcheng District* ☎ *10/6400–4875* ▭ *AE, MC, V* ✛ *D2.*

$$
CANTONESE
✗**Crystal Jade Palace** 翡翠皇宫酒家. Don't let the dark granite floors and crystal chandeliers intimidate you—the food at this Cantonese favorite is familiar, and the service is sincere. Weekdays see wheeler-dealers closing deals over dim sum, while the weekends bustle with families from Singapore and Hong Kong lingering over many pots of excellent teas. Plenty of pricey seafood dishes are on the menu, but you can opt for the less expensive stir-fry dishes and dim sum. ✉ *Oriental Plaza, 1 Dongchang'an Jie, Dongcheng District* ☎ *010/8515–0238* ▭ *AE, DC, MC, V* ✛ *E4.*

$$$$
YUNNAN
✗**Dali Courtyard** 大理. Yunnan's tranquility and bohemian spirit are captured in this enchanting traditional courtyard house, just a short walk from the Drum and Bell towers. On breezy summer nights the best seats are in the central courtyard with its overflowing greenery. The set menus, ranging from Y100 to Y300, change on a daily basis. Meals are designed for sharing, with numerous generously sized dishes. The staff is memorably friendly and efficient. ✉ *67 Xiaojingchang Hutong,*

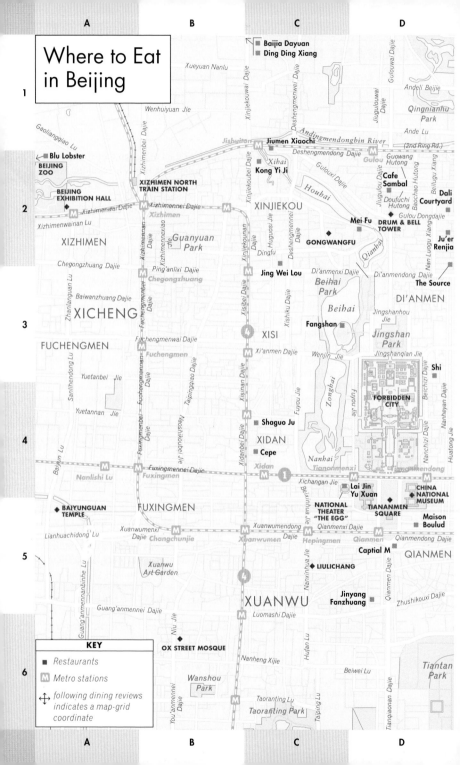

Where to Eat in Beijing

KEY

■ Restaurants

Ⓜ Metro stations

↔ following dining reviews indicates a map-grid coordinate

Labels

■ Baijia Dayuan
■ Ding Ding Xiang

← Blu Lobster
BEIJING ZOO
BEIJING EXHIBITION HALL

Jiumen Xiaochi
■ Xihai
Kong Yi Ji

XINJIEKOU

Cafe Sambal
Dali Courtyard
Mei Fu
DRUM & BELL TOWER
Ju'er Renjia

GONGWANGFU

Jing Wei Lou

The Source

Fangshan

DI'ANMEN

Jingshan Park

Shi

XIZHIMEN NORTH TRAIN STRAIN

Guanyuan Park

XIZHIMEN

XICHENG

FUCHENGMEN

XISI

FORBIDDEN CITY

■ Shaguo Ju
XIDAN
■ Cepe

Lai Jin Yu Xuan
CHINA NATIONAL MUSEUM

NATIONAL THEATER "THE EGG"
TIANANMEN SQUARE
Maison Boulud

BAIYUNGUAN TEMPLE

FUXINGMEN

Captial M
QIANMEN

♦ LIULICHANG

XUANWU

Jinyang Fanzhuang

Xuanwu Art Garden

OX STREET MOSQUE

Wanshou Park

Tiantan Park

Taoranting Park

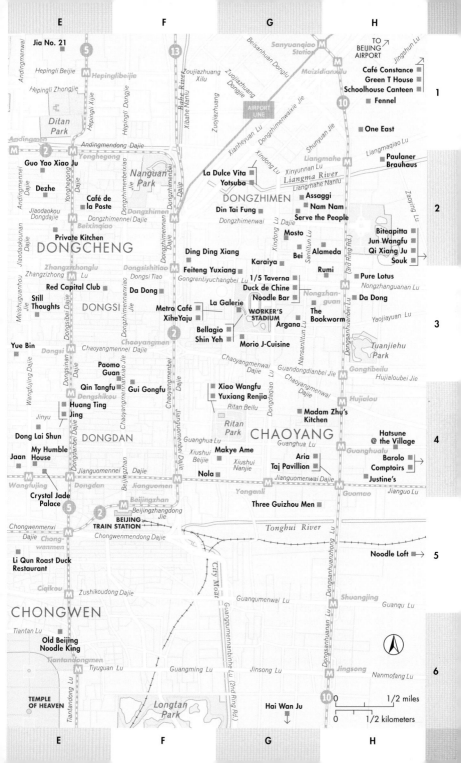

CHINESE CUISINE

To help you navigate China's cuisines, we have used the following terms in our restaurant reviews.

Beijing: As the seat of government for several dynasties, Beijing cuisine has melded the culinary traditions of many cultures. Specialties include Peking duck, *ma doufu* (spicy tofu), zhajiang noodles, flash-boiled tripe, and a wide variety of snack food.

Cantonese: A diverse cuisine that roasts and fries, braises and steams. Spices are used in moderation. Dishes include steamed fish, sweet-and-sour pork, and roasted goose.

Chinese: Catchall term used for restaurants that serve cuisine from multiple regions of China.

Chinese fusion: Any Chinese cuisine with international influences.

Chiu chow: Known for its vegetarian and seafood dishes, which are mostly poached, steamed, or braised. Specialties include *popiah* (non-fried spring rolls) and fish-ball noodle soup.

Hunan: Flavors are spicy, with chili peppers, ginger, garlic, and dried salted black beans and preserved vegetables. Signature dishes are Mao's braised pork, steamed fish head with coarse chopped salted chilies, and cured pork with smoked bean curd.

Guizhou: The two most important cooking condiments that are used to prepare Guizhou's fiery hot cuisine are *zao lajiao* (pounded dried peppers brined in salt) and fermented tomatoes. The latter are used to make sour fish soup, the region's hallmark dish.

Northern Chinese (Dongbei): Staples are lamb and mutton, preserved vegetables, noodles, steamed breads, pancakes, stuffed buns, and dumplings.

Sichuan (central province): Famed for bold flavors and spiciness from chilies and numbing Sichuan peppercorns. Dishes include kong pao chicken, mapo bean curd, "dan dan" spicy noodles, twice-cooked pork, and tea-smoked duck.

Shanghainese and Jiangzhe: Cuisine characterized by rich flavors produced by braising and stewing, and the use of rice wine in cooking. Signature dishes are steamed hairy crabs and "drunken chicken."

Taiwanese: Diverse cuisine centers on seafood. Specialties include "three cups chicken" with a sauce made of soya, rice wine, and sugar; oyster omelets; cuttlefish soup; and dried tofu.

Tibetan: Cuisine reliant on foodstuffs grown at high altitudes including barley flour, yak meat, milk, butter, and cheese.

Tan Family Cuisine: Tan family cuisine originated in the home of Tan Zongjun (1846–1888), a native of Guangdong, who secured a high position in the Qing inner court in Beijing. He added other regional influences into his cooking, which resulted in this new cuisine.

Yunnan (southern province): This region's cuisine is noted for its use of vegetables, bamboo shoots, and flowers in its spicy preparations. Dishes include rice noodle soup with chicken, pork, and fish; steamed chicken with ginseng and herbs; and cured Yunnan ham.

Gulou Dong Dajie, Dongcheng District ☎ *010/8404–1430* ⊟ *No credit cards* ✛ *D2.*

$$
SICHUAN

✕ **Dezhe Xiaoguan** 得着. This simple, rustic, and adorable restaurant is appropriately named *Dezhe* or "you got it"—a local phrase which means the best of something. Dezhe serves up a memorable poached chicken dish drenched in aromatic young and green Sichuan peppercorns, which permeate the entire dish. Other standard Sichuan fare includes kong pao chicken, classic twice-cooked pork, and mapo tofu. ⊠ *1Beijixiang Hutong, Jiaodaokou Nan Dajie, Dongcheng District* ☎ *010/6407–8615* ⊟ *AE, V* ✛ *H4, F2.*

$$
BEIJING

✕ **Dong Lai Shun** 东来顺. Dating to 1903, this is one of Beijing's oldest Hui (Chinese Muslim) restaurants. Their specialty is a mutton dish famous for three attributes: paper-thin slices, high-quality meat, and an excellent dipping sauce. The hotpot dishes are amazingly flavorful: the best part is near the end, when the broth reaches a tongue-tingling climax. If you like, drop some cilantro into the bowl. *Zhima shaobing* (small baked sesame bread) is the perfect accompaniment. ⊠ *5/F Xin Dongan Plaza, Wangfujing Dajie, Dongcheng District* ☎ *010/6528– 0932* ⊟ *MC, V* Ⓜ *Wangfujing* ✛ *E4.*

$$$$
TAN FAMILY
CUISINE

✕ **Guo Yao Xiao Ju** 国肴小居. Tucked inside a small hutong, the style of food served in this restaurant, which dates back to the Qing dynasty, is phenomenal. The Beijing Culinary Association named this small family eatery the best restaurant for private cuisine in 2005. The owner's brother-in-law is a veteran of the Beijing Hotel and the fourth generation trained in Tan cooking. Chef Guo has also prepared state banquets for U.S. presidents Nixon and Clinton, and for Chinese leaders such as Deng Xiaoping. Go for the Tan cuisine set menu for a thorough experience of China's haute cuisine. An à la carte menu is also available. Try the homemade wine-flavored sausages, tender bamboo shoots tossed in chili oil, baked codfish, or spaetzle in rich tomatoey soup. ⊠ *58 Jiaodaokou Bei Santiao, Andingmennei, Dongcheng District* ☎ *010/6403– 1940* ⊟ *AE, MC, V* ✛ *E2.*

$$$$
CANTONESE
Fodor's Choice
★

✕ **Huang Ting** 凰庭. Beijing's traditional courtyard houses, facing extinction as entire neighborhoods are demolished to make way for highrises, provide the theme here. The walls are constructed from original hutong bricks taken from centuries-old courtyard houses that have been destroyed. This is arguably one of Beijing's best Cantonese restaurants, serving southern favorites such as braised shark fin with crab meat, seared abalone with seafood, and steamed scallop and bean curd in black-bean sauce. The dim sum is delicate and refined, and the deep-fried taro spring rolls and steamed pork buns are not to be missed. ⊠ *The Peninsula, 8 Jinyu Hutong, Wangfujing, Dongcheng District* ☎ *010/6512–8899 Ext. 6707* ⊟ *AE, DC, MC, V* Ⓜ *Dongdan* ✛ *E4.*

$$$$
FRENCH

✕ **Jaan** 家安. If you're looking for old-world elegance, this is the place. You'll be transported back to the 1920s, complete with wood-plank floors, an antique piano, and graceful arched doorways. The French-influenced dishes have yet to disappoint, and crossover classics such as caramelized foie gras terrine with Sichuan peppercorns are a pleasant discovery. The wine list is staggeringly long and befits a place that has been around since 1917. ✉ *33 East Chang'an Avenue, Wangfujing, Dongcheng District* ☎ *010/6526–3388* 🖃 *AE, DC, MC, V* ✛ *E4.*

$$$$ ✕ **Jing** 京. Consistently rated among the city's best, Jing serves up East–
INTERNATIONAL West fusion cuisine in an ultramodern setting replete with polished
★ red wooden floors, cream-colored chairs, and gauzy curtain dividers. Signature appetizers include outstanding duck rolls, tiger prawns, and fragrant coconut soup. The fillet of barramundi and risotto with seared langoustines are standout main courses. For dessert, don't miss the warm chocolate cake with almond ice cream. There's also an excellent selection of international wines. ✉ *The Peninsula Beijing, 8 Jinyu Hutong, Wangfujing, Dongcheng District* ☎ *010/6523–0175 Ext. 6714* 🖃 *AE, DC, MC, V* Ⓜ *Dongdan* ✛ *E4.*

$ ✕ **Ju'er Renjia** 菊儿人家. This modest little eatery offers only one set meal
CHINESE for less than $3, a tasty lurou fan, or rice with an aromatic ground pork topping complemented with flavorful boiled egg, mixed pickled vegetable and a delicious clear soup. The home-brewed teas are excellent, especially the red date, longan, and ginger selections. Not to be missed is the homemade chilled milk custard called *shuang pi nai*, or double-skin milk. ✉ *63 Xiao Ju'er Hutong, Dongcheng District* ☎ *010/6400–8117* 🖃 *No credit cards* ✛ *D2.*

$$ ✕ **Lai Jin Yu Xuan** 来今雨轩. A gem tucked inside Zhongshan Park on the
BEIJING west side of the Forbidden City, Lai Jin is known for its Red Mansion banquet, based on dishes from Cao Xueqin's classic 18th-century novel, *The Dream of the Red Chamber*. The two-level restaurant sits beside a small pond amid willow and peach trees. The two daily dishes are *qie xiang* (eggplant with nuts) and *jisi haozigan* (shredded chicken with crown-daisy chrysanthemum). After your meal, take a lazy stroll across the park to the nearby teahouse with the same name, where you can enjoy a cup of tea in the courtyard surrounded by ancient cypress and scholar trees. ✉ *Inside Zhongshan Park, on the west side of the Forbidden City, Dongcheng District* ☎ *010/6605–6676* 🖃 *No credit cards* ✛ *C4.*

$$ ✕ **Lei Garden** 利苑. Bright and bustling on any day of the week, Lei
CANTONESE Garden really packs them in on Sunday afternoons for dim sum. The pan-fried turnip pudding is juicy and topped with generous amounts of grated veggies, and the shrimp dumplings are bursting with sweet plump shrimp and crunchy bamboo shoots. A platter of roast pork, with bite-size pieces laced with buttery fat and capped with crisp, crunchy skin, hits the spot. Private dining rooms offer sanctuary from the crowd. ✉ *Jinbao Tower, 89 Jinbao Jie, Dongcheng District* ☎ *010/8522–1212* 🖃 *AE, DC, MC, V.*

$$$$ ✕ **Maison Boulud** 布鲁宫法餐厅. Internationally acclaimed chef Daniel
FRENCH Boulud's first foray in China is this restaurant in the historic Legation Quarter. Arrive early for your reservation to sip an aperitif in the parlor and admire the chic colonial decor. Entering the understated dining room, you'll find yourself in the company of the city's movers and shakers. Peruse the concise à la carte menu for all the usual suspects—steak, king crab, foie gras—or opt for the four-course prix-fixe menu for Y428. ✉ *23 Qian Men Dong Dajie, Dongcheng District* ☎ *010/6559–9200* 🖃 *AE, DC, MC, V* ✛ *D5.*

Continued on page 111

A CULINARY TOUR OF CHINA

For centuries the collective culinary fragrances of China have drifted far beyond its borders and tantalized the entire world. Now with China's arms open to the world, a vast variety of Chinese flavors—from the North, South, East, and West—are more accessible than ever.

In dynasties gone by, a visitor to China might have to undertake a journey of a thousand li just to feel the burn of an authentic Sichuanese hotpot, and another to savor the crispy skin and juicy flesh of a genuine Beijing roast duck. Luckily for us, the vast majority of regional Chinese cuisines have made successful internal migrations. As a result, Sichuanese cuisine can be found in Guangzhou, Cantonese dim sum in Urumuqi, and the cumin-spiced lamb-on-a-stick, for which the Uigher people of Xinjiang are famous, is now grilled all over China.

Four corners of the Middle Kingdom

Before you begin your journey, remember, a true scholar of Middle Kingdom cuisine should first eliminate the very term "Chinese food" from their vocabulary. It hardly encompasses the variety of provincial cuisines and regional dishes that China has to offer, from succulent Shanghainese dumplings to fiery Sichuanese hotpots.

To guide you on your gastronomic journey, we've divided the country's gourmet map along the points of the compass—North, South, East, and West. Bon voyage and bon appétit!

Following the revolution, it was hard to find authentic Chinese cuisine.

NORTH

THE BASICS

Cuisine from China's Northeast is called dongbei cai, and it's more wheat than rice based. Vegetables like kale, cabbage, and potatoes are combined with robust, thick soy sauces, garlic (often raw), and scallions.

Even though many Han Chinese from southern climates find mutton too gamey, up north it's a regular staple. In many northern cities, you can't walk more than a block without coming across a small sidewalk grill with yang rou chua'r, or lamb-on-a-stick.

Peking duck sliced table-side.

NOT TO BE MISSED

The most famous of all the northern dishes is Peking duck, and if you've ever had it well prepared, you'll know why Beijingers are proud of the dish named for their city.

The fowl is cleaned, stuffed with burning millet stalks and other aromatic combustibles, and then slow-cooked in an oven heated by a fire made of fragrant wood. Properly cooked, Peking duck should have crispy skin, juicy meat, and none of the grease. Peking duck is served with pancakes, scallions, and a delicious soy-based sauce with just a hint of sweetness.

LEGEND HAS IT

Looking for the best roast duck in Beijing? You won't find it in a luxury hotel. But if you happen to find yourself wandering through the Qianmendong hutong just south of Tiananmen Square, you may stumble upon a little courtyard home with a sign in English reading LI QUN ROAST DUCK. This small and unassuming restaurant is widely considered as having the best Peking roast duck in the capital. Rumor has it that the late leader Deng Xiaoping used to send his driver out to bring him back Li Qun's amazing ducks.

THE CAPITAL CITY'S NAMESAKE DISH

A perfectly prepared duck

Scallions

Soy based hoisin sauce

Pancakes

SOUTH

(left) Preparing for the feast. (top right) Dim sum as art. (bottom right) Place your order.

THE BASICS

The dish most associated with Southern Chinese cuisine is dim sum, which is found in great variety and abundance in Guangdong province, as well as Hong Kong and Macau. Bite-size dim sum is usually eaten early in the day. Any good dim sum place should have dozens of varieties. Some of the most popular dishes are *har gao*, a shrimp dumpling with a rice-flour skin, *siu maai*, a pork dumpling with a wrapping made of wheat flour, and *chaa-habao*, a steamed or baked bun filled with sweetened pork and onions. Adventerous eaters should order the chicken claws. Trust us, they taste better than they look.

The Cantonese saying *"fei qin zou shou"* roughly translates to *"if it flies, swims or runs, it's food."*

For our money, the best southern food comes from Chaozhou (Chiuchow), a coastal city only a few hours' drive north of its larger neighbors. Unlike dim sum, Chaozuo cuisine is extremely light and understated. Deep-fried bean curd is also a remarkably fresh Chaozuo dish.

NOT TO BE MISSED

One Chaozuo dish that appeals equally to the eye and the palate is the plain-sounding mashed vegetable with minced chicken soup. The dish is served in a large bowl, and resembles a green-and-white yin-yang. As befitting a dish resembling a Buddhist symbol, a vegetarian version substituting rice gruel for chicken broth is usually offered.

SOUTHWEST AND FAR WEST

Southwest

THE BASICS

When a person from the Southwest asks you if you like spicy food, consider your answer well. Natives of Sichuan and Hunan take the use of chilies, wild pepper, and garlic to blistering new heights. These two areas have been competing for the "spiciest province in China" title for centuries. The penchant for fiery food is likely due to the weather—hot and humid in the summer and harshly cold in the winter. But no matter what the temperature, if you're eating Sichuan or Hunan dishes, be prepared to sweat.

Southwest China shares some culinary traits with both Southeast Asia and India. This is likely due to the influences of travelers from both regions in centuries past. Traditional Chinese medicine also makes itself felt in the regional cuisine. Theory has it that sweating expels toxins and equalizes body temperature.

As Chairman Mao's province, Hunan has a number of dishes with revolutionary names. The most popular are red-cooked Hunan fish (*hongshao wuchangyu*) and red-cooked pork (*hongshao rou*), which was said to have been a personal favorite of the Great Helmsman.

Sichuan pepper creates a tingly numbness.

NOT TO BE MISSED

One dish you won't want to miss out on in Sichuan is *mala zigi*, or "peppery and hot chicken." It's one part chicken meat and three parts fried chilies and a Sichuanese wild pepper called *huajiao* that's so spicy it effectively numbs the tongue. At first it feels like eating Tiger Balm, but the hot-cool-numb sensation produced by crunching on the pepper is oddly addictive.

KUNG PAO CHICKEN

One of the most famous Chinese dishes, Kung Pao chicken (or gongbao jiding), enjoys a legend of its own.

Though shrouded in myth, its origin exemplifies the improvisational skills found in any good Chinese chef. The story of Kung Pao chicken has to do with a certain Qing Dynasty era (1644–1911) provincial governor named Ding Baozhen, who arrived home unexpectedly one day with a group of friends in tow. His cook, caught in between

shopping trips, had only the chicken breast and a few vegetables he was planning to cook for his own dinner. The crafty chef diced the chicken into tiny bits and fried it up with everything he could find in the cupboard—some peanuts, sugar, onion, garlic, bits of ginger, and a few handfuls of dried red peppers—and hoped for the best.

(top left) Tibetan dumplings. (center left) Uyghur-style pilaf. (bottom left) Monk stirring tsampa barley. (right) Juggling hot noodles in the Xinjiang province.

Far West

THE BASICS

Religion is the primary shaper of culinary tradition in China's Far West. Being a primarily Muslim province, chefs in Xinjiang don't use pork products of any kind. Instead, meals are likely to be heavy on spiced lamb. Baked flat breads coated in sesame seeds are a specialty. Whole lamb roasted on a spit, fine spicy tomato salads, and lightly spiced mutton and vegetable soups are also favorites.

NOT TO BE MISSED

In Tibet, climate is the major factor dictating cuisine. High and dry, the Tibetan plateau is hardly suited for rice cultivation. Whereas a Han meal might include rice, Tibetan cuisine tends to include tsampa, a ground barley usually cooked into a porridge. Another staple that's definitely an acquired taste is yak butter tea. Dumplings, known as *momo,* are wholesome and filling. Of course, if you want to go all out, order the yak penis with caterpillar fungus.

EAST

(top left) Cold tofu with pork and thousand-year-old eggs. (top right) Meaty dumplings. (bottom right) Letting off the steam of Shanghai: soup dumplings. (bottom left) Steamed Shanghai hairy crabs.

THE BASICS

The rice, seafood, and fresh vegetable-based cooking of the southern coastal provinces of Zhejiang and Jiangsu are known collectively as huiyang cai. As the area's biggest city, Shanghai has become a major center of the culinary arts. Some popular dishes in Shanghai are stir-fried freshwater eels and finely ground white pepper, and red-stewed fish—a boiled carp in sweet and sour sauce. Another Shanghai favorite are xiaolong bao, or little steamer dumplings. Similar to Cantonese dim sum, xiaolong bao tend to be more moist. The perfect steamed dumpling is meant to explode in your mouth in a juicy burst of meat.

NOT TO BE MISSED

Drunken anything! Shanghai chefs are known for their love of cooking with wine. Dishes like drunken chicken, drunken pigeon, and drunken crab are all delectable meals cooked with prodigious amounts of Shaoxing wine. People with an aversion to alcohol should definitely avoid these. Another meal not to be missed is hairy freshwater crabs, which only come into season in October. One enthusiast of the dish was 15th-century poet and essayist Li Yu, who wrote of the dish in near-erotic terms. "Meat as white as jade, golden roe . . . to use seasoning to improve its taste is like holding up a torch to brighten the sunshine."

$$$$
INTERNATIONAL

✕**My Humble House** 寒舍. From its decor to the dinnerware, there's nothing humble about this fusion restaurant. The main dining area is designed around a pool covered with rose petals; gingko leaves scatter the hallway. Many find this to be one of the few restaurants that successfully creates fusion dishes, tapping Western ingredients while retaining a distinct Chinese flavor. The lightly fried crispy prawn glazed with wasabi-mayonnaise sauce is unforgettable. For dessert, try cool lemongrass jelly served with red wolfberries. ✉ *W307 Oriental Plaza, 1 Dong Changan Jie, Dongcheng District* ☏ *010/8518–8811* ⊟ *AE, DC, MC, V* Ⓜ *Wangfujing* ✛ *E4.*

> **ON THE MENU**
>
> Peking duck is the capital's best-known dish, but there's much more to the city's cuisine than just the famous fowl. Beijing-style eateries offer many little-known but excellent specialties, such as *dalian huoshao* (meat- and vegetable-filled dumplings) and *zhajiangmian* (thick noodles with meat sauce). If you're adventurous, sample a bowl of intestines brewed in an aromatic broth mixed with bean curd, baked bread, and chopped cilantro.

¢
NORTHERN
CHINESE

✕**Paomo Guan** 泡馍馆. The bright red-and-blue bamboo shading on the front porch of this adorable spot will immediately catch your eye. Paomo Guan focuses on *paomo*—a Shaanxi trademark dish. Guests break a large piece of unleavened flat bread into little pieces and then put them in their bowl. After adding condiments, the waiter takes your bowl to the kitchen where broth—simmered with spices, including star anise, cloves, cardamom, cinnamon sticks, and bay leaves—is poured over the bread bits. ✉ *59 Chaoyangmennei Nanxiaojie, Dongcheng District* ☏ *010/6525–4639* ⊟ *No credit cards* ✛ *F3.*

$
SOUTHWEST-
ERN CHINESE

✕**Private Kitchen No. 44** 44号私家厨房. This place is worth the risk of getting lost in the maze of alleyways in which it is located. Call ahead to order the signature dish called *suantang yu*, meaning fish in a sour tomato broth. Fermented tomatoes brought from western China are essential to achieve the bright tanginess of this dish. Ask the waiter for the day's recommendations, or try the generous Y68 prix-fixe menu, which might include spicy plump shrimps and savory chicken wings. The service is notoriously slow but sincere. You may find your patience increases with a cup of house-made rice wine. ✉ *44 Xiguan Hutong, Dongcheng District* ☏ *010/6400–1280* ⊟ *No credit cards* ✛ *E2.*

¢
NORTHERN
CHINESE

✕**Qin Tangfu** 秦唐府. Authentic Shaanxi fare, including *roujia mo* (bread stuffed with meat), noodles, and dumplings, is served up next to the traditional stove, which produces hot, fresh baked goods. The low tables and chairs here reflect the lifestyle of Shaanxi people. Lending a bit of charm are framed paper cuts (a form of Chinese folk art in which red paper is cut into animal, flower, or human shapes), traditional handicrafts, and big baskets (where you can store your purse or bags while you eat). ✉ *69 Chaoyangmennei Nanxiaojie, Dongcheng District* ☏ *010/6559–8135* ⊟ *No credit cards* ✛ *F4.*

3

CLOSE UP

Fast Food: Beijing's Best Street Snacks

Part of the fun of exploring Beijing's lively hutongs is the chance to munch on the city's traditional snacks, served up by itinerant food sellers. Sweet-potato sellers turn their pedicabs into restaurants on wheels. An oil drum, balanced between the two rear wheels, becomes a makeshift baking unit, with small cakes of coal at the bottom roasting sweet potatoes strung around the top. In fall and winter, sugarcoated delicacies are a popular treat. Crab apples, water chestnuts, grapes, and yams are placed on skewers, about a half-dozen to a stick; the fruit is then bathed in syrup that hardens into a shiny candy coating, providing a sugar rush for those all-day walks.

The Donghuamen night market is more fun for photographers than gourmets. Located on the north end of the Wangfujing pedestrian street, the market has an extensive lineup of cooked-food stalls, many selling food items designed to shock. Sure, it's extremely touristy, and you'll be elbow-to-elbow with wide-eyed travelers from tour buses, but it is also an incredibly fun place. Cheerful vendors call out to potential customers, their wares glowing under red lanterns. Kebabs are the main attraction here, and it seems as though anything under the sun can be skewered and fried. There are the outlandish skewers of scorpion, silkworm cocoons, and even starfish, all fried to a crisp and covered with spices. There are also the more palatable (and more authentic) lamb kebabs flavored with cumin and chili flakes.

Worried about hygiene? The turnover at vendor carts and street-side stands is rapid, so it's unusual that anything has been sitting around long. It's easy to tell if the food is fresh, because it will be furiously hot when served. If you have any doubts, ask the vendor to cook yours to order, rather than accepting the ready-made skewers on display.

On the banks of Houhai, near the historical residence of Soong Ching-ling, is the entrance to Xiaoyou Hutong. Down this narrow alley you'll find Jiumen Xiaochi, a traditional courtyard house occupied by famous family eateries forced to relocate because of urban redevelopment plans. Some of these small eateries have been producing the same specialty dishes for decades. Look out for *lu dagun*, a pastry made of alternate layers of glutinous rice and red bean paste; *dalian huoshao*, northern-style pork potstickers; and *zha guanchang*, deep-fried slices of cooked sweet potato starch dipped in a raw garlic sauce.

Some modern snacks are ubiquitous, such as the *jiangbing*, a hearty crepe made from mung bean flour and stuffed with egg and a crispy piece of fried batter. Briny fermented bean paste and hot chili sauce are spread on thick before they are topped with a sprinkling of cilantro and spring onions. Also on the streets: *baozi*, fluffy white buns filled with all manners of meat and vegetables, and *xianbing*, wheat flour pockets typically stuffed with chives and eggs. When the weather turns colder, expect fruit covered in syrup and roasted sweet potatoes. These snacks satisfy cold-weather cravings, and are an important part of the city's street-food extravaganza.

3

$$$$ ✕ **Red Capital Club** 新红资俱乐部. Occupying a meticulously restored
CHINESE courtyard home in one of Beijing's few remaining traditional neigh-
Fodor's Choice borhoods, the Red Capital Club oozes nostalgia. Cultural Revolution
★ memorabilia and books dating from the Great Leap Forward era adorn
every nook of the small bar, while the theme of the dining room is imperial. The fancifully written menu reads like a fairy tale, with dreamily
named dishes. South of Clouds is a Yunnan dish of fish baked over bamboo—it's said to be a favorite of a former Communist marshal. Dream
of the Red Chamber is a fantastic eggplant dish cooked according to
a recipe in the classic novel by the same name. ✉ *66 Dongsi Jiutiao,
Dongcheng District* ☎ *010/6402–7150* ✍ *Reservations essential* ▭ *AE,
DC, MC, V* ⊘ *No lunch* ✛ *E3.*

$$ ✕ **Shi** 食. Tucked away in an alley adjacent to the Forbidden City, Shi is
CHINESE FUSION nestled among traditional temples and courtyard houses. Contemporary
renditions of eight classic dishes come with a story, told by your server,
that link the recipe to a specific Chinese emperor. A side of garlic bread
balances the Poison Soup, a chicken broth infused with Chinese herbs,
and the Concubine Fragrance Grilled Lamb Chops is a piquant favor-
ite from Emperor Qianlong's rule. There is also a collection of vintage
Chinese rice wines. ✉ *33 Qihelou Hutong, Tian'anmen, Dongcheng
District* ☎ *010/6526–5566* ▭ *AE, DC, MC, V* ✛ *D3.*

$$$$ ✕ **The Source** 都江源. The Source serves a set menu of Sichuan specialties,
SICHUAN which completely changes every two weeks. The menu includes several
Fodor's Choice appetizers, both hot and mild dishes, and a few surprise concoctions
★ from the chef. On request, the kitchen will tone down the spiciness.
The Source's location was once the backyard of a Qing Dynasty gen-
eral regarded by the Qing court as "The Great Wall of China" for his
military exploits. The grounds have been painstakingly restored; an
upper level overlooks a small garden filled with pomegranate and date
trees. The central yard's dining is serene and acoustically protected
from the hustle and bustle outside. ✉ *14 Banchang Hutong, Kuanjie,
Dongcheng District* ☎ *010/6400–3736* ✍ *Reservations essential* ▭ *AE,
DC, MC, V* ✛ *D2.*

$ ✕ **Still Thoughts** 静思素食坊. Soft Buddhist chants hum in this clean, cheer-
VEGETARIAN ful restaurant. Even though there is no meat on the menu, carnivores
★ may still be happy here as much of the food is prepared to look and taste
like meat. Try the crispy Peking "duck," or a "fish" (made of tofu skin)
that even has scales carved into it. *Zaisu jinshen,* another favorite, has
a filling that looks and tastes like pork. It is wrapped in tofu skin, deep-
fried, and coated with a light sauce. ✉ *18A Dafosi Dongjie, Dongcheng
District* ☎ *010/6400–8941* ▭ *No credit cards* ✛ *E3.*

¢ ✕ **Yue Bin** 悦宾饭馆. Located on a narrow alley opposite the National
BEIJING Museum of Art, Yue Bin's home-style cooking attracts neighborhood
residents as well as hungry museumgoers. In business since 1949, it
has managed to maintain its popularity throughout decades. The no-
frills dining room is just big enough for half a dozen spotless tables.
Don't leave without trying *suanni zhouzi,* pork elbow in a marinade of
raw garlic and vinegar; the *guota doufuhe,* bite-size tofu stuffed with
minced pork; or the *wusitong,* a roll of duck and vegetables. ✉ *43
Cuihua Hutong, Dongcheng District* ☎ *010/6524–5322* ▭ *No credit
cards* ✛ *E3.*

XICHENG DISTRICT 西城区

Xicheng extends north and west of the Forbidden City, and includes Beihai Park and Houhai. Dive into the hutongs here and try one of the excellent local restaurants, such as **Jiumen Xiaochi**, which serves Old Beijing favorites, or **Kong Yi Ji**, for its huixiang dou, boiled bean with star anise, and *Dongpo rou*, or red braised pork belly.

$$$$ ✕**Cepe** 意味轩. The Ritz-Carlton's
ITALIAN flagship restaurant serves some of the city's best Italian food. As the name implies, the kitchen is proficient in dishes using a variety of mushrooms, such as homemade beef and porcini mushroom ravioli with a black truffle sauce. An in-house humidor stores seasonal mushrooms that can be transformed into various risottos and pastas. Taking the fungi theme a step further, about 1,000 mushroom-shaped sculptures are suspended from the ceiling, adding a touch of whimsy to the otherwise unaffected interior. ✉ *Ritz-Carlton Beijing, 8 Beijing Financial St., Xicheng District* ☎ 10/6601–6666 ▭ *AE, DC, MC, V* ✛ *C4.*

$$$$ ✕**Fangshan** 仿膳. In a traditional courtyard villa on the shore of Beihai,
BEIJING you can get a taste of China's imperial cuisine. Established in 1925 by
★ three royal chefs, Fangshan serves dishes once prepared for the imperial family, based on recipes gathered across China. The place is best known for its filled pastries and steamed breads—traditional snack foods developed to satisfy Empress Dowager Cixi's sweet tooth. To experience Fangshan's exquisite imperial fare, order one of the banquet-style set meals at Y500 per person. Be sure to make reservations two or three days in advance. ✉ *Beihai Park, northwest of the Forbidden City, Xicheng District* ☎ *010/6401–1879* ⌖ *Reservations essential* ▭ *AE, DC, MC, V* Ⓜ *Tiananmen West* ✛ *C3.*

$ ✕**Jing Wei Lou** 京味楼. Always crowded with locals, this "House of
BEIJING Beijing Flavors" focuses on traditional local fare. Dishes include *ma doufu* (sautéed mung-bean pulp), *zhagezha* (fried mung-bean paste), and a variety of mutton dishes. The two-story building has red pillars; the entrance is guarded by a statue of a man traditionally dressed and holding a birdcage—check out his Manchu queue (the hair braid men were forced to wear during the Qing Dynasty). A semi-open kitchen around the inner dining room gives the restaurant the flavor of an Old Beijing courtyard house. ✉ *181 A Di'anmen Xidajie, Xicheng District* ☎ *010/6617–6514* ▭ *No credit cards* ✛ *C2.*

Street snacks at Wangfujing, Beijing's premier shopping spot.

$
SHANGHAINESE
AND JIANGZHE

✕ **Kong Yi Ji** 孔乙己. Named for the down-and-out protagonist of a short story by Lu Xun (one of China's most famous writers), this restaurant is set behind a small bamboo forest. Upon entering, the first thing you'll see is a bust of Lu Xun. The old-fashioned menu, which is bound with thread in a traditional fashion, features some of the dishes made famous in the story, such as *huixiang dou*, or aniseed-flavored broad beans. A wide selection of *huangjiu*, sweet rice wine, is served in heated silver pots; it's sipped from a special ceramic cup. ⊠ *South shore of Shichahai, Deshengmennei Dajie, Xicheng District* ☎ *010/6618–4915* ☰ *AE, MC, V* ✛ *C2.*

$$$$
CHINESE
Fodor's Choice
★

✕ **Mei Fu** 梅府. In a plush, restored courtyard on Houhai's south bank, Mei Fu oozes intimate elegance. The interior is filled with antique furniture and velvet curtains punctuated by pebbled hallways and waterfalls. Black-and-white photos of Mei Lanfang, China's famous opera star, who performed female roles, hang on the walls. Diners choose from set menus, starting from Y300 per person, which feature typical Jiangsu and Zhejiang cuisine, such as fried shrimp, pineapple salad, and tender leafy vegetables. A Y200 (per person) lunch is also available. ⊠ *24 Daxiangfeng Hutong, south bank of Houhai Lake, Xicheng District* ☎ *010/6612–6845* ☖ *Reservations essential* ☰ *MC, V* ✛ *D2.*

$
BEIJING

✕ **Shaguo Ju** 沙锅居. Established in 1741, Shaguo Ju serves a simple Manchu favorite—*bairou,* or white-meat pork, which first became popular 300 years ago. The first menu pages list all the dishes cooked in the *shaguo* (the Chinese term for a casserole pot). The classic *shaguo bairou* consists of strips of pork neatly lined up, concealing bok choy and glass noodles below. Shaguo Ju emerged as a result of ceremonies held by imperial officials and wealthy Manchus in the Qing Dynasty,

CLOSE UP

Legendary Eats in the Xiaoyou Hutong

A dozen well-known restaurants, some dating back more than a century and threatened by the urban renewal of the old Qianmen business district, have found refuge in a large traditional courtyard house in **Xiaoyou Hutong**. Some of Beijing's oldest and most famous eateries have regrouped here under one roof. Our favorites are:

Baodu Feng. This vendor specializes in tripe. The excellent accompanying dipping sauce is a long-guarded family secret. You'll see upon entering that this stall has the longest line.

Chatang Li. On offer here is *miancha*, a flour paste with either sweet or salty toppings. Miancha was created by an imperial chef who ground the millet, poured boiling water into it, mixed it into a paste, and added brown sugar and syrup. The imperial family loved it, and it soon became a breakfast staple.

Niangao Qian. This stall makes sticky rice layered with red-bean paste. It's the most popular sticky rice snack made by the Hui, or Chinese Muslims.

Yangtou Ma. Known for thin-sliced meat from boiled lamb's head, this shop was once located on Ox Street, in the old Muslim quarter.

Doufunao Bai. These folks sell soft bean curd, recognized for its delicate

texture. It's best topped with braised lamb and mushrooms.

En Yuan Ju. Sample the *chaogeda*, which are small, stir-fried noodles with vegetables and meat.

Yue Sheng Zhai. Line up for excellent *jiang niurou* (braised beef), *shao yangrou* (braised lamb), and *zasui tang* (mutton soup).

Xiaochang Chen. The main ingredient of this vendor's dish is intestines, complemented with pork, bean curd, and *huoshao* (unleavened baked bread). The contents are simmered slowly in an aromatic broth.

Dalian Huoshao. This stall serves pot stickers in the shape of old-fashioned satchels that the Chinese once wore. These pot stickers were the creation of the Yao family of Shunyi, who set up their small restaurant in the old Dong'an Market in 1876.

The Jiumen Xiaochi (Nine Gates Snacks). The archway by the lake in front of Xiaoyou Hutong refers to the former nine gates in the inner city of the Forbidden City. The private dining rooms in the courtyard are named after these gates.

✉ *1 Xiaoyou Hutong, Xicheng District* ☎ *010/6402–5858* ▭ *No credit cards* ✛ *C1.*

which included sacrificial offerings of whole pigs. The meat offerings were later given away to the nightwatch guards, who shared the "gifts" with friends and relatives. Such gatherings gradually turned into a small business, and white meat became very popular. ✉ *60 Xisi Nan Dajie, Xicheng District* ☎ *010/6602–1126* ▭ *No credit cards* Ⓜ *Xidan* ✛ *C4.*

SOUTHERN DISTRICTS: CHONGWEN AND XUANWU 崇文区 AND 宣武区

These two districts stretch south of the Forbidden City and Tiananmen Square. Once a bustling center of commerce and street life, with opera theaters, street performers, and many of Beijing's *laozihao*, or famous old name-brand shops, both Chongwen and Xuanwu are undergoing major renovations nowadays. Venture here to sample some of the city's most famous eateries, such as Li Qun Roast Duck Restaurant and Jinyang Fanzhuang, which serves Shanxi specialties.

$
ECLECTIC
Fodor's Choice
★

✕ **Capital M.** One of the few restaurants in the capital with both stunning views and a chef with versatile culinary skills. The Aussie-bred-and-trained chef, Robert Cunningham, prepares a menu that is contemporarily innovative and unique in taste. Try his subtle and complex Kashgar-inspired chicken, served with chickpeas, currants, pistachios, and infused with a mix of spices. The hearty weekend brunch should not be missed. The backdrop to this culinary experience is a bold and colorful muraled wall sandwiched between the ornate ceiling and the starkly contrasting black-and-white-tiled floors, which when combined create a vibrant and cheerful atmosphere. The imposing Arrow and Zhengyang towers at the southern end of Tiananmen Square provide romantic views. ✉ *2 Qianmen Pedestrian Street, Chongwen District* ☎ *010/6702–2727* ✍ *Reservations essential* ▬ *AE, DC, MC, V* ✛ *D5.*

$
NORTHERN
CHINESE

✕ **Jinyang Fanzhuang.** Reliable, standard Shaanxi fare is the order of the day here, alongside famous crispy duck and cat-ear-shaped pasta stir-fried with meat and vegetables. End your meal with a "sweet happiness" pastry. Jinyang Fangzhuang is attached to the ancient courtyard home of Ji Xiaolan, a Qing Dynasty scholar, the chief compiler of the *Complete Library of the Four Branches of Literature.* You can visit the old residence without admission fee and see Ji Xiaolan's study, where he wrote his famous essays. The crab-apple trees and wisteria planted during his lifetime still bloom in the courtyard. ✉ *241 Zhushikou Xi Dajie, Xuanwu District* ☎ *010/6354–1107* ▬ *No credit cards* ⊘ *No lunch* ✛ *D5.*

$$
BEIJING
Fodor's Choice
★

✕ **Li Qun Roast Duck Restaurant** 利群烤鸭店. Juicy, whole ducks roasting in a traditional oven greet you upon entering this simple courtyard house. This family-run affair, far from the crowds and commercialism of Quanjude, is Beijing's most famous Peking duck eatery. Li Qun is a choice option for those who enjoy a good treasure hunt: the restaurant is hidden deep in a hutong neighborhood. It should take about 10 minutes to walk there from Chongwenmen Xi Dajie, though you may have to stop several times and ask for directions. It's so well known by locals, however, that when they see foreigners coming down the street, they automatically point in the restaurant's direction. Sure, the restrooms

Kebabs are a favorite street food all over China.

and dining room are a bit shabby, but the place is charming. Ask for an English menu and feast to your heart's content! ✉ *11 Beixiangfeng Hutong, Zhengyi Lu, Chongwen District* ☎ *010/6705–5578* ✍ *Reservations essential* ▭ *No credit cards* Ⓜ *Chongwen* ✛ *E5.*

¢ ✕ **Old Beijing Noodle King** 老北京炸酱面大王. Close to the Temple of

NORTHERN CHINESE

Heaven, this noodle house serves hand-pulled noodles and traditional local dishes in a lively old-time atmosphere. Waiters shout across the room to announce customers arriving. Try the tasty *zhajiang* noodle accompanied by meat sauce and celery, bean sprouts, green beans, soybeans, slivers of cucumber, and red radish. ✉ *29 Chongwenmen Dajie, Hongqiao Market, Chongwen District* ☎ *010/6705–6705* ▭ *No credit cards* ✛ *E6.*

CHAOYANG DISTRICT 朝阳区

The huge Chaoyang district extends east from Dongcheng, encompassing Beijing's Jianguomen diplomatic neighborhood, the Sanlitun bar area, the Central Business District, and several outdoor markets and upscale shopping malls. The large foreign population living and working here has attracted a bevy of international restaurants, making this a fine place to sample dishes from around the world. If you're in Sanlitun, try Vietnamese food at Nam Nam or Italian dishes at Assaggi. In Jianguomenwai, head to Madam Zhu's Kitchen for both fiery and mild dishes or Nola for authentic Louisianan fare.

$$ ✕ **1/5 Taverna.** Rustic dishes are a perfect contrast to the industrial-chic

MEDITERRANEAN

interior of this former factory. The young, well-heeled crowd fuels up on roasted lamb and buttery pork belly before heading out into the nightclubs of Sanlitun. The dishes are generously portioned, but the flavors can be a bit underwhelming. Perch yourself on the luxe leather seats against the exposed brick walls and sip on a selection from the modest wine list. There's no need to flinch when the roaming band appears, as the group is partial to unobtrusive ballads—unless you dare request otherwise. ⊠ *Courtyard 4, Gongti Beilu, Chaoyang District* ☎ *010/6501–8882* ▭ *AE, MC, V* ✛ *G3.*

WORD OF MOUTH

"We liked the Li Qun Roast Duck Restaurant, which is in a hutong area south of Tiananmen Square. It's busy, so get your hotel to book you a table—it's a well-known place. At Li Qun, which appeared to be popular with expats and locals, we were able to order in English. Beijing Duck is roasted, but the crispy skin is served separately, along with pancakes, sliced green onions, and a dipping sauce. By the way, I found that rice wasn't always provided as a matter of course, so you may have to ask for it—the word is *mifan*, pronounced mee-FAHN." —Neil_Oz

$$$
BRAZILIAN
Fodor's Choice
★

✕ **Alameda.** Specializing in Brazilian fare, Alameda serves simple but delicious dishes. The weekday Y60 lunch specials are one of the best deals in town. Their menu is light yet satisfying, with plenty of Latin influences. Crowds seek out the *feijoada*—Brazil's national dish—a hearty black-bean stew with pork and rice, served only on Saturdays. The glass walls and ceiling make it a bright, pleasant place to dine but magnify the din of the crowded room. ⊠ *Sanlitun Beijie, by the Nali shopping complex, Chaoyang District* ☎ *010/6417–8084* ▭ *AE, MC, V* ✛ *H2.*

$
MOROCCAN

✕ **Argana.** Beijing's only Moroccan restaurant offers up authentic and mouthwatering dishes such as a slow-cooked chicken *tagine*—the heavy clay pot and cone-shaped lid keep the spices and flavor intact. The couscous is delicious after it soaks up sauces from the chicken. Open your appetite with a fresh salad and close your meal with sweet mint tea. It's a small size restaurant with a limited number of seats, so it would be wise to call ahead of time and book your table. Argana also has a decent range of affordable Spanish wines. ⊠ *55 Xingfu Cun Zhonglu G/F, Jiezuo Daxia, Chaoyang District* ☎ *010/8448–8250* ▭ *AE, MC, V* ✛ *G3.*

$$$$
INTERNATIONAL
★

✕ **Aria** 阿郦雅. Aria's outdoor dining is secluded within neatly manicured bushes and roses, providing a perfectly quiet lunch spot amid Beijing's frenetic downtown. Sample the fish filet topped with crispy pork skin. The best deal at this elegant restaurant is the weekday business lunch: for just Y198 you can enjoy a soup or salad, main course, dessert, and coffee or tea. Renaissance-style paintings decorate the walls. There is a posh dining area and bar on the first floor, and more intimate dining at the top of the spiral staircase. Live jazz enlivens the evenings. ⊠ *2/F China World Hotel, 1 Jianguomenwai Dajie, Chaoyang District* ☎ *010/6505–2266 Ext. 38* ▭ *AE, MC, V* Ⓜ *Guomao* ✛ *H4.*

$$
ITALIAN

✕ **Assaggi** 尝试. Your mood brightens the minute you walk up the sunlightened spiral staircase to the rooftop patio, which includes glassed-in and open-air sections. The flowerbox-lined side of the roof overlooks the tree-lined street below. There is a comprehensive four-course Italian menu, including fish, chicken, pork, ham, and pastas in pesto and tomato sauces. The ravioli, tortellini, and spaghetti with fresh clams and extra-virgin olive oil are all superb. Check out the reasonable prix-fixe business lunches. ⊠ *1 Sanlitun Bei Xiaojie, Chaoyang District* ☎ *010/8454–4508* ☰ *AE, MC, V* ✛ *G2.*

$$$$
ITALIAN

✕ **Barolo 巴罗洛**. This Italian eatery is equally appropriate for a power lunch or a romantic dinner. A love of wine clearly is the inspiration, from the bold burgundies of the decor to the impressive list of Italian vintages to the use of the restaurant's namesake in dishes such as the herb-crusted rack of lamb with glazed shallots. But it's the Parmesan risotto that keeps them coming back for more. Prepared tableside in a hollowed-out wheel of parmeggiano reggiano, it's topped with decadent shaved black truffles. ⊠ *Ritz Carlton Hotel, 83A Jianguo Lu, Chaoyang District* ☎ *010/5908–8888* ☰ *DC, MC, V* ✛ *H4.*

$$$$
ASIAN

✕ **Bei 北**. This little joint has attitude to spare. Perch at the sassy sushi bar or book a sleek wood-paneled private room to enjoy the cuisines of northern Asia. Regional dishes have been transformed by creative presentation and haute techniques, so dishes like Wagyu steak are fit for an emperor. The sashimi is flown in directly from Tokyo, and the silken chocolate tofu is accented with coarse salt. The competent staff will help you navigate their comprehensive list of sakes and wines. ⊠ *The Opposite House, Building 1, 11 Sanlitun Lu, Chaoyang District* ☎ *010/6417–6688* ☰ *AE, DC, MC, V* ✛ *G2.*

$
TAIWANESE
★

✕ **Bellagio 鹿港小镇**. Chic Bellagio is a bright, trendy-but-comfortable restaurant serving up typical Sichuan dishes with a Taiwanese twist. A delicious choice is their *migao* (glutinous rice with dried mushrooms and dried shrimp, stir-fried rice noodles, and meatball soup). You can finish your meal with a Taiwan-style crushed ice and toppings of red bean, green bean, mango, strawberry, or peanut. Bellagio is open until 4 AM, making it a favorite with Beijing's chic clubbing set. The smartly dressed all-female staff—clad in black and white—have identical short haircuts. ⊠ *6 Gongti Xilu, Chaoyang District* ☎ *010/6551–3533* ⌦ *Reservations essential* ☰ *AE, MC, V* ✛ *G3.*

¢
MIDDLE EASTERN

✕ **Biteapitta 吧嗒饼**. Located along a strip of neon-lit bars, this kosher falafel joint serves delicious and filling fare such as hummus, lamb shwarma, and falafel sandwiches brimming with yogurt, cucumbers, and tomatoes. The cheerful room encourages diners to linger. ⊠ *201 Tongli Studio, 43 Sanlitun North, Chaoyang District* ☎ *010/6467–2961* ☰ *AE, MC, V* ✛ *H2.*

$
CAFE
★

✕ **The Bookworm 虫**. We love this Beijing hot spot when we're craving a double-dose of intellectual stimulation and good food. Thousands of English-language books fill the shelves and may be borrowed for a fee or read inside. New books and magazines are also for sale. This is a popular venue for guest speakers, poetry readings, and live-music performances. The French chef offers a three-course set lunch and dinner. For a nibble, rather than a full meal, sandwiches, salads, and a cheese platter are also available. ⊠ *Building 4, Nan Sanlitun Lu, Chaoyang District* ☎ *010/6586–9507* ☰ *No credit cards* ✛ *G3.*

$$
GERMAN

✕ **Café Constance**. The opening of Café Constance, a German bakery, brought excellent rye, pumpernickel, and whole-wheat breads to Beijing. The hearty "small" breakfast begins with coffee, fresh fruit, muesli, unsweetened yogurt, eggs, and bacon; the big breakfast adds several cold cuts and breads and rolls. This is a true winner if you're looking for a good breakfast, simple meal, or a good cup of java and dessert. ⊠ *Lucky St. No. 27, 29 Zaoying Lu, Chaoyang District* ☏ *010/5867–0201* ⊟ *AE, MC, V* ⊹ *H1.*

$
FRENCH
✕ **Comptoirs de France Bakery** 法派. This contemporary French-managed café serves a variety of sandwiches, excellent desserts, coffees, and hot chocolates. Besides the standard Americano, cappuccino, and latte, Comptoirs has a choice of unusual hot-chocolates flavors, including banana and Rhum Vieux and orange Cointreau. In the Sichuan peppercorn–infused hot chocolate, the peppercorns float in the brew, giving it a pleasant peppery aroma. ⊠ *China Central Place, Building 15, N 102, 89 Jianguo Rd. (just northeast of Xiandai Soho), Chaoyang District* ☏ *010/6530–5480* ⊟ *No credit cards* ⊹ *H4.*

$$
NORTHERN
CHINESE
✕ **Da Dong Roast Duck** 北京大董烤鸭店. One taste of the Beijing-style roast duck and the reason for this restaurant's fervent following becomes obvious—crispy, caramel skin over lean but juicy meat. It's intensely aromatic and does justice to this most celebrated of the city's dishes. Other items on their menu are also of consistently high quality, such as the duck liver in brine and stir-fried shrimps. ⊠ *Bldg 3, Tuanjiehu Beikou, Chaoyang District* ☏ *010/6582–2892* ⊟ *AE, MC, V* ⊹ *F3, H3.*

$$$
SHANGHAINESE
AND JIANGZHE
Fodor's Choice
★
✕ **Din Tai Fung** 鼎泰丰. The arrival of Din Tai Fung—one of Taipei's most famous restaurants—was warmly welcomed by Beijing's food fanatics. The restaurant's specialty is *xiaolong bao* (juicy fillings wrapped in a light unleavened-dough skin and cooked in a bamboo steamer), which are served with slivers of tender ginger in a light black vinegar. Xiaolong bao have three different fillings: ground pork, seafood, or crabmeat. If you can, leave some room for the scrumptious tiny dumplings packed with red-bean paste. This restaurant is frequented by both Beijing's up-and-coming middle class and old Taiwan hands, who are fervently loyal to its delicate morsels. ⊠ *24 Xinyuan Xili Zhongjie, Chaoyang District* ☏ *010/6462–4502* ⊟ *AE, MC, V* ⊹ *G2.*

$$
BEIJING
✕ **Duck de Chine** 全鸭季. This duck eatery is located in 1949 Hidden City, a large complex that consists of Duck de Chine and a gallery, open coffee bar, noodle bar, wine club, and Western restaurant. The restaurant is set up in a traditional structure with a skylight running across the roof ridge so that the room is bathed in natural light. Large windows offer views of the green landscaped complex, while the red bricks and wooden floor give the venue a rustic feel. The duck sauce is the creation of Chef Lam, who adds a dash of hoisin and oyster sauce to fermented soybean sauce. It's the perfect melding of flavors, neither too sweet nor too salty. The amazingly rich soup is fortified with tonic herbs such as wolfberries and huaishan. ⊠ *Courtyard 4, Gongti Beilu, Chaoyang District* ☏ *010/6501–1949* ⊟ *AE, MC, V* ⊹ *G3.*

$
SICHUAN
✕ **Feiteng Yuxiang** 沸腾鱼乡. Be warned: Sichuan spices can be addictive. This restaurant's signature dish features sliced fish cooked in broth brimming with scarlet chili peppers and piquant peppercorns. The fish is impossibly delicate, melting in your mouth like butter, while the chilies and peppercorns tingle the lips. It's an overwhelming experience that you'll want to repeat over and over. Red-faced diners test the limits of

their spice-tolerance over dandan noodles and *koushuiji*, or mouthwatering chicken. The service is unfriendly but efficient. ⊠ *1 Gongti Beilu, Chaoyang District* ☎ *010/6417–4988* ▭ *MC, V* ✛ *G3.*

$$$$
MEDITERRANEAN

✕ **Fennel** 茴香. Swiss-born Christian Hoffman is the executive chef of this contemporarily designed restaurant nestled in a chic boutique hotel in what used to be the site of a crystal factory. The black cod fish in ponzu broth is marvelous while the fennel salad is seductively refreshing. The selective selection of desserts is also strikingly impressive. Try the fennel-flavored ice cream clamped between moist and chewy pieces of macaroon—amazing. Also, highly recommended is the cheese platter, which consists of a nice selection of soft and hard cheeses, and the homemade crispy dried fruit bread. The black-and-white images of photograper Marco Beretta's spiritual travels lend an austere but pleasantly peaceful feel to the restaurant. ⊠ *Jiuxianqiao Lu, 2 Hao Yuan, 798 Art District, Chaoyang District* ☎ *010/6436–1818* ▭ *AE, DC, MC, V* ✛ *H1.*

¢
NORTHERN
CHINESE

✕ **Hai Wan Ju** 海碗居. Haiwan means "a bowl as deep as the sea," fitting for this eatery that specializes in crockery filled with hand-pulled noodles. The interior is simple, with traditional wooden tables and benches. A *xiao er* (a "young brother" in a white mandarin-collar shirt and black pants) greets you with a shout, which is then echoed in a thundering chorus by the rest of the staff. The clanking dishes and constant greetings re-create the busy atmosphere of an old teahouse. There are two types of noodles here: *guoshui*, noodles that have been rinsed and cooled; and *guotiao*, meaning "straight out of the pot," which is ideal for winter days. Vegetables, including diced celery, radish, green beans, bean sprouts, cucumber, and scallions, are placed on individual small dishes. Nothing tastes as good as a hand-pulled noodle: it's doughy and chewy, a texture that can only be achieved by strong hands repeatedly stretching the dough. ⊠ *36 Songyu Nanlu, Chaoyang District* ☎ *010/8731–3518* ▭ *AE, MC, V* ✛ *G4.*

$$$$
JAPANESE

✕ **Hatsune @ the Village** 隐泉日本料理. Owned by Alan Wong, a Chinese-American with impeccable taste, this is one of the most popular Japanese restaurants in Beijing. Ultramodern interiors and friendly service make for a pleasant dining experience—be sure to make a reservation. Try the fresh sashimi, tempura, grilled fish, or one of the many innovative California-style sushi rolls. There's also an extensive sake menu. ⊠ *19 Sanlitun Road, 3rd floor, S8-30 Sanlitun Village, Chaoyang District* ☎ *010/6581–3939* ⌕ *Reservations essential* ▭ *AE, MC, V* ✛ *H4.*

$$$$
GUIZHOU

✕ **Jia No. 21** 甲21号. Parked near Beijing's university district, and away from the usual circuit of expat and tourist destinations, Jia No. 21 stands out from its drab neighborhood thanks to its contemporary décor and avant garde paintings and sculptures against a bare wall. The dishes served here are a collection of the best of Guizhou and Yunnan with a Thai twist. Lemongrass is added to the sour fish head soup, lending to another level of sophistication. ⊠ *Jia 21 Bei Tucheng Donglu, Chaoyang District* ☎ *010/6489–5066* ⌕ *Reservations essential* ▭ *No credit cards* ✛ *E1.*

$
CANTONESE

✕ **Jun Wangfu** 君王府. Tucked inside Chaoyang Park, Jun Wangfu excels in classic Cantonese fare; it's frequented by Hong Kong expats. The

comprehensive menu includes steamed tofu with scallops, spinach with taro and egg, crispy goose, roast chicken, and steamed fish with ginger and scallion. The fresh-baked pastry filled with *durian* (a spiny tropical fruit with a smell so notoriously strong it is often banned from being brought aboard airplanes) is actually a mouthwatering rarity—don't be scared off by its overpowering odor. ⊠ *19 Chaoyang Gongyuan Nanlu, east of Chaoyang Park south gate, Chaoyang District* ☎ *010/6507–7888* ⊹ *H2.*

$$$$
FRENCH

✕ **Justine's 杰斯汀.** Classic French cuisine and wine, including foie gras, snails, and Château Haut-Brion, are served with the utmost attention at Beijing's oldest French restaurant. Justine's is well known for its delicious desserts. ⊠ *Jianguo Hotel, 5 Jianguomenwai Dajie, Chaoyang District* ☎ *010/6500–2233 Ext. 8039* ⊟ *AE, MC, V* ⊹ *H4.*

$$$$
HUNAN

✕ **Karaiya Spice House 辣屋.** The tangy smell of chili wafts through the air as you step into this stylish, two-story Hunan eatery, known for its super spicy, inexpensive, and delectable dishes. Stir-fried morning glory with fermented bean curd, tofu with assorted mushrooms, butterflied Mandarin fish with chopped chilies, and spareribs doused in mouthwatering preserved vegetables are among the favorites. ⊠ *Bldg. 8, The Village South, 19 Sanlitun Road Chaoyang District* ☎ *010/6415–3535* ⊟ *AE, DC, MC, V* ⊹ *G2.*

$$
ITALIAN
★

✕ **La Dolce Vita 甜蜜生活.** The food here lives up to the restaurant's name, "the good life." A basket of warm bread is served immediately upon being seated—a nice treat in a city where good bread is hard to come by. You'll have trouble decided between ravioli, tortellini, and oven-fired pizza, all of which are excellent. The rice-ball appetizer, with cheese and bits of ham inside is also fantastic. ⊠ *8 Xindong Lu North, Chaoyang District* ☎ *010/6468–2894* ⊟ *AE, MC, V* ⊹ *G2.*

$$
CANTONESE

✕ **La Galerie 中国艺苑.** Choose between two outdoor dining areas: one a wooden platform facing the bustling Guanghua Road; the other well hidden in the back, overlooking the greenery of Ritan Park. Inspired Cantonese food and dim sum fill the menu: *changfen* (steamed rice noodles) are rolled and cut into small pieces then stir-fried with crunchy shrimp, strips of lotus root, and baby bok choy, accompanied by sweet soybean, peanut, and sesame pastes. The *xiajiao* (steamed shrimp dumplings) envelop juicy shrimp and water chestnuts. ⊠ *South gate of Ritan Park, Guanghua Rd., Chaoyang District* ☎ *010/8563–8698* ⊟ *AE, MC, V* Ⓜ *Jianguomen* ⊹ *G3.*

$$
CHINESE

✕ **Madam Zhu's Kitchen 汉舍.** This sprawling basement dining venue is brightly lit and decked out with sofas, fresh-cut flowers, and fun celebrity photos that line the white walls. While the doors are whitewashed with an antique look and the European cabinets display blue and white china, there is nothing ye olde country inn about this sleek space. The menu features classic regional dishes with new twists—mouthwatering *xun changyu*, smoked fish, scallion chicken and the poached egg white filled with crabmeat are among their best dishes. ⊠ *B, Bldg. D, Vantone Center, 6A Chaoyangmenwai Dajie, Chaoyang District* ☎ *010/5907–1625* ⊟ *AE, DC, MC, V* ⊹ *G4.*

$
TIBETAN

✕ **Makye Ame 玛吉阿米.** Prayer flags lead you to the second floor entrance of this Tibetan restaurant, where a pile of mani stones and a large prayer wheel greet you. Long Tibetan Buddhist trumpets, lanterns, and handicrafts decorate the walls, and the kitchen serves a range of hearty dishes that run well beyond the staples of yak-butter tea and *tsampa* (roasted barley flour). Try the vegetable *pakoda* (a deep-fried dough pocket filled with vegetables), curry potatoes, or roasted lamb spareribs. Heavy wooden tables with brass corners, soft lighting, and Tibetan textiles make this an especially soothing choice. ⊠ *11 Xiushui Nanjie, 2nd floor, Chaoyang District* ☏ *010/6506–9616* ☐ *MC, V* Ⓜ *Jianguomen* ✛ *G4.*

$$$
ITALIAN

✕ **Metro Café** 美特柔. A good assortment of fresh Italian pastas, soups, bruschettas, and meat dishes round out the menu at this informal eatery. Although service is inconsistent, the food is usually very good, and the outdoor tables are wonderful (if you can get one) on spring and summer evenings. ⊠ *6 Gongrentiyuguan Xilu, Chaoyang District* ☏ *010/6552–7828* ☐ *AE, V* ☺ *Closed Mon.* ✛ *G3.*

$$$
JAPANESE

✕ **Morio J-Cuisine.** Named after the chef who owns and operates this restaurant in the chic Hotel G, Morio's interior is a blend of modern design with very Japanese tones. The striking black décor with chrome and silver is stunning—an ideal place for an intimate dinner. Chef Morio Sakayori is known for his innovative and contemporary take on Japanese cuisine with an international flair. The cheese tofu with green tea jelly topping, layered vegetable mousse, and peach immersed in Moscato Asti Pio Cesare are all brilliant choices. ⊠ *Hotel G, 7 Gongti Xilu, Chaoyang District* ☏ *010/6551–6999* ⊕ *www.moriobj.com* ☐ *AE, MC, V* ✛ *G3.*

$$$
INTERNATIONAL

✕ **Mosto.** This Latino-inspired restaurant is a popular dining venue located in the Nali Garden complex, in the Sanlitun district. The restaurant serves innovative contemporary cuisine that stimulates your palate. Venezuelan chef Daniel Urdaneta cleverly weaves in diverse oils, foams, and mousses to create uniquely flavored dishes with infinite possibilities. The interior design is a cross between traditional and industrial with exposed cement ceilings, candle-lit brick walls, and a central open kitchen, which gives it a smart-looking and cosmopolitan chicness. But, foremost is the food. The eggplant ravioli and Sichuan pepper–flavored ice cream are absolutely wonderful. ⊠ *81 Sanlitun Beilu, D308 Nali Patio, Chaoyang District* ☏ *010/5208–6030* ☐ *MC, V* ✛ *G2.*

$
VIETNAMESE

✕ **Nam Nam** 那 那. A sweeping staircase to the second floor, a tiny indoor fish pond, wooden floors, and posters from old Vietnam set the scene in this atmospheric restaurant. The light, delicious cuisine is paired with speedy service. Try the chicken salad, beef noodle soup, or the raw or deep-fried vegetable or meat spring rolls. The portions are on the small side, though, so order plenty. Finish off your meal with a real Vietnamese coffee prepared with a slow-dripping filter and accompanied by condensed milk. ⊠ *7 Sanlitun Jie, Sanlitun, Chaoyang District* ☏ *010/6468–6053* ☐ *AE, MC, V* ✛ *G2.*

$
AMERICAN

✕ **Nola.** The only place in the capital to get genuine New Orleans grits, cornbread, and other Creole fare. Don't miss the pork tenderloin served with plums wrapped in bacon. For dessert, try the warm apple cobbler with a scoop of homemade nutmeg-flavored ice cream. Park yourself on the lovely rooftop terrace for romantic alfresco dining overlooking

3

Dishing up hotpot

the surrounding green. ✉ *A 11 Xiushui Street South, Ritan, Chaoyang District* ☎ *010/8563–6215* ▭ *AE, MC, V* ✛ *G4.*

$ **CANTONESE** ✕ **Noodle Bar** 面吧. With a dozen seats surrounding the open kitchen, this petite dining room is a giant when it comes to flavor. The stark menu lists little more than beef brisket, tendon, and tripe, which are stewed to chewy perfection and complemented with noodles hand-pulled right before your eyes. For those seeking a moment of respite in Beijing's busy Sanlitun district, this is the place for a light lunch and a quick noodle-making show. The service is efficient and friendly. ✉ *Courtyard 4, Gongti Beilu, Chaoyang District* ☎ *010/6501–8882* ▭ *AE, MC, V* ✛ *G3.*

$ **NORTHERN CHINESE** ✕ **Noodle Loft** 面酷. A first-floor noodle bar is surrounded by stools, where several dough masters are working in a flurry, snipping, shaving, and pulling dough into noodles. The stainless-steel stairway leads to a second dining space, this one spacious, with high ceilings. The black-and-white color scheme plays backdrop to a trendy crowd. Do as they do and order yummy fried "cat ears," which are actually small nips of dough, boiled and then topped with meat, scrambled eggs, and shredded cabbage. ✉ *18 Baiziwan, Chaoyang District* ☎ *010/6774–9950* ▭ *AE, MC, V* ✛ *H5.*

$$$ **AMERICAN** ✕ **One East** 东方路一号. Contemporary American-style fine dining brings business travelers to the Hilton's flagship restaurant. With an emphasis on seasonal ingredients, the kitchen serves dishes that are fresh and light, such as sea bass with a sweet garlic puree. You'll find one of Beijing's best wine lists here sampled by a crowd that is a mix of longtime residents and hotel guests drifting down from their rooms. ✉ *2/F, Beijing*

Hilton Hotel, Dong Sanhuan Beilu, 1 Dongfang Lu, Chaoyang District ☎ *010/5865–5000 Ext. 5030* ▭ *AE, MC, V* ✛ *H1.*

$$ ✕ **Paulaner Brauhaus** 普 拉那啤酒坊餐厅. Traditional German food is
GERMAN dished up in heaping portions at this spacious, bright restaurant in the Kempinski Hotel. Wash it all down with delicious Bavarian beer made right in the restaurant: try the Maibock served in genuine German steins. In summer, you can enjoy your meal outdoors in the beer garden. ✉ *Kempinski Hotel, 50 Liangmaqiao Lu, Chaoyang District* ☎ *010/6465–3388* ▭ *AE, MC, V* ✛ *H2.*

$ ✕ **Pure Lotus** 净心莲. You'd never guess, but this glamorous vegetarian
VEGETARIAN haven is owned and operated by Buddhist monks. The warm jewel tones and traditional artwork will calm and restore frazzled nerves. The exhaustive menu amply transcends the typical tofu and salad offerings by including mock meat dishes such as Sichuan-style fish or Beijing-style duck. (It's all made from wheat gluten and soy protein.) These dishes will also win over sworn carnivores with their surprising similarity to the real thing. Alcohol is not served, but a wide range of rare teas and fruit drinks are available. ✉ *Jiangtai Lu Lido Hotel, Chaoyang District* ☎ *010/6592–3627* ▭ *AE, MC, V* ✛ *H3.*

$$ ✕ **Qi Xiang Ju** 其香居. Named after a famous teahouse in Sichuan, the
SICHUAN beautiful stone-carved entrance of this restaurant is flanked by V-shaped screen walls in the style of a high official's residence in the north. The menu's main focus is hot-and-spicy fare, including Rabbit Crossing the River, boiled fish fillet in fiery broth, and delicious duck tongue paired with lotus roots. ✉ *16 Jianguomen Waidajie, Chaoyang District* ☎ *010/6569–1616* ▭ *AE, MC, V* ✛ *H2.*

$ ✕ **Rumi** 入迷. On its best night, Rumi will delight you with the surprising
MIDDLE EASTERN authenticity of its Persian dishes. On its worst, it's still a classy place to get a kebab. Chalky white walls and enormous mirrors decorated with Arabic script create a casually exotic atmosphere. Try the chicken braised in a tangy pomegranate sauce or a platter of generously sized kebabs of meat and seafood. For dessert, take your rosewater and pistachio ice cream to the patio to enjoy the breeze. The Baha'i owner does not offer alcohol, but you are welcome to bring your own. ✉ *1A Gongti Beilu, Chaoyang District* ☎ *010/8454–3838* ▭ *No credit cards* ✛ *H3.*

$$ ✕ **Serve the People** 为人民服务. This eatery—a favorite of Thais living
THAI in Beijing—serves all the traditional Thai dishes. Try the duck salad, pomelo salad, green curry, or one of the plentiful hot-and-spicy soups. ✉ *1 Xiwujie, Sanlitun, across the street from the Spanish embassy, Chaoyang District* ☎ *010/8454–4580* ▭ *AE, MC, V* ✛ *G2.*

$$$ ✕ **Shin Yeh** 欣叶. The focus here is on Taiwanese flavors and freshness.
TAIWANESE *Caipudan* is a scrumptious turnip omelet and *fotiaoqiang* ("Buddha
Fodor's Choice jumping over the wall") is a delicate soup with medicinal herbs and
★ seafood. Last but definitely not least, try the *mashu*, a glutinous rice cake rolled in ground peanuts. Service is friendly and very attentive. ✉ *6 Gongti Xilu, Chaoyang District* ☎ *010/6552–5066* ▭ *AE, MC, V* ✛ *G3.*

$ ✕ **Souk** 苏克. Enjoy Mediterranean and Middle Eastern specialties,
MIDDLE EASTERN and maybe a long toke on a water pipe, while looking out over the green fields of Chaoyang Park from the outdoor dining area at this

eatery beside the park's west gate. In Arabic *souk* means market or bazaar—a place where people gather—and the laid-back ambience here, with lights and music both dimmed, champions the concept. The lamb kebabs, hummus, pita bread, couscous, and falafels are surprisingly delicious. And if it gets too hot or cold outdoors, retreat inside to one of the comfortable daybeds. ⊠ *Chaoyang Park west gate, behind Annie's, Chaoyang District* ☎ *010/6506–7309* ⊟ *No credit cards* ✛ *H2.*

$
INDIAN

✕ **Taj Pavilion** 泰姬楼. Beijing's best Indian restaurant, Taj Pavilion serves up all the classics, including chicken tikka masala, *palak panir* (creamy spinach with cheese), and *rogan josht* (tender lamb in curry sauce). Consistently good service and an informal atmosphere make this a well-loved neighborhood haunt. ⊠ *China World Trade Center, L-1 28 West Wing, 1 Jianguomenwai Dajie, Chaoyang District* ☎ *010/6505–5866* ⊟ *AE, MC, V* Ⓜ *Guomao* ✛ *H4.*

$
GUIZHOU

✕ **Three Guizhou Men** 三个贵州人. The popularity of this ethnic cuisine prompted three Guizhou friends to set up shop in Beijing. There are many dishes here to recommend, but among the best are "beef on fire" (pieces of beef placed on a bed of chives over burning charcoal) accompanied by ground chilies, spicy lamb with mint leaves, and *mi doufu*, a rice-flour cake in spicy sauce. ⊠ *Jianwai SOHO, Bldg. 7, 39 Dong Sanhuan Zhonglu, Chaoyang District* ☎ *010/5869–0598* ⊟ *AE, MC, V* Ⓜ *Guomao* ✛ *G5.*

$
CHINESE

✕ **Xiao Wangfu** 小王府. Beijing residents—locals and expats—enjoy Xiao Wangfu's home-style cooking. Thanks to rampant reconstruction, it has moved from location to location as neighborhoods have been torn down. But fans can now happily find the newest site inside Ritan Park, located in a small, two-story building, with a rooftop area overlooking the park's greenery. The Peking duck is delicious, and the *laziji* (deep-fried chicken smothered in dried red chilies) is just spicy enough. The second-floor dining area overlooks the main floor, with plenty of natural sunlight pouring through the surrounding windows. ⊠ *Ritan Park North Gate, Chaoyang District* ☎ *010/8561–5985* ⊟ *AE, MC, V* Ⓜ *Jianguomen* ✛ *F4.*

$$
CHINESE

✕ **Xiheyaju** 义和雅居. Nestled in Ritan Park, in one of Beijing's embassy neighborhoods, Xiheyaju is a favorite of diplomats and journalists, many of whom live and work nearby. The outdoor courtyard is perfect on a sunny spring day. Not many places can do as well as Xiheyaju in four regional cuisines: Sichuan, Shandong, Cantonese, and Huaiyang. The tasty *ganbian sijidou* (stir-fried green beans), *mapou doufu* (spicy bean curd), and *gongbao jiding* (chicken with peanuts) are all great choices. ⊠ *Northeast corner of Ritan Park, Chaoyang District* ☎ *010/8561–7643* ⊟ *AE, MC, V* ✛ *G3.*

$$$$
JAPANESE
Fodor's Choice
★

✕ **Yotsuba** 四叶. This tiny, unassuming restaurant is arguably the best Japanese restaurant in town. It consists of a sushi counter—manned by a Japanese master working continuously and silently—and two small tatami-style dining areas, evoking an old-time Tokyo restaurant. The seafood is flown in from Tokyo's Tsukiji fish market. Reservations are a must for this dinner-only Chaoyang gem. ⊠ *2 Xinyuan Xili Zhongjie, Chaoyang District* ☎ *010/6467–1837* ⌕ *Reservations essential* ⊟ *AE, MC, V* ☾ *No lunch* ✛ *G2.*

$
SICHUAN
Fodor'sChoice
★

✕**Yuxiang Renjia**渝乡人家 . There are many Sichuan restaurants in Beijing, but if you ask native Sichuan residents, Yuxiang Renjia is their top choice. Huge earthen vats filled with pickled vegetables, hanging bunches of dried peppers and garlic, and simply dressed servers evoke the Sichuan countryside. The restaurant does an excellent job of preparing provincial classics such as *gongbao jiding* (diced chicken stir-fried with peanuts and dried peppers) and *ganbian sijidou* (green beans stir-fried with olive leaves and minced pork). Thirty different Sichuan snacks are served for lunch on weekends, all at very reasonable prices. ⊠ *5/F, Lianhe Daxia, 101 Chaowai Dajie, Chaoyang District* ☎ *010/6588–3841* ⊟ *AE, MC, V* Ⓜ *Chaoyangmen* ✛ *F4.*

3

HAIDIAN DISTRICT 海淀区

Whether you're visiting the Summer Palace, Beijing's university area, or the electronics mecca of Zhongguancun, you certainly won't go hungry. And if you're hankering for the familiar, wander around the university campuses and pick one of the many Western-style restaurants catering to the local and international student population.

$$$$
BEIJING

✕**Baijia Dayuan** 白家大宅门. Staff dressed in rich-hued, traditional outfits welcome you at this grand courtyard house. Bowing slightly, they'll say *"Nin jixiang"* ("May you have good fortune"). The mansion's spectacular setting was once the garden of Prince Li, son of the first Qing emperor. Cao Xueqin, the author of the Chinese classic *Dream of the Red Chamber,* is said to have lived here as a boy. Featured delicacies include bird's-nest soup, braised sea cucumber, abalone, and authentic imperial snacks. On weekends, diners are treated to short, live performances of Beijing opera. ⊠ *15 Suzhou St., Haidian District* ☎ *010/6265–4186* ⌔ *Reservations essential* ⊟ *MC, V* ✛ *C1*

$$$$
INTERNATIONAL

✕**Blu Lobster** 蓝韵. One of the first restaurants in the city to employ the techniques of "molecular gastronomy," Blu Lobster offers refreshing, Asian-inspired dishes. The lobster bisque is rich with coconut-curry flavors and the intense sweetness of fresh lobster. The spiced crab risotto is served with avocado ice cream and billowing layers of lemongrass foam. The desserts, such as mango and pineapple ravioli served with peppercorn ice cream, are revelatory. Although the sommelier is highly knowledgeable about the wines, service is generally a little rough around the edges. ⊠ *Shangri-La Hotel, 29 Zizhuyuan Lu, Haidian District* ☎ *010/6841–2211* ⊟ *AE, DC, MC, V* ✛ *A2.*

$$
NORTHERN
CHINESE

✕**Ding Ding Xiang** 鼎鼎香. Hotpot restaurants are plentiful in northern China, but few do it better than Ding Ding Xiang. A variety of meats, seafood, and vegetables can be cooked in a wide selection of broths (the wild mushroom broth is a must for mycophiles). Should you be visiting Beijing in the bitter winter months, look forward to paper-thin lamb slices dipped in a bubbling pot of broth. Despite the surly service and gaudy decor, this place is perennially crowded. ⊠ *Bldg 7, Guoxing Jiayuan, Shouti Nanlu, Haidian District* ☎ *010/8835–7775* ⊟ *No credit cards* ⊠ *14 Dongzhong Jie, Dongzhimenwai, Dongcheng District* ☎ *010/6417–2546* ⊟ *AE, MC, V* ✛ *C1.*

ENGLISH	PINYIN	CHINESE
1/5 Taverna	n/a	n/a
Alameda	n/a	n/a
Argana	n/a	n/a
Aria	Ālìyǎ	阿郦雅
Assaggi	Chángshì	尝试
Baijia Dayuan	Báijiā dà zháimén	白家大宅门
Barolo	Bāluóluò	巴罗洛
Bei	Běi	北
Bellagio	Lùgǎng xiǎo zhèn	鹿港小镇
Biteapitta	Batà bǐng	吧嗒饼
Blu Lobster	Lányùn	蓝韵
The Bookworm	Shūchóng	书虫
Café Constance	n/a	n/a
Café de la Poste	Yúnyóu yì	云游驿
Café Sambal	n/a	n/a
Capital M	n/a	n/a
Cepe	Yìwèi xuān	意味轩
Comptoirs de France Bakery	Fǎpài	法派
Crystal Jade Palace	Fěicuì huánggōng jiǔjiā	翡翠皇宫酒家
Da Dong Roast Duck	Běijīng Dàdǒng kǎoyā diàn	北京大董烤鸭店
Dali Courtyard	Dàlǐ	大理
Dezhe Xiaoguan	Dézhé	得着
Din Tai Fung	Dīngtàifēng	鼎泰丰
Ding Ding Xiang	Dīngdīngxiāng	鼎鼎香
Dong Lai Shun	Dōngláishùn	东来顺
Duck de Chine	Quányājì	全鸭季
Fangshan	Fǎngshàn	仿膳
Feiteng Yuxiang	Fèiténgyúxiāng	沸腾鱼乡
Fennel	Huíxiāng	茴香
Guo Yao Xiao Ju	Guó yáo xiǎo jū	国肴小居
Hai Wan Ju	Hǎiwǎnjū	海碗居
Hatsune @ the Village	Yǐnquán Rìběn liàolǐ	隐泉日本料理
Huang Ting	Huángtíng	凰庭
Jaan	Jiāān	家安

ENGLISH	PINYIN	CHINESE
Jia No. 21	Jiǎ èrshíyī hào	甲21号
Jing	Jīng	京
Jing Wei Lou	Jngwèilóu	京味楼
Jinyang Fanzhuang	n/a	n/a
Ju'er Renjia	Júér rénjia	菊儿人家
Jun Wangfu	Jūnwángfǔ	君王府
Justine's	Jiésītīng	杰斯汀
Karaiya Spice House	Làwū	辣屋
Kong Yi Ji	Kǒngyǐjǐ	孔乙己
La Dolce Vita	Tiánmìshēnghuó	甜蜜生活
La Galerie	Zhōngguó yìyuàn	中国艺苑
Lai Jin Yu Xuan	Láijīn yǔxuān	来今雨轩
Lei Garden	Lìyuán	利苑
Li Qun Roast Duck Restaurant	Lìqún kǎoyādiàn	利群烤鸭店
Madam Zhu's Kitchen	Hànshè	汉舍
Maison Boulud	Bùlǔgōng fǎ cāntīng	布鲁宫法餐厅
Makye Ame	Mǎjíāmǐ	玛吉阿米
Mei Fu	Méi fǔ	梅府
Metro Café	Měitèróu	美特柔
Morio J-Cuisine	n/a	n/a
Mosto	n/a	n/a
My Humble House	Hánshè	寒舍
Nam Nam	Nàmenàme	那么那么
Nola	n/a	n/a
Noodle Bar	Miàn bā	面吧
Noodle Loft	Miànkù	面酷
Old Beijing Noodle King	Lǎo Běijīng zhájiàngmiàn dàwáng	老北京炸酱面大王
One East	Dōngfāng lù yīhào	东方路一号
Paomo Guan	Pào mó guǎn	泡馍馆
Paulaner Brauhaus	Pǔlānà píjiǔ fāng cāntīng	普 拉那啤酒坊餐厅
Private Kitchen No. 44	Sìshísìháo sījiā chúfáng	44号私家厨房
Pure Lotus	Jìngxīnliányu	净心莲
Qi Xiang Ju	Qíxiāngjū	其香居
Qin Tangfu	Tíntáng fǔ	秦唐府

ENGLISH	PINYIN	CHINESE
Red Capital Club	Xīnhóngzī jùlèbù	新红资俱乐部
Rumi	Rùmí	入迷
Serve the People	Wèirénmínfúwù	为人民服务
Shaguo Ju	Shāguō jū	沙锅居
Shi	Shí	食
Shin Yeh	Xīnyè	欣叶
Souk	Sūkè	苏克
Still Thoughts	Jìngsī sùshí fāng	静思素食坊
Taj Pavilion	Tàijī lóu	泰姬楼
The Source	Dōujiāngyuán	都江源
Three Guizhou Men	Sāngeguìzhōurén	三个贵州人
Xiao Wangfu	Xiǎowángfǔ	小王府
Xiheyaju	Yìhéyǎjū	义和雅居
Yotsuba	Sìyè	四叶
Yue Bin	Yuèbīn fànguǎn	悦宾饭馆
Yuxiang Renjia	Yúxiāngrénjiā	渝乡人家

Where to Stay

WORD OF MOUTH

"After we got into the cab, I gave the driver the phone number for the hotel, which he seemed to appreciate since he promptly pulled over and called the hotel for directions."

—Wiselindag

Updated by
Eileen Wen
Mooney

The hotel scene in Beijing today is defined by a multitude of polished palaces. You can look forward to attentive service, improved amenities—such as conference centers, health clubs, and nightclubs—and, of course, rising prices. "Western-style" comfort, rather than history and character, is the main selling point for Beijing's hotels. Gone forever is the lack of high-quality hotels that distinguished Beijing in the 70s.

If you're looking for something more intimate and historical, check out the traditional courtyard houses that have been converted into small hotels—they offer a quiet alternative to the fancier establishments.

There are a few things you should know before you book. Beijing's busiest seasons are spring and fall, with summer following closely behind. Special rates can be had during the low season, so make sure to ask about deals involving weekends or longer stays. If you are staying more than one night, you can often get some free perks—ask about free laundry service or free airport transfers.

The local rating system does not correspond to those of any other country. What is called a five-star hotel here might only warrant three or four elsewhere. This is especially true of the state-run hotels, which often seem to be rated higher than they deserve. And lastly, children 16 and under can normally share a room with their parents at no extra charge—although there may be a modest fee for adding an extra bed. Ask about this when making your reservation.

WHAT IT COSTS IN YUAN				
	¢	$	$$	$$$	$$$$
For two people	under Y700	Y700–Y1,100	Y1,101–Y1,400	Y1,401–Y1,800	over Y1,800

Prices are for two people in a standard double room in high season, excluding the 10% to 15% service charge.

BEST BETS FOR BEIJING LODGING

Fodor's offers a selective listing of quality lodging experiences in every price range, from the city's best budget beds to its most sophisticated luxury hotels. Here we've compiled our top recommendations by price and experience. The very best properties—in other words, those that provide a particularly remarkable experience in their price range—are designated in the listings with the Fodor's Choice logo.

Fodor'sChoice ★

- Banqiao No. 4, p. 136
- Beijing Sihe Courtyard Hotel, p. 137
- The Emperor, p. 140
- Hotel G, p. 151
- Hotel Kapok, p. 143
- Legendale, p. 143
- Park Hyatt Beijing, p. 153
- Red Capital Residence, p. 145
- St. Regis, p. 154

Best by Price

¢

- Dongtang Inn, p. 140

$

- Autumn Garden, p. 147
- Day's Inn Forbidden City Beijing, p. 140
- Park Plaza Beijing, p. 144

$$

- Aman Summer Palace, p. 157

- Haoyuan Hotel, p. 141
- Hilton Beijing, p. 150
- Kerry Centre Hotel, p. 152
- Novotel Peace Hotel, p. 144
- Traders Hotel, p. 156
- Yi House, p. 156

$$$

- The Emperor, p. 140
- Grand Millennium Beijing Hotel, p. 149
- Hotel G, p. 151
- Peninsula Beijing, p. 144
- Shangri-La Hotel, p. 159
- Sofitel Wanda, p. 154
- Westin Beijing, p. 147

$$$$

- Park Hyatt Beijing, p. 153
- Ritz-Carlton Beijing, Financial Street, p. 146
- St. Regis, p. 154
- The Opposite House, p. 153

Best by Experience

BEST CONCIERGE

- JW Marriott, p. 151
- St. Regis, p. 154

BEST SPA

- Park Hyatt Beijing, p. 153
- Peninsula Beijing, p. 144
- Ritz-Carlton Beijing, Financial Street, p. 146

MOST KID-FRIENDLY

- Commune by the Great Wall, p. 158
- Double Tree by Hilton Beijing, p. 148
- Grandma's Place, p. 158
- Holiday Inn Lido, p. 150
- Kerry Centre Hotel, p. 152
- Sino-Swiss Hotel, p. 159

BEST FOR BUSINESS

- Courtyard by Northeast Beijing, p. 149
- China World Hotel, p. 148
- Ritz-Carlton Beijing, Financial Street, p. 146

BEST INTERIOR DESIGN

- China World Summit Wing, p. 149
- Hotel G, p. 151
- Hotel Kapok, p. 143
- Ritz-Carlton Beijing, Financial Street, p. 146
- The Opposite House, p. 153
- Yi House, p. 156

BEST COURTYARD

- Banqiao No. 4, p. 136
- Du Ge, p. 140
- Red Capital Residence, p. 145

BEST HOTEL BARS

- Grand Hyatt Beijing, p. 141
- Kerry Centre Hotel, p. 152
- Park Hyatt Beijing, p. 153
- St. Regis, p. 154

BEST LOCATION

- Crowne Plaza Beijing, p. 137
- Day's Inn Forbidden City, p. 140
- Hotel Kapok, p. 143
- Peninsula Beijing, p. 144
- Raffles Beijing Hotel, p. 145
- St. Regis, p. 154

4

DONGCHENG DISTRICT 东城区

Dongcheng District lies north and east of the Forbidden City and incorporates the city's most important historic sites and temples. The hotels off Dongchang'an Jie and Wangfujing Dajie are within walking distance of Tiananmen Square.

Use the coordinate (✛ A1) at the end of each listing to locate a site on the corresponding map.

LOCALE CON-CERNS

As traffic conditions worsen, more travelers are choosing hotels closer to their interests. That said, Beijing's new subway lines are providing good alternatives to reaching distant places without getting stuck in traffic.

$$$ 🖥 **3+1 bedroom.** Located in a quaint *hutong* (alleyway) near the Drum and Bell towers, this is one of the smallest boutique hotels in Beijing. Each room offers five-star amenities, including iPod stereos, detached bathtubs and standing showers, and a large outdoor patio. **Pros:** spacious rooms with Apple MP3 players. **Cons:** no health club, restaurants, or other facilities. ✉ *17 Zhangwang Hutong, Jiu Gulou Dajie, Drum Tower,Dongcheng District* ☎ *010/6404–7030* ⊕ *www.3plus1bedrooms. com* 🛏 *4 rooms* ⚘ *In-room: a/c, safe, refrigerator, no TV, Wi-Fi. In-hotel: room service, bar* ▭ *AE, DC, MC, V* ⃝⃝ *BP* ✛ *C2.*

¢–$ 🖥 **Banqiao No. 4 板桥4号.** It may seem impossible, but Banqiao No. 4 is a well-preserved courtyard house with an unbeatable central location.

Fodor's Choice You might expect this stylish lodging to be expensive, but the rates are ★ quite reasonable. Set in an old neighborhood with many intertwined alleyways, this hotel is only a few minutes walk from the subway station, and a 20-minute bike ride from the Lama Temple, Confucian Temple, and Beihai Park. In addition to tastefully furnished rooms, Banqiao 4 offers thoughtful extras like Wi-Fi access. The hotel has two suites that are perfect for families, with a large bed and a sofa bed. There is no restaurant, but the hotel is a 10-minute walk from Gui Jie and its dozens of eateries. **Pros:** reasonable prices; large rooftop terrace. **Cons:** some bathrooms are small. ✉ *4 Banqiao Hutong, Beixinqiao, Dongcheng District* ☎ *010/8403–0968* 🛏 *16 rooms, 2 suites* ⚘ *In-room: Wi-Fi* ▭ *AE, DC, MC, V* ⃝⃝ *BP* Ⓜ *Beixinqiao* ✛ *E3.*

$$ 🖥 **Beijing Guxiang 20 Hotel 北京古乡20号.** This hotel is in one of the city's most interesting old hutong districts, so there's plenty to do. The modern rooms are simple but stylish, with traditional-style furnishings. Sepia-tone photographs of Old Beijing hang on the restaurant walls next to carved wall stones with traditional flower motifs. This is one of the best deals in town in terms of comfort, location, and price. **Pros:** reasonable rates; near plenty of shops and restaurants. **Cons:** some rooms are windowless; plumbing problems; poor food. ✉ *20 Nanluoguxiang, Dongcheng District* ☎ *010/6400–5566* ⊕ *www.guxiang20.com* 🛏 *487 rooms* ⚘ *In-room: safe, refrigerator, Internet. In-hotel: restaurant, bar, tennis court* ▭ *AE, DC, MC, V* ⃝⃝ *EP* Ⓜ *Gulou, Beixinqiao, Zhangzizhonglu* ✛ *D2.*

$$$–$$$$ 🖥 **Beijing Hotel 北京饭店.** One of the capital's oldest hotels, this property opened in 1900 as the Hotel de Pekin. Within sight of Tiananmen Square, it has housed countless foreign delegations, diplomatic missions, and celebrities. China's longtime premier Zhou Enlai stayed and worked in room #1735. The rooms retain an old-fashioned splendor with French-classic touches. This is the place for people in search of some history or proximity to nearby tourist sites, such as Tiananmen Square and the Forbidden City. **Pros:** a short walk from the Forbidden City; close to shopping. **Cons:** mediocre restaurants. ⌧ *33 Dongchang'an Jie, off Wangfujing Dajie, Dongcheng District* ☎ *010/6513–7766* 🖷 *010/6523–2395* ⊕ *www.chinabeijinghotel.com. cn* 🛏 *800 rooms, 51 suites* ♙ *In-room: refrigerator, Internet. In-hotel: 5 restaurants, room service, tennis court, pool, gym, Wi-Fi hotspot* ▤ *AE, DC, MC, V* ⍓EP Ⓜ *Wangfujing* ✛ *D5.*

$$$ 🏨 **Beijing International** 北京国际饭店. This white monolith symbolized the revitalization of the country's tourism industry. Nowadays, the comfortable rooms and reliable service here attract many tour groups. Opposite the Beijing train station, the hotel is a few minutes' drive from Tiananmen Square. Many great restaurants—including Qin Tangfu, Paomo Guan, and Gui Gongfu—are close by. **Pros:** near popular sites; close to restaurants. **Cons:** mediocre restaurants; lacks character. ⌧ *9 Jianguomennei Dajie, off Wangfujing Dajie, Dongcheng District* ☎ *010/6512–6688* ⊕ *www.bih.com.cn* 🛏 *916 rooms, 60 suites* ♙ *In-hotel: 8 restaurants, bar, gym, salon, massage, Wi-Fi hotspot* ▤ *AE, DC, MC, V* ⍓EP Ⓜ *Dongdan* ✛ *F5.*

$$–$$$ 🏨 **Beijing Marriott Hotel City Wall** 北京万豪酒店. At the edge of a restored section of the city wall (there are great views from the lobby coffee shop), this hotel has a very good location near the sites. The spacious rooms have nice touches like flat-screen TVs and bathrooms equipped with both bathtubs and showers. The hotel has three dining rooms offering Cantonese, Mediterranean, and Southeast Asian cuisines. **Pros:** close to tourist sites; near city wall. **Cons:** some rooms have odd shapes; lacks an intimate feel. ⌧ *7 Jianguomen Nanlu, Dongcheng District* ☎ *010/5811–8888* 🛏 *1,312 rooms* ⊕ *www.marriott.com* ♙ *In-room: safe, Wi-Fi. In-hotel: 3 restaurants, pool, gym, spa, Wi-Fi hotspot* ▤ *AE, D, DC, MC, V* ⍓EP Ⓜ *Beijing Station* ✛ *F5.*

$–$$ 🏨 **Beijing Sihe Courtyard Hotel** 北京四合宾馆. This lovely courtyard hotel
Fodor's Choice is tucked inside one of the city's quaint hutongs. This old house, with a
★ centuries-old date tree, was once the home of Mei Lanfang, the legendary male opera star known for playing female roles. Even though the hotel does not have its own kitchen, food service is provided by several restaurants in the neighborhood. The VIP room is the largest and best room and is worth reserving in advance. If that is not available, ask for one of the executive rooms. All rooms are furnished with rosewood beds, antique bureaus, and modern gadgets like satellite TV. Bicycles are available for free. **Pros:** lots of privacy; homey atmosphere. **Cons:** not many rooms have courtyard views; no restaurant. ⌧ *5 Dengcao Hutong, Dongcheng District* ☎ *010/5169–3555* 🛏 *12 rooms* ♙ *In-room: Internet* ▤ *AE, DC, MC, V* ⍓BP Ⓜ *Dongsi (Exit C)* ✛ *E4.*

$$$ 🏨 **Crowne Plaza Beijing** 北京国际艺苑. Located on Wangfujing, the Crowne Plaza puts you in the center of Beijing's tourist, shopping, and business districts. The lobby's champagne bar serves light Japanese and Vietnamese food. Huang Yue, on the second floor, is a stylish Cantonese

4

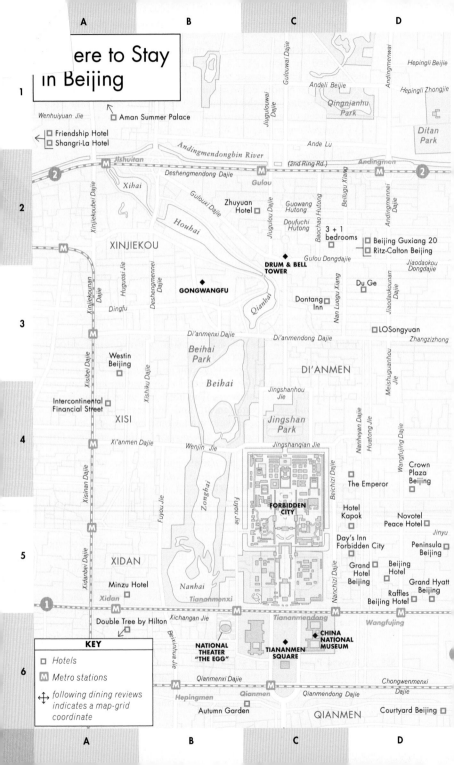

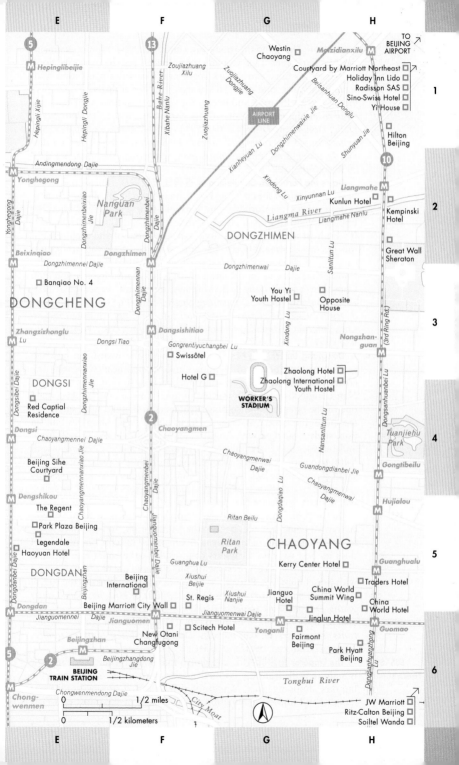

restaurant. The standard rooms are small, but have top-notch amenities like flat-screen TVs. Craving more space? Try the executive floor, where rooms have extra work space and sprawling bathrooms with separate showers and tubs. This is one of the better deals in town, providing a great location and luxury for your dollar. **Pros:** near the sites; close to shopping; good value. **Cons:** chain-hotel feel. ⊠ *48 Wangfujing Dajie, Dongcheng District* ☎ *010/5911–9999* ⊕ *www.crownplaza.com/ beijingchn* ↗ *360 rooms, 27 suites* ⌂ *In-room: safe, refrigerator, Internet. In-hotel: 2 restaurants, pool, gym, spa* ▭ *AE, DC, MC, V* ⊓⊙⊢ *BP* Ⓜ *Wangfujing* ⊹ *D4.*

$ 🏨 **Day's Inn Forbidden City Beijing** 北京香江戴斯酒店. This is one of the best hotel deals in the city. The Day's Inn offers a lot of pluses: it's inexpensive, clean, comfortable, and located just a few minutes from the Imperial Wall Ruins Park, the Forbidden City, and Tiananmen Square. It's built in a contemporary style but has some of the architectural touches of a courtyard house. The brick walls are inlaid with traditional carvings of chrysanthemums—the Chinese national flower. **Pros:** fantastic price; close to tourist sites; near great restaurants; free Internet. **Cons:** lower-level rooms lack windows; restaurant is average at best. ⊠ *99 Nanheyan Dajie, Dongcheng District* ☎ *010/6512–7788* ⊕ *www. daysinn.cn* ↗ *164 rooms* ⌂ *In-room: safe, Internet. In-hotel: restaurant, Internet terminal, parking (free)* ▭ *AE, DC, MC, V* Ⓜ *Wangfujing* ⊹ *D5.*

¢ 🏨 **Dongtang Inn** 东堂客栈. This small, privately owned inn has two types of rooms: ones with windows and ones without windows. The crowd here is quite young—mainly backpackers and students. It's along Nan Luogu Xiang, a 700-year-old hutong. This area is fast becoming one of the latest up-and-coming nightspots in Beijing, with small coffee shops and good restaurants. The in-house coffee shop has built-in bookshelves stacked with English-language guidebooks, a television, and Internet terminals. Bikes are available for rental (Y200/day with Y400 deposit). **Pros:** very inexpensive; lots of free travel advice. **Cons:** small rooms; some lack windows. ⊠ *85 Nan Luogu Xiang, Dongcheng District* ☎ *010/8400–2429* ↗ *20 rooms* ⌂ *In-room: no TV. In-hotel: bar, laundry service* ▭ *No credit cards* ⊹ *C3.*

$$$–$$$$ 🏨 **Du Ge** 杜革. This carefully renovated hotel is located within an old courtyard home that goes back to the 18th century, and was once home to three generations of Qing dynasty officials. This chic boutique hotel does its best to make its guests comfortable—the room rate includes airport pickup service, refreshments, bicycles, and use of a mobile phone with preset numbers. **Pros:** great location; free soft drinks at the bar all day. **Cons:** small rooms. ⊠ *26 Qian Yuan En Si Hutong, Nan Luogu Xiang Dongcheng District* ☎ *010/6406–0686* ⊕ *www.dugecourtyard. com* ↗ *6 rooms* ⌂ *In-room: a/c, safe, DVD, Wi-Fi. In-hotel: 2 restaurants, room service, bar, bicycles, laundry facilities, laundry service, some pets allowed.* ▭ *AE, DC, MC, V* ⊹ *D3.*

$$$–$$$$ 🏨 **The Emperor** 皇家驿栈. Located on a tree-lined avenue, The Emperor
Fodor's Choice is a short walk from the Forbidden City, Tiananmen Square, and the
★ famous shopping area, Wangfujing. It's nestled among traditional temples and houses, making it a tranquil oasis in the midst of a fast-

evolving metropolis. Though fronted by a classical brick facade, the hotel features a cutting-edge interior created by a team of internationally renowned designers. Its rooms boast a modern aesthetic, and have wall-mounted flat-screen TVs, wireless Internet connections, and butler service. On the roof, the chic restaurant Shi serves fusion cuisine creatively prepared by Chinese chef, John Hao, who puts a modern spin on traditional local dishes. Both the Yin bar and Shi offer breathtaking views over the Forbidden City. Also on the roof is the hotel's spa, an all-glass structure with amazing city views. **Pros:** best rooftop terrace in the city; views of the Forbidden City; unique design of rooms. **Cons:** restaurant on the expensive side. ⊠ *33 Qihelou Jie, Dongcheng District* ☎ *010/6526–5566* ⊕ *www.theemperor.com.cn* ⇘ *46 rooms, 9 suites* ♨ *In-room: safe, Wi-Fi. In-hotel: restaurant, bar, spa, Wi-Fi hotspot* ⊟ *AE, D, DC, MC, V* ⊺○⫴ *EP* Ⓜ *Tiananmen Dong* ✛ *D4.*

4

$$$$ 🏨 **Grand Hotel Beijing** 北京贵宾楼饭店. This lovely hotel on the north side of Chang'an Avenue blends ancient traditions with modern comforts. It's close to Tiananmen Square and the Forbidden City, and some rooms have views of the latter. The Red Wall Café, Ming Yuan Dining Room, Rong Yuan Restaurant, and Old Peking Grill provide a range of cuisines, but the non-Chinese food isn't up to snuff. The service also doesn't compare to some other überfancy foreign-managed hotels. Even if you don't stay here, visit the rooftop terrace at sunset. The terrace is open only from May through October, from 5 PM to 9:30 PM. **Pros:** good location; classic decor; great rooftop views. **Cons:** disappointing dining; confusing layout; little atmosphere. ⊠ *35 Dongchang'an Jie, Dongcheng District* ☎ *010/6513–7788* 🖷 *010/6513–0048* ⊕ *www. grandhotelbeijing.com* ⇘ *217 rooms, 50 suites* ♨ *In-room: safe, Internet. In-hotel: 2 restaurants, bars, gym, Wi-Fi hotspot* ⊟ *AE, DC, MC, V* ⊺○⫴ *EP* Ⓜ *Wangfujing* ✛ *D5.*

$$$$ 🏨 **Grand Hyatt Beijing** 北京东方君悦酒店. This mammoth complex ★ includes an upscale shopping mall, a cinema screening films in English, and a wide range of inexpensive eateries. Rooms and suites, many with floor-to-ceiling windows, are decorated with comfortable cherry-wood furnishings. The hotel's Olympic-size swimming pool is surrounded by lush vegetation, waterfalls, statues, and comfortable teak chairs and tables. Over the pool a "virtual sky" ceiling imitates different weather patterns. The gym is equipped with state-of-the-art exercise equipment. The Red Moon on the lobby level is one of the city's chicest bars and has live music every night. The hotel is within walking distance of Tiananmen Square and the Forbidden City. **Pros:** efficient service; plenty of shopping; impressive pool. **Cons:** small rooms; hard mattresses; pricey Internet. ⊠ *1 Dongchang'an Jie, corner of Wangfujing, Dongcheng District* ☎ *010/8518–1234* ⊕ *www.beijing.grand.hyatt.com* ⇘ *825 rooms, 155 suites* ♨ *In-room: safe, refrigerator, Wi-Fi. In-hotel: 3 restaurants, bar, pool, gym, spa, Wi-Fi hotspot* ⊟ *AE, DC, MC, V* ⊺○⫴ *EP* Ⓜ *Wangfujing* ✛ *D5.*

$$ 🏨 **Haoyuan Hotel** 好园宾馆. Tucked away in a hutong, the tiny Haoyuan Hotel has rooms surrounding a pair of pretty courtyards. Try to book one of the larger rooms in the tranquil back courtyard, where you can sit under the date trees and listen to the evening chorus of cicadas on

Red Capital Residence

Hotel G Beijing

Hotel Kapok

summer evenings. The hotel's small restaurant serves good Sichuan, Guangdong, and Shandong dishes. Nearby Nan Luogu Xiang, with its many restaurants, coffee shops, bars, and boutiques, is reason enough to stay here. **Pros:** nice atmosphere; near restaurants and shops; bicycles are available for Y30 per day—the best bargain in the city. **Cons:** furnishings need updating; uninspired service. ⊠ *53 Shijia Hutong, Dongsi Nan Dajie, Dongcheng District* ☎ *010/6512–5557* ⊕ *www. haoyuanhotel.com* ↪ *19 rooms* ♺ *In-hotel: restaurant, laundry service, Wi-Fi hotspot* ⊟ *AE, MC* ⦿ *BP* Ⓜ *Dengshikou* ✛ *E5.*

$ Ⓣ **Hotel Kapok** 木棉花酒店. Just a few blocks from the east gate of **Fodor'sChoice** the Forbidden City, this hotel is quite a find. One of a growing num-★ ber of boutique hotels in Beijing, it's the work of local architect, Pei Zhu, who came up with the minimalist design. Rooms are large and nicely designed, and have all the modern amenities of more expensive hotels. The entrances to some rooms face small bamboo and pebble gardens. **Pros:** cozy and comfortable rooms; near top tourist sites; close to shopping. **Cons:** no pool. ⊠ *16 Donghuamen, Dongcheng District* ☎ *010/6525–9988* ⊕ *www.kapokhotelbeijing.com* ↪ *89 rooms* ♺ *In-room: Wi-Fi. In-hotel: restaurant, Wi-Fi hotspot* ⊟ *AE, D, DC, MC, V* ⦿ *EP* Ⓜ *Tiananmen East* ✛ *D5.*

$$$$ Ⓣ **Legendale** 励骏酒店. Those fond of a classic ambience will be drawn **Fodor'sChoice** to the Legendale, surrounded by some of the city's best-preserved ★ hutongs. The hotel's palatial architecture is done up in rich blues, golds, and burgundies, exuding an old-world elegance. The breathtaking gilded staircase winds upward, creating a theaterlike ambience with balconies at each level and a domelike atrium drawing in an abundance of natural light. Sparkling and ornate crystal chandeliers dangle from the high ceilings; an antique Parisian fireplace is the centerpiece in the opulent lobby. Camoes, with its hand-painted white and blue mural depicting a seafaring scene from old Portugal, offers Macanese and Portuguese cuisine. Petrus, a French restaurant, has a large wine collection, and Macao focuses on Chinese fare. **Pros:** plenty of pampering; in a great neighborhood. **Cons:** stratopheric prices. ⊠ *90-92 Jinbao Street, Dongcheng District* ☎ *010/8511–3388* ⊕ *www.legendalehotel. com* ↪ *390 rooms, 81 suites* ♺ *In-room: safe, refrigerator, Internet. In-hotel: 3 restaurants, pool, laundry service, Wi-Fi hotspot* ⊟ *AE, DC, MC, V* ⦿ *EP* Ⓜ *Dengshikou* ✛ *E5.*

¢–$ Ⓣ **LüSongyuan** 侣松园宾馆. In 1980, the China Youth Travel Service set up this delightful courtyard hotel on the site of an old Mandarin's residence. The traditional wooden entrance is guarded by two *menshi* (stone lions). Inside are five courtyards decorated with pavilions, rockeries, and greenery. Rooms are basic, with large windows. There are no self-service cooking facilities, but it has a reasonable Chinese restaurant. It's all about location here: you're in the middle of an ancient neighborhood, within walking distance of Houhai, and just a block away from many restaurants on Nan Luogu Xiang. **Pros:** convenient location; near restaurants. **Cons:** cluttered courtyard; unenthusiastic service. ⊠ *22 Banchang Hutong, Kuanjie, Dongcheng District* ☎ *010/6401–1116* ↪ *55 rooms* ♺ *In-hotel: restaurant, bar, Internet terminal, Wi-Fi hotspot* ⊟ *AE, DC, MC, V* ⦿ *EP* ✛ *D3.*

$$ 🏨 **Novotel Peace Hotel** 和平宾馆.
⏱ This tower of shimmering glass has rooms with floor-to-ceiling windows affording stellar city views. The location is great, just a stroll away from plenty of shops and restaurants, as well as Tiananmen Square. Although the service is fairly basic, and the ambience is decidedly low-key, the hotel is a good value for the location. For dinner you might try one of the three Chinese restaurants or Le Cabernet, a French-style brasserie. Our vote? Head out onto the street and try one of the many restaurants in the bustling neighborhood. **Pros:** near plenty of restaurants; close to the sites. **Cons:** not much ambience; lackluster service. ⊠ *3 Jinyu Hutong, Wangfujing Dajie, Dongcheng District* ☎ *010/6512–8833* ⊕ *www.accorhotels-asia.com* ⤻ *337 rooms, 25 suites* ⚡ *In-room: safe, refrigerator, Wi-Fi. In-hotel: 2 restaurants, bar, pool, gym, laundry service, Wi-Fi hotspot* ⊟ *AE, DC, MC, V* Ⓞ❘ *EP* Ⓜ *Wangfujing.*

$–$$ 🏨 **Park Plaza Beijing** 北京丽亭酒店. Known for its excellent service, the Park Plaza has good amenities for business travelers. The beige rooms are equipped with executive-size desks and wireless Internet connections. The garden is perfect for open-air dining, offering tranquillity in the center of a bustling city. Sit under a canopy of scholar trees with a glass of cold beer and nibble on salty snacks before retiring to your comfortable room. **Pros:** close to the Forbidden City; relaxing garden. **Cons:** lobby is small and dark. ⊠ *97 Jinbao Street, Dongcheng District* ☎ *010/8522–1999* ⊕ *www.parkplaza.com/beijingcn* ⤻ *216 rooms, 16 suites* ⚡ *In-room: safe, Internet. In-hotel: 2 restaurants, room service, gym, laundry service* ⊟ *AE, D, DC, MC, V* Ⓞ❘ *EP* Ⓜ *Dengshikou* ✛ *E3.*

$$$–$$$$ 🏨 **Peninsula Beijing** 王府半岛酒店. Guests at the Peninsula Beijing enjoy
★ an impressive combination of modern facilities and traditional luxury. A waterfall cascades through the spacious lobby, which is decorated with well-chosen antiques. Rooms have teak and rosewood flooring, colorful rugs, and gorgeous wood furnishings. There are high-tech touches like custom bedside control panels that let you adjust lighting, temperature, and the flat-screen TVs. Food fanatics, take note: one on-site restaurant, Jing, serves delicious East-meets-West fusion food. Huang Ting, a second restaurant, provides a rustic setting for some of Beijing's tastiest dim sum. Work off the meals in the fully equipped gym or swimming pool—or take the 10-minute walk to the Forbidden City. If you're less ambitious, relax in the hotel's spa. The Peninsula's arcade has designer stores, including Chanel, Jean Paul Gaultier, and Tiffany & Co. **Pros:** near the Forbidden City; close to sightseeing, restaurants, and shopping; rooms are impeccable. **Cons:** lobby is too dark; hectic atmosphere. ⊠ *8 Jinyu Hutong (Goldfish La.), Wangfujing, Dongcheng District* ☎ *010/8516–2888* ⊕ *www.peninsula.com* ⤻ *525 rooms, 59 suites* ⚡ *In-room: safe, refrigerator, Wi-Fi. In-hotel: 2 restaurants, room service, bar, tennis court, pool, gym, spa, laundry service, Wi-Fi hotspot* ⊟ *AE, DC, MC, V* Ⓞ❘ *EP* Ⓜ *Dongdan* ✛ *D5.*

$$$$ ⊡ **Raffles Beijing Hotel** 北京饭店莱佛士. Singaporean designer Grace Soh and her team transformed this hotel into a vivid, modern space while retaining its history. Crystal chandeliers illuminate the lobby, and the grand white staircase is enveloped in a royal-blue carpet. The atrium is adorned with 13 large cloth lanterns in olive green, plum, purple, and yellow—a welcome change from the ubiquitous red. The presidential suite is one of the largest, most luxurious accommodations in Beijing. For dining, choose between French and Italian restaurants. The Writer's Bar is replete with large leather armchairs and dark, polished floors. This is a great location for visitors who plan to do some sightseeing: Tiananmen Square, the Forbidden City, and Wangfujing are all nearby. **Pros:** near the Forbidden City; close to night market; wonderful French cuisine. **Cons:** restaurants very pricey; poor service. ✉ *33 Dongchang'an Jie, off Wangfujing Dajie, Dongcheng District* ☎ *010/6526–3388* ⊕ *www.beijing.raffles.com* ⇨ *171 rooms, 24 suites* △ *In-room: refrigerator, Wi-Fi. In-hotel: 2 restaurants, room service, bar, pool, Wi-Fi hotspot* ⊟ *AE, DC, MC, V* Ⓜ *Wangfujing* ⊹ *D5.*

$–$$ ⊡ **Red Capital Residence** 新红资客栈. Beijing's first boutique courtyard
Fodor's Choice hotel is located in a carefully restored home in Dongsi Hutong. Each
★ of the five rooms is decorated with antiques and according to different themes, including the Chairman's Suite, the two Concubine's Private Courtyards, and the two Author's Suites (one inspired by Edgar Snow, an American journalist who lived in Beijing in the 1930s and 1940s, and the other by Han Suyin, a famous Japanese novelist). There is a cigar lounge where you can sit on original furnishings used by China's early revolutionary leaders, as well as a wine bar in a Cultural Revolution–era bomb shelter. Special arrangements can also be made for guests to tour Beijing at night in Madame Mao's Red Flag limousine. **Pros:** intimate feel; friendly service; plenty of atmosphere. **Cons:** small rooms; limited facilities. ✉ *9 Dongsi Liutiao, Dongcheng District* ☎ *010/6402–7150* ⊕ *www.redcapitalclub.com.cn* ⇨ *5 rooms* △ *In-hotel: bar, laundry service, AE, DC, MC, V* ⊗ *CP* ⊹ *E4.*

$$$–$$$$ ⊡ **The Regent** 北京丽晶酒店. The Regent has an excellent location a
★ block from the Wangfujing shopping district and a short walk from the Forbidden City. The hotel has an imposing lobby decorated with beautiful carved furniture and a huge window overlooking the lobby lounge. The impressive rooms have plenty of natural light and king-size beds. Traveling executives will appreciate the large desks and wireless Internet connections. The hotel has good restaurants, including Li Jing Xuan, which offers excellent Cantonese dishes, Daccapo, which serves contemporary Italian, and Grill Bar, known for its thick and juicy steaks. **Pros:** convenient location; close to the metro. **Cons:** stained carpets; mediocre service. ✉ *99 Jinbao Street, Dongcheng District* ☎ *010/8522–1888* ⊕ *www.regenthotels.com* ⇨ *500 rooms* △ *In-room: safe, Wi-Fi. In-hotel: 3 restaurants, laundry service, Wi-Fi hotspot* ⊟ *AE, D, DC, MC, V* ⊗ *EP* Ⓜ *Dengshikou* ⊹ *E5.*

$ ⊡ **Zhuyuan Hotel** (*Bamboo Garden Hotel*) 竹园宾馆. This charming hotel was once the residence of Kang Sheng, a sinister character responsible for "public security" during the Cultural Revolution. Kang nevertheless had fine taste in art and antiques, some of which are on display. The Bamboo

Garden cannot compete with the high-rise crowd when it comes to amenities, but its bamboo-filled gardens make it a treasure for those looking for a true Chinese experience. It's within walking distance of the colorful Houhai, or Rear Lakes, area. The neighborhood is perfect if you want to experience the lifestyles of ordinary Beijingers. **Pros:** traditional feel; interesting neighborhood. **Cons:** courtyard is underused; pricey for what you get. ⊠ *24 Xiaoshiqiao Hutong, Jiugulou Dajie, Dongcheng District* ☎ *010/5852–0088* ⊐ *40 rooms, 4 suites* ♺ *In-hotel: restaurant, bar, bicycles (Y50/day), laundry service* ▭ *AE, DC, MC, V* Ⓜ *Gulou* ✛ *H3.*

> **WORD OF MOUTH**
>
> "Really enjoyed our stay at the Ritz-Carlton Beijing. We were at the Ritz Financial Street, about a 10-minute walk from the subway. First class all the way." —Shar

XICHENG DISTRICT 西城区

Xicheng District, north and west of the Forbidden City, lies opposite Dongcheng. This is the place to lose yourself among Beijing's old hutong alleyways and take long walks by Qianhai and Houhai.

Use the coordinate (✛ A1) at the end of each listing to locate a site on the corresponding map.

\$\$\$–\$\$\$\$ ▦ **InterContinental Financial Street Beijing** 金融洲际酒店. At this massive chain hotel the large rooms have contemporary designs and hints of traditional Chinese art. There's a 24-hour business center that makes it perfect for traveling executives. An indoor pool, a spa, and state-of-the-art fitness facilities complete the package. There are sizzling steaks at the Steak Exchange and excellent buffet meals in the café. **Pros:** convenient location; great for business travelers. **Cons:** pricey Internet; glass-walled bathrooms lack privacy. ⊠ *11 Financial Street, Xicheng District* ☎ *010/5852–5888* ⊕ *www.ichotelsgroup.com* ⊐ *332 rooms, 10 suites* ♺ *In-room: safe, refrigerator (some), Wi-Fi. In-hotel: 2 restaurants, pool, gym, spa* ▭ *AE, D, DC, MC, V* ⦿ *EP* Ⓜ *Fuchengmen (Exit C)* ✛ *A4.*

\$\$ ▦ **Minzu Hotel** 民族饭店. When it opened in 1959, the Minzu was labeled one of the 10 great buildings in Beijing. This paean to the unity of the country's different peoples has welcomed many prominent foreign dignitaries over the years. It's been renovated into yet another shiny pleasure dome but maintains its original local appeal. The hotel lies on western Chang'an Jie, 10 minutes from Tiananmen Square and next to the Nationalities' Cultural Palace. With the rise in the number of luxury hotels around Beijing, the hotel no longer attracts prominent visitors, and the only reason to stay here—other than price—is if you have business in the immediate area. **Pros:** close to shopping. **Cons:** medicore service; pricey food. ⊠ *51 Fuxingmennei Dajie, Xicheng District* ☎ *010/6601–4466* ⊕ *www.minzuhotel.cn* ⊐ *509 rooms, 40 suites* ♺ *In-room: safe. In-hotel: restaurant, bar* ▭ *AE, DC, MC, V* ⦿ *EP* Ⓜ *Xidan* ✛ *A5.*

\$\$\$–\$\$\$\$ ▦ **Ritz-Carlton Beijing, Financial Street** 北京金融街丽思卡尔顿酒店. With
★ an inspired East-meets-West decor, the Ritz-Carlton is ideal for travelers looking for a little extra. With ample amounts of glass and chrome,

the Ritz-Carlton could be mistaken for many of the city's sleek financial buildings. The interior is stylish and contemporary, with crystal mythological animals to provide good luck. Greenfish Café offers a great contemporary buffet that offers low-calorie fare, and the chef at Cepe produces homemade pasta with phenomenal sauces and other Italian fare. The enormous health club has an indoor pool and a spa with six treatment rooms. The hotel is located in the western part of the

city on the up-and-coming Financial Street, which is being touted as the city's Wall Street. **Pros:** impeccable service; luxurious atmosphere; spacious rooms. **Cons:** far from the city's attractions. ⊠ *18 Beijing Financial St., Xicheng District* ☎ *010/6601–6666* ⊕ *www.ritzcarlton.com* ⤶ *253 rooms, 33 suites* ⚘ *In-room: safe, Wi-Fi. In-hotel: 3 restaurants, room service, bar, pool, gym, spa, Wi-Fi hotspot* ☐ *AE, DC, MC, V* ⅼ⊚ⅼ *EP* Ⓜ *Fuchengmen*

$$$ ⌂ **Westin Beijing** 威斯汀酒店. In the middle of Financial Street, the city's new Wall Street, the Westin Beijing has a notable location. The comfortable rooms have many up-to-the-minute features such as flat-screen TVs and wireless connections. The lobby bar is one of the hippest places in Beijing. Chocolates and fruit are waiting for you when you return from the office. **Pros:** sumptuous beds; high-tech gadgets. **Cons:** glass between bathroom and bedroom not for the timid. ⊠ *9B Financial Street, Xicheng District* ☎ *010/6606–8866* ⊕ *www.westin.com/beijingfinancial* ⤶ *486 rooms* ⚘ *In-room: safe, Wi-Fi. In-hotel: 3 restaurants, bars, pool, spa* ☐ *AE, D, DC, MC, V* ⅼ⊚ⅼ *EP* Ⓜ *Fuchengmen* ✛ *A3.*

CHONGWEN AND XUANWU 崇文区 AND 宣武区

The Chongwen and Xuanwu districts, just south of the Forbidden City, are two of Beijing's oldest neighborhoods, with beautiful Chinese and Western architecture. A stroll through Source of Law Temple or Liulichang on a quiet afternoon is sure to remind you of the city's past.

Use the coordinate (✛ A1) at the end of each listing to locate a site on the corresponding map.

$ ⌂ **Autumn Garden** 春秋园宾馆南园. The Autumn Garden is a family-★ oriented courtyard guesthouse hidden in one of the alleyways of Qianmen, an old business district. The hotel is difficult to find, but the staff will send a tricycle out to pick you up at a nearby landmark. The three wells in front of the building are the sign that you've reached your destination. The 300-year-old courtyard is well preserved, with persimmon and date trees providing shade. The location is excellent, as Tiananmen Square is only a couple of hundred steps to the east. There are many things to recommend this hotel, including the free cell phones loaned to every guest, tea and coffee set out every evening, and free classes in cooking, mahjong, and calligraphy. If it's booked up, there's a sister hotel called Spring Garden. **Pros:** great location; plenty of atmosphere. **Cons:** neighborhood is confusing for newcomers; difficult to find. ⊠ *23 Sanjing Hutong, Xuanwu District* ☎ *010/6303–4232* ⊕ *www.springgardenhotel.com* 🛏 *8 rooms* ⚹ *In-room: Wi-Fi. In-hotel: laundry service* ▭ *AE, DC, MC, V* ⵙ *BP* Ⓜ *Qianmen* ✛ *C6.*

$ 🏨 **Courtyard Beijing** 北京万怡酒店. Blending Eastern and Western styles, the Courtyard is situated in the Chongwen District. One problem is that this is a super-congested part of the city. However, there's a subway station just one block away, making quick escapes to quieter areas quite easy. You have a direct connection to the huge New World Shopping Center, one of the busiest malls in the city. **Pros:** convenient location; close to shopping and historic sites. **Cons:** in a traffic-clogged area; drab lobby. ⊠ *3C Chongwenmenwai Dajie, Chongwen District* ☎ *010/6708–1188* ⊕ *www.courtyard.com/bjscy* 🛏 *283 rooms, 16 suites* ⚹ *In-room: safe, refrigerator, Wi-Fi. In-hotel: restaurant, pool, gym, laundry service, Wi-Fi hotspot* ▭ *AE, DC, MC, V* ⵙ *EP* Ⓜ *Chongwenmen* ✛ *D6.*

$$$ 🏨 **Double Tree by Hilton Beijing** 北京希尔顿逸林酒店. The most modern building in this part of the city, the Double Tree soars 22 stories into the air. You are welcomed with warm chocolate-chip cookies at check-in. The whirlpool and swimming pool on the third-floor terrace are shaded by trees, calling to mind a desert oasis. The spacious rooms are bright and have a wide range of amenities. **Pros:** near government agencies; pretty pool area. **Cons:** a little too remote. ⊠ *168 Guang'anmenwai Dajie, Xuanwu District* ☎ *010/6338–1888* ⊕ *www.beijing.doubletreebyhilton.com* 🛏 *547 rooms, 118 suites* ⚹ *In-room: safe, Wi-Fi. In-hotel: 2 restaurants, bar, pool, gym* ▭ *AE, DC, MC, V* ⵙ *EP* Ⓜ *None* ✛ *A6.*

WORD OF MOUTH

"Go to Beijing! I took my eight-year-old son one October a couple of years ago, and we did it all on our own. I asked the hotel concierge to write out directions in Chinese. We hired a guide through the hotel for a day at the Great Wall. The guide was superb and the whole day was quite economical (probably $100). You can also join half-day tours. I hope you have a joyous time." —EllenLM

CHAOYANG DISTRICT 朝阳区

Chaoyang District is outside the old-city wall, so there is little of historical interest here. The district extends east of Dongcheng and includes the Central Business District. You'll also find some of the city's best restaurants, bars, and shopping malls here. The hotels in this urban district are nearly all modern towers.

Use the coordinate (✛ A1) at the end of each listing to locate a site on the corresponding map.

$$$$ 🏨 **China World Hotel** 中国大饭店. One of the finest hotels in Beijing, China World has a lobby with marble floors and gold accents. Upstairs are comfortable, contemporary rooms with marble baths. The dining choices are diverse and enticing: Scene a Café is a casual eatery featuring

eight different cuisines, Aria serves a wonderful and inexpensive business lunch, Summer Palace serves dim sum, and Nadaman has superb Japanese seafood teppanyaki (cooked on an iron griddle). The hotel is quite popular with business travelers, who crowd here during conferences and exhibitions. **Pros:** convenient location for business travelers; close to subway. **Cons:** busy, big, and impersonal; rooms are quite small. ☒ *1 Jianguomenwai Dajie, Chaoyang District* ☎ *010/6505–2266* ⊕ *www.shangri-la.com* ⮌ *716 rooms, 26 suites* ⌂ *In-room: safe, refrigerator, Wi-Fi. In-hotel: 4 restaurants, bars, gym, laundry service, Wi-Fi hotspot, parking (paid)* ▭ *AE, DC, MC, V* Ⓜ *Guomao* ✛ *H5.*

$$$$ ⌂ **China World Summit Wing** 北京国贸大酒店. This is Beijing's newest international hotel, and at 330 meters, also the tallest. This hotel is situated from Levels 64 to 77, and all the rooms have floor-to-ceiling windows and stunning city views. Rooms average 700 square feet, each with complimentary wired and wireless broadband Internet access, 40-inch flat-screen TVs, DVD players, bathroom LCD televisions, iPod docking stations, and Nespresso coffee machines. **Pros:** magnificent views. **Cons:** nearby streets often jammed with traffic. ☒ *1 Jianguomenwai Avenue, Chaoyang District* ☎ *010/6505–2299* ⊕ *www.shangri-la. com* ⮌ *278* ⌂ *In-room: a/c, safe, kitchen (some), refrigerator (some), DVD, Wi-Fi. In-hotel: 4 restaurants, room service, 3 bars, pools, gym, spa, laundry facilities, laundry service, Wi-Fi hotspot, parking (free).* ▭ *AE, DC, MC, V* ✛ *H5.*

$–$$ ⌂ **Courtyard by Northeast Beijing**北京人济万怡酒店. Located between the
★ Lido Commercial District and Wangjing High Tech Park, this hotel has a good location for business travelers. The spacious and stylish rooms are equipped with high-tech touches like LCD TVs and high-speed Internet access. The 24-hour fitness center features an indoor swimming pool and whirlpool bathed in natural light. Upgrade to the executive level and you can get free Continental breakfast and evening cocktails. The open-kitchen MoMo Café serves a variety of international dishes, while MoMo 2 Go offers sandwiches and salads. **Pros:** good value; ideal location for people doing business in the city's northeast. **Cons:** far from the tourist sights. ☒ *101 Jingshun Road, Chaoyang District* ☎ *010/5907–6666* ⊕ *courtyardbeijingnortheast.com* ⮌ *258 rooms, 43 suites* ⌂ *In-room: refrigerator, Wi-Fi. In-hotel: restaurant, bar, pool, gym* ▭ *AE, DC, MC, V* �○i *EP* Ⓜ *None* ✛ *H1.*

$$$$ ⌂ **Fairmont Beijing** 北京华彬费尔蒙酒店. Fairmont Beijing is surrounded by high-end office towers in Beijing's diplomatic and commercial district. The sun-filled interiors are highlighted by contemporary artwork that creates a nice East-meets-West ambience. The hotel's restaurant, The Cut, offers wood-roasted duck and Wagyu beef. **Pros:** in the heart of the Central Business District. **Cons:** limited dining facilities. ☒ *8 Yong An Dong Li, Chaoyang District* ☎ *010/8511–7777* ⊕ *www.fairmont. com* ⮌ *222 rooms* ⌂ *In-room: a/c, safe, DVD, Wi-Fi. In-hotel: 2 restaurants, room service, 2 bars, pools, gym, spa, bicycles, laundry facilities, laundry service, Wi-Fi hotspot, parking (free).* ▭ *AE, DC, MC, V* i○i *EP* Ⓜ *Yong An Li* ✛ *G6.*

$$$ ⌂ **Grand Millennium Beijing Hotel** 北京千禧大酒店. In the heart of the Central Business District, this glass tower is designed for corporate travelers. It's close to the city's business and commercial districts and exhibition centers. Rooms have a contemporary style, with a chic black-and-white color scheme. Yao Chi's open kitchen lets you watch the chef prepare a wide range of Cantonese dishes. **Pros:** centrally located; near subway. **Cons:** food outlets expensive. ⊠ *7 Dongsanhuan Zhonglu, Chaoyang District* ☎ *010/8587–6888* ⊕ *www.millenniumhotels.com* ⤻ *521 rooms, 118 suites* ♨ *In-room: safe. In-hotel: restaurant, bar, pool* ▤ *AE, DC, MC, V* ⍾⍈ *EP* Ⓜ *Jintai Xizhao.*

$ 🏨 **Great Wall Sheraton** 北京长城饭店. The oldest luxury hotel in Beijing, the Great Wall Sheraton is still going strong because of its popularity with tour groups. The rooms are comfortable, though no different from those in any other chain hotel. The top-floor restaurant has pleasing city views and serves decent Sichuan and Cantonese food. The hotel also has two restaurants serving French and Italian cuisine. Although the Sheraton is an old standby, the service is uneven. **Pros:** in the embassy district; lovely views. **Cons:** far from the sights; service is uneven. ⊠ *10 Dongsanhuan Beilu, Chaoyang District* ☎ *010/6590–5566* ⊕ *www. sheraton.com* ⤻ *827 rooms, 83 suites* ♨ *In-room: safe, refrigerator, Internet. In-hotel: 3 restaurants, 2 bars, pool, gym, Internet terminal* ▤ *AE, DC, MC, V* ⍾⍈ *EP* ⊹ *H2.*

$$ 🏨 **Hilton Beijing** 北京稀尔顿酒店. One of the city's oldest and most comfortable hotels, the Hilton Beijing lies at the city's northeast corner; it's a good choice for those wanting easy access to the airport, which is about a 20-minute drive away. Rooms are simply furnished, and most have two large picture windows and balconies. One East on Third is designed to resemble an antebellum mansion, with dark wood and louvered windows, and offers light American cuisine and an extensive wine list. The Zeta Bar has a retro-cool ambience, with Bauhaus chairs and Chinese-inspired birdcages hanging above the crescent-shaped bar. A resident DJ spins here every night. **Pros:** easy drive to airport; near embassies in the northeast part of the city. **Cons:** far from the sights; neighborhood lacks charm. ⊠ *1 Dongfang Lu, Dongsanhuan Beilu, Chaoyang District* ☎ *010/5865–5000* ⊕ *www.beijing.hilton.com* ⤻ *375 rooms, 12 suites* ♨ *In-room: safe, refrigerator. In-hotel: 2 restaurants, bar, pool, bicycles* ▤ *AE, DC, MC, V* ⍾⍈ *EP* ⊹ *H1.*

$ 🏨 **Holiday Inn Lido** 丽都假日饭店. This enormous hotel is part of Lido ↻ Place, a commercial and residential complex northeast of the city center. With a high concentration of international businesses, Lido Place is home to an ever-increasing number of expats. You won't have an authentic Chinese experience here: there's an Italian restaurant called Pinocchio, a steak restaurant called the Texan Bar & Grill, and a British-style pub called the Pig and Thistle. Located in the northeast of the city, this isn't our top choice for sightseers, as it's far from all the major attractions. However, it's a good location if you want to get to and from the airport quickly. **Pros:** not far from the airport; plenty of dining options. **Cons:** far from the sights. ⊠ *Jichang Lu at Jiangtai Lu, Chaoyang District* ☎ *010/6437–6688* ⊕ *www.beijing-lido.holiday-inn.com* ⤻ *433 rooms, 89 suites* ♨ *In-room: refrigerator, Internet. In-hotel: 4 restaurants, room service, bar, pool, gym, laundry service, Internet terminal, Wi-Fi hotspot, parking (free)* ▤ *AE, DC, MC, V* ⍾⍈ *EP* Ⓜ *None* ⊹ *H1.*

$$$

Fodor's Choice

★

Hotel G 北京极栈. This vibrant and stylishly designed hotel is just minutes from the major commercial district. The midcentury modern design uses subtle Chinese accents to add an understated glamour. Its 110 rooms have designations that are easy to remember when booking: Good (studio), Great (deluxe studio), Greater (suite), and Greatest (deluxe suite). Rooms have a colorful and almost funky atmosphere. There's a split-level rooftop Mediterranean restaurant with a Tibetan-style tent and open fireplace, a sleek Japanese restaurant, and a glamorous lobby bar for cocktails. Hotel G claims to make the best hamburgers in town, using Argentinian premium beef with a choice of more than a dozen cheeses and sauce toppings. **Pros:** adjacent to one of the hottest nightlife areas; chic design. **Cons:** too colorful for some; can be noisy. ⊠ *7 Gongti Xilu, Chaoyang District* ☎ *010/6552–3600* ⊕ *www.hotel-g.com* ⇆ *110 rooms* ⚹ *In-room: safe, refrigerator, Wi-Fi. In-hotel: 3 restaurants, gym* ▭ *AE, D, MC, V* ⍾ *EP* Ⓜ *None* ✛ *F3.*

$$

Jianguo Hotel 建国饭店. The Jianguo Hotel has maintained its friendly feel for years and continues to attract many diplomats, journalists, and business executives. Nearly half the rooms have balconies overlooking busy Jianguomenwai Dajie. The sunny atrium lobby is furnished with comfortable cushioned rattan sofas and chairs. Charlie's Bar, a longtime favorite, has a good lunch buffet, and Flo Justine's is one of the city's best French restaurants. The gym and pool facilities, however, are very basic. The hotel is a reasonably priced alternative for those attending conferences at the more expensive China World Hotel, just one block away. **Pros:** central location; reasonable rates. **Cons:** limited amenities; rooms are small. ⊠ *5 Jianguomenwai Dajie, Chaoyang District* ☎ *010/6500–2233* ⊕ *www.hoteljianguo.com* ⇆ *462 rooms, 54 suites* ⚹ *In-room: safe, refrigerator. In-hotel: 4 restaurants, bar, pool, laundry service, Wi-Fi hotspot* ▭ *AE, DC, MC, V* ⍾ *EP* Ⓜ *Yongli* ✛ *G5.*

$$

Jinglun Hotel 京伦饭店. The rooms of the elegantly refurbished Jinglun Hotel are decorated in a minimalist style. Just a 10-minute drive from Tiananmen Square and a few minutes from the China World Trade Center, the Jinglun is a well-appointed business and leisure hotel with competitive prices. The tiny, crowded lobby gives way to simple rooms with white-linen beds accented by dark purple, olive green, and yellow cushions. **Pros:** sleek design; unimpeded city views; great location. **Cons:** small rooms. ⊠ *3 Jianguomenwai Dajie, Chaoyang District* ☎ *010/6500–2266* ⊕ *www.jinglunhotel.com* ⇆ *642 rooms, 126 suites* ⚹ *In-room: safe, refrigerator, Wi-Fi. In-hotel: restaurant, bar, pool, gym, Wi-Fi hotspot* ▭ *AE, DC, MC, V* ⍾ *BP* Ⓜ *Yongli* ✛ *G5.*

$$$

JW Marriott 北京万豪酒店. One of the city's luxury hotels, the JW Marriott pampers guests with thick mattresses, rich linens, and fluffy pillows. The hotel has an indoor pool, a lovely spa, and one of the largest ballrooms in Beijing. It's adjacent to a shopping mall filled with high-end stores and interesting restaurants. **Pros:** sleek style; spectacular service; attention to detail. **Cons:** hallways are dark; glass walls on bathrooms; traffic-clogged area. ⊠ *83 Jianguo Road, Chaoyang District* ☎ *010/5908–6688* ⊕ *jwmarriottbeijing.com* ⇆ *549 rooms, 39 suites* ⚹ *In-room: refrigerator, Internet. In-hotel: restaurant, bar, pool, gym, spa, Wi-Fi hotspot* ▭ *AE, DC, MC, V* ⍾ *EP* Ⓜ *Dawanglu* ✛ *H6.*

4

$$ 🏨 **Kempinski Hotel** 凯宾斯基饭店. This fashionable hotel is part of the Lufthansa Center, so you're close to shopping. It's also within walking distance of the Sanlitun neighborhood, with its dozens of bars and restaurants. There is an excellent German restaurant here, the Paulaner Brauhaus, which has its own microbrewery. A deli, with an outstanding bakery frequented by expats, is also on-site. We love Kranzler's Coffee Shop, which has an excellent Sunday brunch. A gym and swimming pool are on the 18th floor. **Pros:** excellent service; easy access to the airport. **Cons:** far from attractions. ✉ *50 Liangmaqiao Lu, Chaoyang District* ☎ *010/6465–3388* ⊕ *www.kempinski.com* ⤴ *526 rooms, 114 suites* ♿ *In-room: safe, Internet. In-hotel: 6 restaurants, room service, bars, pool, gym, bicycles, laundry service* ▭ *AE, DC, MC, V* �ⓄⅠ *EP* Ⓜ *Liangmaqiao* ✛ *H2.*

$$ 🏨 **Kerry Centre Hotel** 北京嘉里中心饭店. This hotel is close to the city's
★ embassy and business districts, making it an excellent choice for busi-
🕐 ness travelers. It's also well situated for anyone who wants to be near ample shopping. What really distinguishes the Kerry from the rest of the pack is the amazing health club. With a full-service fitness center, a jogging track, squash and tennis courts, a spa, and, of course, a pool, it's *the* health club of choice for expats living in Beijing. Centro, the lobby bar, is arguably the most popular hotel bar in the city. The free wireless Internet throughout the lobby, including in the bar and restaurants, is an added plus. **Pros:** Reasonably priced luxury, great location, first-class swimming pool and sports facilities. **Cons:** Small rooms, poor food, congested area. ✉ *1 Guang Hua Lu, Chaoyang District* ☎ *010/6561–8833* ⊕ *www.shangri-la.com* ⤴ *487 rooms, 23 suites* ♿ *In-room: safe, refrigerator, Internet. In-hotel: 2 restaurants, bar, tennis courts, pool, gym, Wi-Fi hotspot* ▭ *AE, DC, MC, V* ⓄⅠ *EP* Ⓜ *Guomao* ✛ *H5.*

$$–$$$ 🏨 **Kunlun Hotel** 北京昆仑饭店. Topped by a revolving restaurant, this 28-story tower is a bit over the top. The hotel was named for the Kunlun Mountains, a range between northwestern China and northern Tibet that features prominently in Chinese mythology. The lovely rooms are spacious, with nice touches like slippers and robes. The superior suites, with hardwood floors, marble baths, and chic furnishings, are the most attractive. The hotel restaurant serves great Shanghai-style food as well as reliable Thai and Japanese fare in very nicely designed venues. The Kunlun, close to Beijing's rising new diplomatic area, is popular with Chinese business travelers. This shouldn't be your top choice if sightseeing is your priority. **Pros:** imposing lobby; restful rooms. **Cons:** far from the sights. ✉ *2 Xinyuan Nanlu, Sanlitun, Chaoyang District* ☎ *010/6590–3388* ⊕ *www.hotelkunlun.com* ⤴ *701 rooms, 50 suites* ♿ *In-room: Internet. In-hotel: 6 restaurants, bar, pool, gym, Wi-Fi hotspot* ▭ *AE, DC, MC, V* ⓄⅠ *EP* ✛ *H2.*

$$$$ 🏨 **New Otani Changfugong** 北京长富宫饭店. This Japanese-run hotel is renowned for its crisp service. It enjoys a great downtown location near the Friendship Store and the Ancient Observatory. Overlooking a lovely garden where guests can participate in morning exercises, the lobby's coffee shop serves Chinese meals as well as Western dishes. Or you can try the excellent Japanese restaurant. The hotel is popular with business travelers and large groups from Japan. ■ **TIP→** It's also accessible for people with disabilities—sadly, not always the norm for Beijing. **Pros:** close to the sights; efficient staff. **Cons:** pricey food; worn-out carpets. ⊠ *26 Jianguomenwai Dajie, Chaoyang District* ☎ *010/6512–5555* ⊕ *www. cfgbj.com* ↪ *500 rooms, 18 suites* ♿ *In-room: safe, refrigerator, Internet. In-hotel: 2 restaurants, bar, tennis court, pool, gym, bicycles, laundry service* ⊟ *AE, DC, MC, V* ⍐ *BP* Ⓜ *Jianguomen* ⊹ *F6.*

$$$$
★
The Opposite House 瑜舍. This boutique hotel has loftlike studios and a two-level penthouse with a private rooftop terrace. The contemporary and uncluttered style and the casually dressed staff make you feel right at home. The sunny atrium lobby has two large ponds and is decorated with contemporary artworks, such as an emperor's robe made from transparent plastic. The rooms are designed to convey a sense of space and warmth by using a lot of natural wood. Everything is operated with a touch panel. **Pros:** bright common areas; spacious rooms. **Cons:** one of the city's most expensive hotels. ⊠ *Bldg. 1, 11 Sanlitun Lu, Chaoyang District* ☎ *010/6417–6688* ↪ *98 studios, 1 penthouse* ⊕ *www.theoppositehouse.com* ♿ *In-room: refrigerator, Wi-Fi. In-hotel: 3 restaurants, bars, pool* ⊟ *AE, D, DC, MC, V* ⍐ *CP* Ⓜ *None* ⊹ *H3.*

$$$$
Fodor's Choice
★
Park Hyatt Beijing 北京柏悦酒店. This 63-story tower hotel offers plenty of pampering. Imagine your own spa-inspired bathroom with an oversize rain showerhead, deep-soaking tub, and heated floors. The rooms themselves are large and functional, with expansive desks fitted with international power outlets and wireless access. The rooftop bar, designed to resemble a Chinese lantern, has dramatic views of the city. The restaurant features international cuisine and 360-degree views of Beijing. **Pros:** spectacular views of the city; centrally located. **Cons:** pricey. ⊠ *2 Jianguomenwai Dajie., Chaoyang District* ☎ *010/8567–1234* ↪ *237 rooms, 18 suites.* ⊕ *beijing.park.hyatt.com* ♿ *In-room: safe, refrigerator, Wi-Fi. In-hotel: restaurant, bar, pool, laundry service, Wi-Fi hotspot* ⊟ *AE, D, DC, MC, V* ⍐ *EP* Ⓜ *Guomao* ⊹ *H6.*

$$$$
Radisson SAS 北京皇家大饭店. A big box near the international exhibition center in northeast Beijing, this high-end hotel receives business travelers from around the world. The rates, moderate for a business hotel, reflect the slightly out-of-the-way location. You can choose between rooms decorated in Chinese or Italian style. The restaurants—one alfresco—offer good food, including a Western-style Sunday brunch with music. Located beside the China Exhibition Center, in a congested area far from most attractions, the Radisson only makes sense if you're here on business. **Pros:** excellent dining options; good for business travelers. **Cons:** out-of-the-way location. ⊠ *6A Beisanhuan Donglu, Chaoyang District* ☎ *010/5922–3388* ⊕ *www.radisson.com* ↪ *362 rooms, 16 suites* ♿ *In-room: safe, refrigerator. In-hotel: 3 restaurants, bar, tennis court, pool, gym, bicycles* ⊟ *AE, DC, MC, V* ⍐ *EP* ⊹ *H1.*

$$$$
The Ritz-Carlton, Beijing 北京丽思卡尔顿酒店. In the Central Business District, the Ritz-Carlton sits near an upscale mall occupied by the likes of Juicy Couture, Ferragamo, Marc Jacobs, and Chanel. The press of a button closes the drapes and lowers the blackout shades; you won't know if it's day or night, which is handy if you're jet-lagged. Yu turns out marvelous Cantonese fare, especially the crispy chicken. **Pros:** superior service; great location. **Cons:** small lobby; dark public

areas; expensive food and wine. ✉ *83A Jianguo Lu, Chaoyang District* ☎ *010/5908–8888* ⊕ *www.ritzcarlton.com* ⇗ *305 rooms* ⚇ *In-room: refrigerator, Wi-Fi. In-hotel: 3 restaurants, bars, pool, gym* ▭ *AE, D, DC, MC, V* ⦿ *EP* Ⓜ *Dawanglu* ⊹ *D2, H6.*

$$$–$$$$ ⊞ **Scitech Hotel** 塞特饭店. This hotel is part of the Scitech complex, so there's a popular shopping center downstairs. The hotel enjoys a good location on busy Jianguomenwai Dajie, opposite the Friendship Store. There's a small fountain in the lobby and a small teahouse off to one side. The rooms are nondescript, and the service is nothing to write home about. **Pros:** central location; easy access to public transportation; near restaurants. **Cons:** tobacco odors throughout; worn carpets. ✉ *22 Jianguomenwai Dajie, Chaoyang District* ☎ *010/6512–3388* ⊕ *www. scitechhotel.com* ⇗ *294 rooms, 32 suites* ⚇ *In-room: safe, refrigerator. In-hotel: 2 restaurants, room service, bar, tennis court, pool, gym, laundry service, parking (paid)* ▭ *AE, DC, MC, V* ⦿ *EP* Ⓜ *Yonganli* ⊹ *F6.*

$$$ ⊞ **Sofitel Wanda** 北京万达索菲特大饭店. Tang Dynasty–style mixes with contemporary-French flair at this hotel. The plush rooms and suites are enlivened with subtle Asian motifs. They're outfitted with built-in LCD TVs in both the bedrooms and bathrooms and have complimentary broadband access. The fitness center has a 25-meter swimming pool and a state-of-the-art gym. Le Pré Lenôtre offers fabulous French cuisine. **Pros:** nice design; plenty of high-tech touches; near subway. **Cons:** traffic-clogged area. ✉ *97 Jianguo Road, Tower C, Chaoyang District* ☎ *010/8599–6666* ⊕ *www.sofitel-wanda-beijing.com* ⇗ *417 rooms, 43 suites* ⚇ *In-room: safe, refrigerator, Wi-Fi. In-hotel: 4 restaurants, spa, Wi-Fi hotspot* ▭ *AE, D, DC, MC, V* ⦿ *EP* Ⓜ *Dawanglu* ⊹ *H6.*

$$$$ ⊞ **St. Regis** 北京国际俱乐部饭店. Considered by many to be the best
Fodor's Choice hotel in Beijing, the St. Regis is a favorite of business travelers and vis-
★ iting dignitaries. This is where Uma Thurman and Quentin Tarantino relaxed during the filming of *Kill Bill*. You won't be disappointed: the luxurious interiors combine classic Chinese elegance and modern furnishings. The Press Club Bar, with its wood paneling, overflowing bookcases, and grand piano, feels like a private club. The Japanese restaurant has tasty, moderately priced lunch specials. The Astor Grill is known for its steak and seafood dishes, and Danielli's serves authentic Italian food. Don't miss the waffles with fresh blueberries at the incredible breakfast buffet. The St. Regis health club is arguably the most unique in Beijing: the equipment is state-of-the-art; the Jacuzzi is supplied with natural hot spring water pumped up from deep beneath the hotel; and the glass-atrium swimming pool, with plenty of natural light, is a lovely place for a relaxing swim. An added plus is that it's just a 10-minute taxi ride to the Forbidden City. If you can afford it, this is the place to stay. **Pros:** ideal location; near public transportation; lots of restaurants nearby. **Cons:** the little extras really add up here. ✉ *21 Jianguomenwai Dajie, Chaoyang District* ☎ *010/6460–6688* ⊕ *www.stregis.com/beijing* ⇗ *156 rooms, 102 suites* ⚇ *In-room: refrigerator, Wi-Fi. In-hotel: 5 restaurants, bar, tennis court, pool, gym, spa, bicycles, laundry service, Wi-Fi hotspot, parking (paid)* ▭ *AE, DC, MC, V* Ⓜ *Jianguomen* ⊹ *F5.*

$$$–$$$$ ⊞ **Swissôtel** 港澳中心瑞士酒店. In the large, impressive marble lobby you can enjoy jazz every Friday and Saturday evening. Rooms have

Park Hyatt Beijing

St. Regis

high-quality, European-style furnishings in cream and light grey, plus temperature controls and coffeemakers. The hotel health club has an atrium-style swimming pool and an outdoor tennis court. The Western coffee shop has one of the best hotel buffets in Beijing. It's a short walk to the bustling Sanlitun bar area and the Nanxincang complex of restaurants, which are housed in a former Ming Dynasty granary. A subway entrance is just outside the hotel's front door. **Pros:** lovely lobby; great amenities. **Cons:** far from most sites; mediocre food. ⊠ *2 Chaoyangmennei Dajie, Dongsishiqiao Flyover Junction (Second Ring Rd.), Chaoyang District* ☎ *010/6553–2288* 🖷 *010/6501–2501* ⊕ *www. swissotel-beijing.com* ↩ *430 rooms, 50 suites* ♨ *In-room: safe, refrigerator, Internet. In-hotel: 2 restaurants, room service, bar, tennis court, pool, gym, laundry service* ☰ *AE, DC, MC, V* Ⓜ *Dongsi Shitiao* ✛ *F3.*

$$ 🏨 **Traders Hotel** 国贸饭店. Inside the China World Trade Center complex, this hotel is connected to a shopping mall. The hotel is a favorite of international business travelers who appreciate its central location, good service, and top-notch amenities. On top of all that, it's an excellent value. Rooms are done up in muted colors and have queen- or king-size beds. Guests have access to an excellent health club. **Pros:** moderately priced for a business hotel; near plenty of shopping. **Cons:** small lobby. ⊠ *1 Jianguomenwai Dajie, Chaoyang District* ☎ *010/6505–2277* ⊕ *www.shangri-la.com* ↩ *570 rooms, 27 suites* ♨ *In-room: safe, refrigerator, Internet. In-hotel: 2 restaurants, bar* ☰ *AE, DC, MC, V* ⏹⊙⏹ *EP* Ⓜ *Guomao* ✛ *H5.*

$$$$ 🏨 **Westin Beijing Chaoyang** 金茂北京威斯汀大饭店. With 550 spacious guest rooms, the new Westin Beijing Chaoyang isn't exactly a small affair. But what the hotel lacks in intimacy, it more than makes up for in luxury. Highlights include the heavenly beds and rainforest showers, flat-screen interactive televisions, and IP wireless phones. Rooms are decorated with warm colors and contemporary furnishings. **Pros:** convenient location near airport expressway; beautiful atrium-style swimming pool. **Cons:** in northeast corner of the city far from tourist sites. ⊠ *1 Xinyuan Nanlu, Chaoyang District* ☎ *010/5922–8888* ⊕ *www. westin.com/chaoyang* ↩ *550 rooms* ♨ *In-room: a/c, safe, refrigerator, DVD, Wi-Fi. In-hotel: 2 restaurants, room service, bar, pool, gym, spa, children's programs (ages 6 and under), laundry facilities, laundry service, Internet terminal, Wi-Fi hotspot, parking (free)* ☰ *AE, DC, MC, V* ⏹⊙⏹ *EP* Ⓜ *Liangmaqiao* ✛ *G1.*

$–$$ 🏨 **Yi House** 一驿. Yi House is arguably Beijing's most interesting concept hotel. The venue sits on the grounds of the Dashanzi Art District, better known as 798. The redbrick Bauhaus structure, once the site of an old crystal factory, has been rebuilt to accommodate visitors to Beijing's most popular art district. On the inside the design has a French colonial and art deco touch. Artwork hangs in the rooms, from nostalgic black-and-white photos to the works of avant-garde artist Chi Peng. The restaurant features Mediterranean cooking. **Pros:** unique themed hotel; in the 798 Art District. **Cons:** 798 is off the beaten track. ⊠ *D-Park, Jiuxianqiao Lu 2 Hao Yuan, 798 Art District, Chaoyang District* ☎ *010/6436–1818* ⊕ *www.yi-house.com* ↩ *30 rooms* ♨ *In-room: a/c (some), no phone (some), safe, kitchen (some), refrigerator,*

DVD, Wi-Fi. In-hotel: restaurant, room service, bar, laundry facilities, laundry service, Internet terminal, Wi-Fi hotspot, parking (paid). ⊟ *AE, DC, MC, V* ✦ *H1.*

¢ ⊡ **You Yi Youth Hostel** 北京友谊青年酒店. Backpackers who don't mind that this youth hostel (also called the Friendship Youth Hostel) is attached to one of Beijing's most popular bars (Poachers) should stay here. Rooms sleep two to four people and are well kept, with clean white walls and dark-wood trim. Best of all, the hostel is located smack in the middle of Beijing's bar-street area. **Pros:** very cheap; ideal for party animals. **Cons:** very basic. ⊠ *43 Beisanlitun Nan, Sanlitun, Chaoyang District* ☏ *010/6417–2632* ⊕ ↳ *35 rooms with shared bath* ⌂ *In-room: no TV (some). In-hotel: restaurant, bar, laundry service* ⊟ *AE, MC, V* �aⁱ *BP* ✦ *G3.*

$–$$ ⊡ **Zhaolong Hotel** 兆龙饭店. This building was a gift to the nation from Hong Kong shipping magnate Y.K. Pao, who named it for his father. Located at the intersection of Gongti Beilu and the Third Ring Road, the Zhaolong is next door to a great Cantonese restaurant, De Luxe, and L'Isola, an Italian restaurant. The Bookworm, a popular expat coffee shop and restaurant, is a few blocks away. Its location puts you close to the capital's nightlife. The back of the hotel houses a youth hostel. **Pros:** near restaurants and nightlife; close to shopping. **Cons:** uninspired decor; lackluster service. ⊠ *2 Gongren Tiyuchang Beilu, Chaoyang District* ☏ *010/6597–2299* ⊕ *www.zhaolonghotel.com.cn* ↳ *270 rooms, 16 suites* ⌂ *In-room: Internet. In-hotel: 3 restaurants, bar, pool, gym* ⊟ *AE, DC, MC, V* �aⁱ *EP* ✦ *C2.*

¢ ⊡ **Zhaolong International Youth Hostel** 兆龙青年旅. If partaking in Beijing's lively nightlife scene is on your itinerary, consider this comfortable youth hostel in Sanlitun for your stay. The hostel offers spic-and-span rooms with two to six beds each, a reading room, a kitchen, and bicycle rentals. **Pros:** as cheap as it gets; clean and comfortable. **Cons:** just the basics. ⊠ *2 Gongti Beilu, Sanlitun, Chaoyang District* ☏ *010/6597–2299 Ext. 6111* ⊕ *www.zhaolonghotel.com.cn* ↳ *30 rooms* ⌂ *In-room: no phone, no TV. In-hotel: bar, laundry facilities* ⊟ *AE, MC, V* �aⁱ *CP* Ⓜ *Tuanjiehu/Nongzhanguan* ✦ *H3.*

HAIDIAN DISTRICT 海淀区

The Haidian District, in the far northwestern corner of Beijing, is where you'll find the university district, the city zoo, and numerous parks. The main attractions here for visitors are the Summer Palace and Old Summer Palace.

Use the coordinate (✦ A1) at the end of each listing to locate a site on the corresponding map.

$$ ⊡ **Aman Summer Palace** 北京颐和安缦. This luxury hotel sprawls out across a series of carefully renovated ancient Qing Dynasty courtyards. The resort sits against a side of the Summer Palace with its own private gate providing guests easy access to this historic landmark. Rooms are decorated in restful earth tones and feature traditional wooden screens and bamboo blinds. Suites have roomy bathrooms with island bath-tubs and separate shower and toilet areas. Guests can enjoy breakfast

looking over a reflecting lotus pool. **Pros:** right next to the Summer Palace. **Cons:** pricey; far from city sights. ⊠ *15 Gongmen Qian Street, Summer Palace, Haidian District* ☎ *010/5987–9999* ⊕ *www.amanresorts. com* ▭ *8 rooms, 25 suites* ⌂ *In-room: a/c, safe, DVD, Wi-Fi. In-hotel: 3 restaurants, bar, room service, pool, gym, spa, laundry facilities, laundry service, Internet terminal, Wi-Fi hotspot, parking (free)* ▭ *AE, DC, MC, V* Ⓜ *Yiheyuan* ♦ *A1.*

$$$$ 🏨 **Commune by the Great Wall** 长城脚下公社. An hour from Beijing, the
★ Commune by the Great Wall offers modern comfort in a rural setting. There's plenty of space, so it's an ideal place for families and groups of friends. Bamboo House and Suitcase House are the most popular of the 11 houses designed by renowned Asian architects; each of the houses offers views of the Great Wall and the distant mountains. While mom indulges in spa treatments, the children can go off to the kids' club, the pool, or even the library. The Terrace Lounge offers Chinese and Western food, while 24 Cafe has light meals. **Pros:** rustic environment; comfortable accommodations; near the Great Wall. **Cons:** you will likely share the villa with other guests. ⊠ *Exit 20 at Shuiguan, Badaling Highway, Beijing* ☎ *010/8118–1888* ⊕ *www.communebythegreatwall. com* ▭ *11 houses* ⌂ *In-room: Wi-Fi. In-hotel: restaurant, pool, gym* ▭ *AE, MC, V* ⏐○⏐ *BP.*

$$$$ 🏨 **Eagle's Rest** 鹰之巢. This hotel was designed by Jim Spear, a long-
★ time resident of Mutianyu Village. Take your time wandering through the peaceful village of Yingbeigou and exploring the surrounding lush hills. It's here that you'll find Eagle's Rest retreat (be sure to spend time on the patio overlooking the village and the Mutianyu Great Wall). Even though the hotel melds perfectly with the village, it still provides modern comforts. Enjoy the luxury of solitude and an aerie retreat above the fray. **Pros:** rustic setting; near the Great Wall. **Cons:** need a car to get around. ⊠ *12 Mutianyu Village, Beijing* ☎ *010/6162–6282* ⊕ *www.chinacountrysidehotels.com* ▭ *2 rooms* ⌂ *In-hotel: Wi-Fi hotspot* ▭ *AE, MC, V* ⏐○⏐ *CP.*

$ 🏨 **Friendship Hotel** 友谊宾馆. The name is telling, as the hotel was built in 1954 to house foreigners, mostly Soviets, who had come to help rebuild the nation. This is one of the largest garden-style hotels in Asia. The architecture is traditional Chinese, and the public spaces are classic and elegant. Rooms are large, but they are filled with somewhat outdated furnishings. With 14 restaurants, an Olympic-size pool, and a driving range, the hotel aims to be a one-stop destination. Its location far from the main tourist trail means that it's better situated for people who need to be close to the university area. **Pros:** a bit of history; good location in northwest Beijing. **Cons:** away from the city center. ⊠ *3 Baishiqiao Lu, Haidian District* ☎ *010/6849–8888* ⊕ *www. bjfriendshiphotel.com* ▭ *1,700 rooms, 200 suites* ⌂ *In-room: refrigerator, Internet. In-hotel: 14 restaurants, bar, tennis courts, pool, gym* ▭ *AE, DC, MC, V* ⏐○⏐ *EP* ♦ *A1.*

$$$ 🏨 **Grandma's Place** 奶奶家. This rural inn was constructed using stones
☾ salvaged from Ming and Qing Dynasty structures, as well massive beams torn from a village landlord's house. The original peasant family's furniture is still used in the strikingly contemporary interior.

There is a traditional *kang*—a brick bed heated from beneath—in the master bedroom, a very private garden with fruit trees, and a terrace with clear views of the Great Wall. There are two bedrooms with en-suite bathrooms, wireless broadband, a kitchen, and laundry facilities. Grandma's Place is located near The Schoolhouse (where the restaurant is). **Pros:** a wonderful rustic getaway with views of the Great Wall. **Cons:** guests must hire a car to reach the hotel. ⊠ *The Schoolhouse, 12 Mutianyu Village, Huairou District* ☏ *010/6162–6282* ⊕ *www. grandmasplaceatmutianyu.com* ⇆ *2 rooms* ⚑ In-hotel: Wi-Fi hotspot ⊙ *EP* ⊟ *No credit cards.*

$$$$ ⛫ **The Schoolhouse Homes** 小园. The Schoolhouse Homes, designed by Jim Spear, a long-time resident of Mutianyu Village, include 11 custom-designed luxurious venues with spectacular views of the Great Wall. The Schoolhouse Homes was awarded the best sustainable communities development in Asia-Pacific and also awarded 4 Green Stars by Eco Hotels of the World. **Pros:** fresh air; laid-back atmosphere. **Cons:** far from other historical sites. ⊠ *12 Mutianyu Village, Huairou101405* ☏ *010/6162–6282* ⊕ *www.theschoolhouseatmutianyu.com* ⇆ *30 rooms* ⚑ In-room: *a/c, safe, kitchen, Wi-Fi. In-hotel: 2 restaurants, pool, children's programs (6–17), Wi-Fi hotspot, parking (free)* ⊟ *AE, DC, MC, V* ⊙ *EP.*

$$$ ⛫ **Shangri-La Hotel** 北京香格里拉饭店. Set in delightful landscaped gardens, the Shangri-La is a wonderful retreat for business travelers and those who don't mind being far from the city center. A new tower, called the Valley Wing, was completed in 2007. Each room is designed to have a garden or city view. The hotel's Blu Lobster is headed by Chef de Cuisine Brian McKenna, and offers exciting molecular gastronomy and innovative cuisine. **Pros:** lovely gardens; excellent amenities. **Cons:** far from the city center. ⊠ *29 Zizhuyuan Lu, Haidian District* ☏ *010/6841–2211* ⊕ *www.shangri-la.com* ⇆ *670 rooms, 32 suites* ⚑ In-room: *safe, refrigerator, Wi-Fi. In-hotel: 7 restaurants, room service, pool, gym, laundry service, Wi-Fi hotspot, parking (free)* ⊟ *AE, DC, MC, V* ⊙ *EP* ⊹ *A1.*

BEIJING AIRPORT AREA

$$ ⛫ **Sino-Swiss Hotel** 北京国都大饭店. This contemporary hotel overlooks a gorgeous outdoor pool surrounded by trees, shrubs, and colorful umbrellas. All the rooms and public areas are completely up-to-date. The restaurant Mongolian Gher offers barbecue and live entertainment inside a traditional yurt (a tentlike structure), whereas the Swiss Chalet serves familiar Continental food on the outdoor terrace. Just five minutes from the airport, the Sino-Swiss Hotel is convenient if you have an early-morning flight or get stuck at the airport. **Pros:** good dining options; near the airport. **Cons:** far from the downtown attractions. ⊠ *9 Xiao Tianzhu Nanlu, Beijing Capital Airport, Shunyi County* ☏ *010/6456–5588* ⊕ *www.sino-swisshotel.com* ⇆ *408 rooms, 35 suites* ⚑ In-room: *safe, refrigerator, Internet. In-hotel: 4 restaurants, bars, tennis courts, pool, gym, laundry service* ⊟ *AE, DC, MC, V* ⊙ *BP* ⊹ *H1.*

ENGLISH	PINYIN	CHINESE
3+1 bedroom		n/a
Autumn Garden	Chūnqiūyuán bīnguǎn nányuán	春秋园宾馆南园
Aman Summer Palace	Běijīng yíhé ānmàn	北京颐和安缦
Banqiao No. 4	Bǎnqiáo sì hào	板桥4号
Beijing Guxiang 20 Hotel	Běijīng Gǔxiāng èrshí hào	北京古乡20号
Beijing Hotel	Běijīng fàndiàn	北京饭店
Beijing International	Běijīng guójì fàndiàn	北京国际饭店
Beijing Marriott Hotel City Wall	Běijīng Wànháo jiǔdiàn	北京万豪酒店
Beijing Sihe Courtyard Hotel	Běijīng Sìhé bīnguǎn	北京四合宾馆
China World Hotel	Zhōngguó dàfàndiàn	中国大饭店
China World Summit Wing	Běijīng guómào dànjiǔdiàn	北京国贸大酒店
Courtyard by Northeast Beijing	běijīng rénjì wànyí jiǔdiàn	北京人济万怡酒店
Commune by the Great Wall	Chánghéng jiǎoxià gōngshè	长城脚下公社
Courtyard Beijing	Běijīng Wànyí jiǔdiàn	北京万怡酒店
Crowne Plaza Beijing	Běijīng guójì yìyuàn	北京国际艺苑
Day's Inn Forbidden City Beijing	Běijīng Xiāngjiāng Dàisī jiǔdiàn	北京香江戴斯酒店
Dongtang Inn	Dōngtáng kèzhàn	东堂客栈
Double Tree by Hilton Beijing	Běijīng Xīěrdùnyìlín jiǔdiàn	北京希尔顿逸林酒店
Du Ge	Dù gé	杜革
Eagle's Rest	Yīngzhī cháo	鹰之巢
The Emperor	Huángjiā yìzhàn	皇家驿栈
Fairmont Beijing	Běijīng huábīn ěrméng jiǔdiàn	北京华彬费尔蒙酒店
Friendship Hotel	Yǒuyì bīnguǎn	友谊宾馆
Grand Hotel Beijing	Běijīng Guìbīn lóu fàndiàn	北京贵宾楼饭店
Grand Hyatt Beijing	Běijīng Dōngfāngjūnyuè jiǔdiàn	北京东方君悦酒店
Grand Millennium Beijing Hotel	Běijīng Qiānxǐ dà jiǔdiàn	北京千禧大酒店
Grandma's Place	Nǎinaijiā	奶奶家
Great Wall Sheraton	Běijīng Chángchéng fàndiàn	北京长城饭店
Haoyuan Hotel	Hǎoyuán bīnguǎn	好园宾馆
Hilton Beijing	Běijīng Xīěrdùn jiǔdiàn	北京稀尔顿酒店
Holiday Inn Lido	Lìdū jiàrì fàndiàn	丽都假日饭店
Hotel G	Běijīng jí zhàn	北京极栈
Hotel Kapok	Mùmiánhuā jiǔdiàn	木棉花酒店

ENGLISH	PINYIN	CHINESE
InterContinental Financial Street Beijing	Jīnróng zhōujì jiǔdiàn	金融洲际酒店
Jianguo Hotel	Jiànguó fàndiàn	建国饭店
Jinglun Hotel	Jīnglún fàndiàn	京伦饭店
JW Marriott Hotel Beijing	Běijīng Wànháo jiǔdiàn	北京万豪酒店
Kempinski Hotel	Kǎibīnsījī fàndiàn	凯宾斯基饭店
Kerry Centre Hotel	Běijīng Jiālǐ zhōngxīn fàndiàn	北京嘉里中心饭店
Kunlun Hotel	Běijīng Kūnlún fàndiàn	北京昆仑饭店
Legendale	Lìjùn jiǔdiàn	励骏酒店
LüSongyuan	Lǚsōngyuán bīnguǎn	侣松园宾馆
Minzu Hotel	Mínzú fàndiàn	民族饭店
New Otani Changfugong	Běijīng Chángfùgōng fàndiàn	北京长富宫饭店
Novotel Peace Hotel	Hépíng bīnguǎn	和平宾馆
The Opposite House	Yúshě	瑜舍
Park Hyatt Beijing	Běijīng Bòyuè jiǔdiàn	北京柏悦酒店
Park Plaza Beijing	Běijīng Lìtíng jiǔdiàn	北京丽亭酒店
Peninsula Beijing	Wángfǔ Bàndǎo jiǔdiàn	王府半岛酒店
Radisson SAS	Běijīng Huángjiā dàfàndiàn	北京皇家大饭店
Raffles Beijing Hotel	Běijīng fàndiàn Láifóshì	北京饭店莱佛士
Red Capital Residence	Xīnhóngzī kèzhàn	新红资客栈
The Regent	Běijīng Lìjīng jiǔdiàn	北京丽晶酒店
The Ritz-Carlton, Beijing	Běijīng Lìsīkǎ'ěrdùn jjiǔdiàn	北京丽思卡尔顿酒店
Ritz-Carlton Beijing, Financial Street	Běijīng Jīnróng jiē Lìsīkǎ'ěrdùn jiǔdiàn	北京金融街丽思卡尔顿酒店
Scitech Hotel	Sāitè fàndiàn	塞特饭店
The Schoolhouse Homes	xiǎoyuán	小园
Shangri-La Hotel	Běijīng Xiānggélǐlā fàndiàn	北京香格里拉饭店
Sino-Swiss Hotel	Běijīng Guódū dàfàndiàn	北京国都大饭店
Sofitel Wanda	Běijīng Wàndásuǒfēitè dà jiǔdiàn	北京万达索菲特大饭店
St. Regis	Běijīng guójì jùlèbù fàndiàn	北京国际俱乐部饭店
Swissôtel	gǎngao zhōngxīn Ruìshì jiǔdiàn	港澳中心瑞士酒店
Traders Hotel	Guómào fàndiàn	国贸饭店
Westin Beijing	Wēisīdtīng jiǔdiàn	威斯汀酒店

4

ENGLISH	PINYIN	CHINESE
Westin Beijing Chaoyang	Jīnmào běijīng wēisīdtīng dàjiǔdiàn	金茂北京威斯汀大饭店
Yi House	Yīyì	一驿
You Yi Youth Hostel	Běijīng yǒuyì qīngnián jiǔdiàn	北京友谊青年酒店
Zhaolong Hotel	Zhàolóng fàndiàn	兆龙饭店
Zhaolong International Youth Hostel	Zhàolóng qīngnián lǚshè	兆龙青年旅
Zhuyuan Hotel	Zhúyuán bīnguǎn	竹园宾馆

Shopping

WORD OF MOUTH

"You should try to get to the Panjiayuan 'Dirt Market' on weekends. I thought that was the best place to shop in Beijing. By far. But you need to go very early (get there by 8 AM if possible) and prepare to bargain fiercely."

—ekscrunchy

Updated by
Helena Iveson

Large markets and malls in Beijing are generally open from 9 AM to 9 PM, though some shops close as early as 7 PM or as late as 10 PM. Weekdays are always less crowded. During rush hour, avoid taking taxis. If a shop looks closed (the lights are out or the owner is resting), don't give up. Many merchants conserve electricity or take catnaps if the store is free of customers. Just knock or offer the greeting "*ni hao*." More likely than not, the lights will flip on and you'll be invited to come in and take a look. Shops in malls have regular hours and will only be closed on a few occasions throughout the year, like Chinese New Year.

Major credit cards are accepted in pricier venues. Cash is the driving force here, and ATMs abound. Before accepting those Mao-faced Y100 notes, most vendors will hold them up to the light, tug at the corners, and rub their fingers along the surface. Counterfeiting is becoming increasingly more difficult, but no one, including you, wants to be cheated. In some department stores, you must settle your bill at a central payment counter.

Shops frequented by foreigners sometimes have an employee with some fluency in English. But money remains the international language. In many cases, whether or not there is a common language—the shop assistant will still whip out a calculator, look at you to see what they think you'll cough up, then type in a starting price. You're expected to counter with your offer. Punch in your dream price. The clerk will come down Y10 or Y20 and so on and so on. Remember that the terms *yuan*, *kuai*, and *RMB* are often used interchangeably.

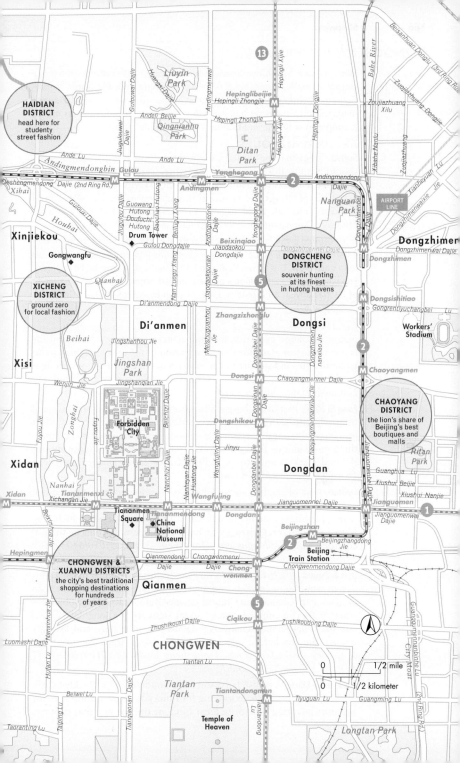

DONGCHENG DISTRICT 东城区

With its tiny boutiques dotted along *hutongs* (alleyways) and glitzy shopping malls, Dongcheng is a key shopping area for those visiting Beijing. Whether searching for souvenirs, silks, or foreign-language magazines, Dongcheng has everything. Its centralized location makes it simple to combine sightseeing with shopping trips.

ART AND ANTIQUES

Sattva. Tibet may be thousands of miles away, but art connoisseurs should head to this art and antique store, a treasure trove of Tibetan crafts tucked away in an interesting hutong. *Thangkas*, Tibetan embroidered silk paintings, are beautiful though expensive. The selection of furniture and yak wool rugs is more affordable. ⊠ *60 Wudaoying Hutong, Dongcheng District* ☎ *138/1116–9101* Ⓜ *Yonghe Gong.*

⚠ Deception is the only real "art" practiced by the charming "art students" who will approach you at tourist destinations and invite you to their college's art show. The artworks are, in fact, usually mass-produced copies. If you want to support Beijing's burgeoning art scene, explore the galleries of Dashanzi, visit an artists' village, or drop by one of the galleries listed in Chapter 6.

BOUTIQUES

Nanluoguxiang's evolution into the center of the city's bohemian life is due in part to plans for the preservation of the area's original architectural style, and in part to the entrepreneurial spirit of local designers. Wudaoying hutong, near the Lama Temple, is now a contender to Nanluoguxiang's hipster crown.

Fang Si 放肆. Part of the burgeoning boutique scene on Gulou, this small but well-edited store features the creations of local designers, including jewelry, clothes and souvenirs. It's also a great place to pick up something more unique than the selection of goods found in more run-of-the-mill markets and stores. ⊠ *96-1 Gulou Dong Dajie, Dongcheng District* ☎ *6403–4165* Ⓜ *Gulou.*

Grifted. One of the first design shops on Nanluoguxiang, Grifted displays socialist-inspired irony in its clothing, accessories, and home-decor items. Highlights include a collection of "socialist dolls," including Mao, Lenin, Marx, Castro, and Che. A percentage of profits go to local charities. ⊠ *28 Nanluoguxiang, Dongcheng District* ☎ *010/6402–0409* Ⓜ *Zhangzizhonglu.*

Lost & Found 失物招领. Tucked down a historic tree-lined hutong, this design boutique is stylish and sensitive to Beijing's past. American designer Paul Gelinas and Chinese partner Xiao Miao salvage objects— whether they're chipped enamel street signs from a long-demolished hutong, a barbershop chair, or a 1950s Shanghai fan—and lovingly remove the dirt before offering them on sale in their treasure trove of a store. ⊠ *42 Guozijian, Dongcheng District* ☎ *010/6401–1855* Ⓜ *Yonghe Gong* ⊕ *lost-and-found.cn*

Plastered T-Shirts. A British lad opened this boutique and it quickly caught the imagination of people looking for quirky souvenirs. Shop here for a T-shirt picturing a favorite local food, or opt for one that captures

One of the many tea shops in Beijing

those nostalgic days of Old Peking, as well as posters, notebooks, and traditional thermoses. Fun and kitschy, everything costs around Y100. It's just north of the Downtown Backpackers Hostel ✉ *Nanluoguxiang, Dongcheng District* ☎ *134/8884–8855* Ⓜ *Zhangzizhonglu.*

Woo 妩. The gorgeous scarves displayed in the windows lure in passersby with their bright colors and luxurious fabrics. In contrast to those of the vendors in the markets, the cashmere, silk, and bamboo used here are 100% natural. The design and construction are comparable to top Italian designers, while the prices are much more affordable. ✉ *110/1 Nanluoguxiang, Dongcheng District* ☎ *010/6400–5395* Ⓜ *Zhangzizhonglu.*

MALLS AND DEPARTMENT STORES

Malls at Oriental Plaza 东方广场购物中心. This enormous shopping complex, which may have newer competition but a location that keeps the crowds coming, originates at the southern end of Wangfujing where it meets Chang'an Jie and stretches a city block east to Dongdan Dajie. A true city within a city, it's conveniently organized by "street" names, such as Gourmet Street (aka the Food Court) and Sky Avenue. Upscale shops include Kenzo and Armani Exchange, which have some of the best men's accessories between Tokyo and Naples. ✉ *1 Dongchang'an Jie, Dongcheng District* ☎ *010/8518–6363* Ⓜ *Wangfujing.*

SHOES

Pi'erman Maoyi 皮尔曼贸易公司. If you've always wanted to have shoes made just for you, this traditional cobbler is highly rated by Beijing expats. If you're in the city for a bit longer—he will take two weeks— you can have a pair of shoes or boots made for very reasonable prices.

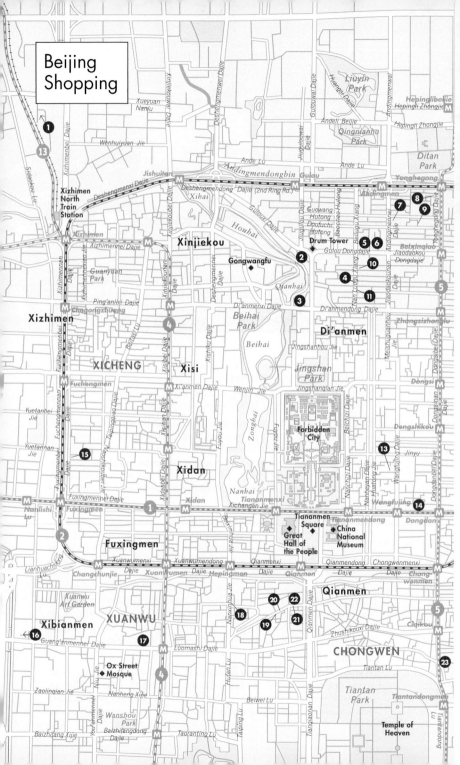

Bring in a photo or a pair that you wish to copy, as the cobbler does not speak much English. ✉ *37 Gulou Dong Dajie, Dongcheng District* ☎ *010/6404–1406.*

⚠ Fakes abound—everything from jade, cashmere, pashminas, silk, and leather to handbags, antiques, and Calvin Klein underwear. Many foreign tourists and local people buy fakes, but it is important to keep in mind that the low price generally reflects poor quality, often in ways that are not immediately apparent. Reserve your big purchases for accredited shops or merchants who can prove the quality of their product. Some countries limit the number of knockoffs you can bring back into the country, so don't go overboard on the handbags or DVDs. If you're buying authentic antiques, you'll need to show customs agents your receipts, embossed with an official red seal.

> **WHEN TO HAGGLE**
>
> Bargaining is acceptable, and expected, in markets and mom-and-pop shops, though not in department stores and malls. Also, an increasing number of higher-end local boutiques follow the lead of their Western peers in not allowing bargaining. The bottom line is to pay what you think is fair.

SILK AND FABRICS

Daxin Textiles Co. 大新纺织. For a wide selection of all types of fabrics, from worsted wools to sensuous silks, head to this shop. It's best to buy the material here and find a tailor elsewhere, as sewing standards can be shoddy. ✉ *Northeast corner of Dongsi, Dongcheng District* ☎ *010/6403–2378* Ⓜ *Dongsi.*

TOYS

Bannerman Tang's Toys and Crafts 北京盛唐轩传统民间玩具开发中心. Step back into the past at this quaint toy store. Wonderfully, it's a world away from today's high-tech toys. Descendants of a legendary Qing Dynasty toymaker make colorful clay puppets, vivid Peking Opera masks, and tiny clay figures to keep and covet. ✉ *38 Guozijian, Dongcheng District* ☎ *010/8404–7179* Ⓜ *Yonghe Gong.*

XICHENG DISTRICT 西城区

Less than 2 km (1 mi) west of the Forbidden City, the massive shopping area of **Xidan,** within Xicheng district, swarms with local shoppers intent on finding knockoffs of obscure brand names and the latest trends from Japan and South Korea. To get here, take subway Line 1 to the Xidan stop (exit A). By taxi, simply show the driver the Chinese characters for "Xidan." The quality has been improving, but foreign shoppers prefer to stick with the Silk and Pearl markets for lower prices, recognizable brands, and Chinese-themed products. But if you're up for this potentially overwhelming jaunt into the crush of young people, you can elbow your way through the labyrinth of malls, markets, and chain stores to find some cheap chic clustered along **Xidan Beidajie,** just north of the Xidan subway stop. The newest mall here, Joy City, is home to international chains like Zara, Uniqlo, and Next.

CLOSE UP

The Ultimate Shopping Tour

Day 1 (weekend): Can't sleep from jet lag? No worries. Rise before dawn and join the hordes at **Panjiayuan,** also known as Dirt Market, for Beijing Shopping 101. Spend some time on a reconnaissance tour of this vast market before making any purchases. Bags in tow, head directly across the street to **Zhaojia Chaowai** for a more manageable experience of shopping for furniture and goodies. Next, direct a pedicab driver to **Beijing Curio City.** From here, take a cab to haggle hard for knockoffs and cheap silk garments at **Silk Alley.** Have lunch, then make the trek to **Qianmen and Dashilan** for a walk down old streets newly renovated for modern shoppers. Travel its length on foot; by this time shops will begin to close and it is time to head back to your hotel.

Day 2: Kick off the day by sampling tea from the seemingly infinite number of vendors pedaling their wares on **Tea Street.** Buy clay or porcelain service sets and tea galore. Then take a cab to **Liulichang.** Linger in this old-time shopping street before entering the modern world at **Wangfujing.** This pedestrian-only shopping

arcade is just east of the Forbidden City. If this mix of malls, snack shops, and souvenir stalls doesn't wipe you out, take a cab to **Hongqiao Market** for a pearl-shopping spree, or to **Shin Kong Place** for some designer purchases.

Day 3: Start the day in the middle of old Beijing's lake district at famous **Yandai Xiejie.** Ethnic garments and Communist memorabilia abound. Walk east past the Bell Tower and down pleasant Gulou Dong Dajie street to reach Nanluoguxiang, Beijing's hippest hutong. There's a range of affordable local designs, cute and ironic T-shirts, and gorgeous scarves and silk garments. Walk the length of the street and choose one of the restaurants for lunch. From here, take a taxi east toward Chaoyang District and hit Sanlitun for a visit to **Yaxiu Market** and next door, **Sanlitun Village.** Designer boutiques and chic malls abound in what used to be just a bar district. Shop, shop, shop, and then drop—wherever you land, a waiter will appear to offer you an ice-cold cola or Tsingtao beer.

5

MALLS AND DEPARTMENT STORES

Seasons Place 金融街购物中心. This ritzy mall is further west in Beijing's Financial Street area. If you're staying at one of the business hotels nearby, Seasons Place will fulfill your shopping needs—as long as you're not on a budget. Designer labels like Louis Vuitton, Gucci, and Versace are here, as well as the Beijing branch of Hong Kong's fab department store, Lane Crawford. ⊠*2 Jinrong Jie, Xicheng District* ☎*010/6622–0088* Ⓜ*Fuxingmen* ⊕*www.seasonsplace.com*

TOYS

Three Stones Kite Store 三石斋风筝店. For something more traditional, go fly a kite. But not the run-of-the-mill type you see anywhere. Here, for three generations, the same family has hand-painted butterflies and birds onto bamboo frames to delight adults and children alike. ⊠*25 Di'anmen Xidajie, Xicheng District* ☎ *010/8404–4505* Ⓜ*Zhangzizhonglu* ⊕*www.cnkites.com.*

SOUTHERN DISTRICTS: CHONGWEN AND XUANWU 崇文区 AND 宣武区

CHINESE MEDICINE

★ **Tongrentang** 同仁堂. A first-time consultation with a Chinese doctor can feel a bit like a reading with a fortune-teller. With one test of the pulse, many traditional Chinese doctors can describe the patient's medical history and diagnose current maladies. China's most famous traditional Chinese medicine shop, Tongrentang, is one of the oldest establishments on Dashilan. Hushed, and dimly illuminated, this 300-year-old old shop even smells healthy. Browse the glassed displays of deer antlers and pickled snakes, dried seahorses and frogs, and delicate tangles of roots with precious price tags of Y48,000. If you don't speak Chinese and wish to have a consultation with a doctor, consider bringing along a translator. ⊠ *24 Dashilan, Qianmen, Exit C, Chongwen District* 🕿 *010/6701–5895* Ⓜ *Qianmen.*

⚠ Chinese medicine is wonderful, but not when practiced by lab-coated "doctors" sitting behind a card table on the street corner. If you're seeking Chinese medical treatment, visit a local hospital, Tongrentang medicine shop, or ask your hotel concierge for a legitimate recommendation.

MARKETS

Pearls, pearls, pearls! Few shoppers visit Beijing without a trip to the Hongqiao Market (aka Pearl Market), where midquality pearls are cheap and plentiful. An afternoon of shopping in Chongwen and Xuanwu can be balanced with a morning tour of the nearby Temple of Heaven.

Baoguosi Temple Antiques Market 报国寺收藏品市场. This little-known market, atmospherically set in the picturesque grounds of the Baoguosi Temple, is a smaller, more manageable version of Panjiayuan. It sees very few foreigners and no one will speak English, but armed with a calculator, stallholders will get their point across. As well as memorabilia from the Cultural Revolution, look out for the stalls that sell original photos, ranging from early-20th century snaps to people posing with their first TVs in the 1970s. ⊠ *Guanganmennei Dajie, Xuanwu District* 🕿 *136/9141–6647.*

☺ **Hongqiao Market** *(Pearl Market)* 红桥市场. Hongqiao is full of tourist
★ goods, knockoff handbags, and cheap watches, but it's best known for its three stories of pearls, hence its nickname. Freshwater, seawater, black, pink, white: the quantity is overwhelming and quality varies by stall. Prices range wildly, though the cheapest items are often fakes. Fanghua Pearls (No. 4318), on the fourth floor, displays quality necklaces and earrings, with photos of Hillary Clinton and Margaret Thatcher shopping there to prove it. Fanghua has a second store devoted to fine jade and precious stones. Stallholders here can be

PACK AN EXTRA BOOK

In general, China has a limited selection of English-language books and magazines, thanks to strict censorship. Upmarket hotels will sell a small selection of international newspapers and magazines, but they rarely stock novels.

Crowded souvenir stalls on the Dashilan Shopping Street

pushy, but accept their haggling in the gamelike spirit it's intended. Or wear headphones to drown them out. ⊠ *Tiantan Lu, between Chongemenwai Lu and Tiyuguan Dajie, east of the northern entrance to Temple of Heaven,Chongwen District* ☎ 010/6711–7630 Ⓜ *Tiantan Dongmen.*

SILK AND FABRICS

Beijing Silk Shop 北京谦祥益丝绸商店. Since 1830 the Beijing Silk Shop has been supplying the city with quality bolts of silks and fabrics. There are tailors on-site to whip up something special and the second floor has ready-to-wear clothing. To reach the shop, walk all the way down Dashilan then head directly onto Dashilan West Street. ■**TIP**➔ Two larger stores on Dashilan specialize in silk. Ruifuxiang, at No. 5, is housed in a beautiful two-story building, as is Century Silk Store at No. 33. ⊠ *50 Dashilan Xi Jie, Xuanwu District* ☎ 010/6301–6658 Ⓜ *Qianmen.*

CHAOYANG DISTRICT 朝阳区

The vast Chaoyang District is *the* area to shop in Beijing, with giant markets, well-stocked malls, and endless boutiques. Highlights include Panjiayuan Antique Market, Silk Alley, and Sanlitun Village.

BOOKS

★ **The Bookworm**书虫. Book lovers, hipsters, and aspiring poets take note: this lending library and bookstore offers a spacious second-story reading room with a full café and bar. All are welcome to browse: the magazine and new-books section are a stupendous sight for English-starved travelers. The store frequently hosts poetry readings and lectures. ⊠ *4 Sanlitun Nan lu, set back slightly in an alley 50 m south of the*

EXPLORING TEA STREET

Tea Street 马连道茶叶批发市场.
Maliandao hosts the ultimate tea
party every day of the week. Literally
a thousand tea shops perfume the
air of this prime tea-shopping district, west of the city center. Midway
down this near-mile-long strip looms
the **Teajoy Market,** the Silk Alley
of teas. Unless you're an absolute
fanatic, it's best to visit a handful of
individual shops, crashing tea parties
wherever you go. Vendors will invite
you to sit down in heavy wooden
chairs to nibble on pumpkin seeds
and sample their large selections of
black, white, oolong, jasmine, and
chrysanthemum teas. Prices range
from a few kuai for a decorative
container of loose green tea to
thousands of yuan for an elaborate
gift set. Tea Street is also the place
to stock up on clay and porcelain
teapots and service sets. Green and
flower teas are sold loose; black
teas are sold pressed into disks and
wrapped in natural-colored paper.
Despite the huge selection of drinking vessels available, you'll find that
most locals prefer to drink their tea
from a recycled glass jar. ⊠ *Located near Guanganmen Wai Dajie,
Xuanwu District* Ⓜ *Xuanwumen.*

Gongti Beilu junction Chaoyang District ☎ *010/6586–9507* ⊕ *www.
beijingbookworm.com* Ⓜ *Tuanjiehu.*

COMPUTERS AND ELECTRONICS

Bainaohui Computer Shopping Mall 百脑会电脑广场. Next door to the
Wonderful Electronic Shopping Mall is Bainao, which means "one
hundred computers." (The Chinese word for computer translates literally as "electric brain.") Home to hundreds of laptops and PCs, this
retail mall is crammed with vendors selling real and knockoff supplies and accessories. ⊠ *10 Chaoyangmenwai Dajie, Chaoyang District*
☎ *010/6599–5912* Ⓜ *Hujialou.*

Tom Shop. Just around the corner from Spin is the best DVD shop in
Beijing (though it's occasionally closed because of police raids). Tom's
offers a bewildering array of the latest films and box sets from Hol-
lywood and beyond. DVDs cost Y10 each, except for DVD 9's (check
the spine). Box sets cost from Y60 to Y500. Phone ahead to make sure
they're open. ⊠ *Hairun International Apartments (Fangyuan Xilu and
Jiangtai Lu intersection, Chaoyang District* ☎ *010/5135–7487.*

Wonderful Electronic Shopping Mall 蓝岛大厦. Cameras, tripods, flash
disks, phones and MP3 players (called MP-San in Chinese) abound. If
you forgot the USB cable for your digital recorder or need extra camera batteries, this is the place. Bargain hard and you'll be rewarded.
⊠ *12 Chaoyangmenwai Dajie, Chaoyang District* ☎ *010/8561–4335*
Ⓜ *Hujialou.*

HOUSEWARES

Spin 旋. This trendy ceramics shop near the 798 Art District features the
work of several talented Shanghainese designers who take traditional
plates, vases, and vessels and give them a unique and delightful twist.
Prices are surprisingly inexpensive. ⊠ *6 Fangyuan Xilu, Chaoyang District* ☎ *010/6437–8649.*

You Can Judge a Pearl by Its Luster

All the baubles of Beijing could be strung together and wrapped around the earth 10 times over—or so it seems with Beijing's abundance of pearl vendors. It's mind-boggling to imagine how many oysters it would take to produce all those natural pearls. But, of course, not all are real: some are cultured and others fake.

The attentive clerks in most shops are eager to prove their product quality. Be wary of salespeople who don't demonstrate, with an eager and detailed pitch, why one strand is superior to another. Keep in mind the following tips as you judge whether that gorgeous strand is destined to be mere costume jewelry or the next family heirloom.

■ **Color:** Natural pearls have an even hue, whereas dyed pearls vary in coloration.

■ **Good Luster:** Pick only the shiniest apples in the bunch. Pearls should have a healthy glow.

■ **Shape:** The strand should be able to roll smoothly across a flat surface without wobbling.

■ **Blemishes:** We hate them on our faces and we hate them on our pearls.

■ **Size:** Smaller pearls are obviously less expensive than larger ones, but don't get trapped into paying more for larger poor-quality pearls just because they're heftier.

The cost of pearls varies widely. A quality strand will generally run around US$50 to $200, but it's possible to buy good-looking but lower-quality pearls much more cheaply. As with any purchase, choose those pearls you adore most, and only pay as much as you think they warrant. After all, we could all use an extra strand of good-looking fakes. Also, if you plan on making multiple purchases and you have time to return to the same shop, go ahead and establish a "friendship" with one key clerk. Each time you return, or bring a friend, the price will miraculously drop.

FASHION DESIGNERS AND BOUTIQUES

Candy & Caviar. Chinese-American fashion designer Candy Lin owns and operates this gem; in just two years her label has attracted a celebrity following, including Will.i.am from the Black Eyed Peas and Taiwanese superstar Jay Chou. From her peaceful and professional store, she designs for both men and women. Expect lots of sharp tailoring, stark colors, and relatively high prices. ⊠ *921, Bldg 16, China Central Place, 89 Jianguo Lu, Chaoyang District* ☎ *010/5203–6581* ⊕ *www. candyandcaviar.com.*

Fei Space 飞. In the 798 Art District, Fei Space more than holds its own against its neighboring galleries with its funky interior design and eclectic selection of clothes, furniture, and housewares. Some of the clothing brands stocked are unique to the store, and all are uniformly stylish—and expensive. ⊠ *B-01, 798 Art District, 4 Jiuxiangqiao Lu, Chaoyang District* ☎ *010/5978–9580*

Heyan'er 何燕服装店. He Yan's design philosophy is stated in her label: BU YAN BU YU, or "NO TALKING." Her linen and cotton tunics and collarless

DID YOU KNOW?

In a country increasingly filled with cars, shopping malls and pedestrian-only streets are becoming all the rage—and for good reason. Not only is the air and noise pollution less oppressive when there are no cars around, but dodging taxis tends to detract from one's shopping enjoyment.

jackets speak for themselves. From earth tones to aubergine hues and peacock patterns, He Yan's designs echo traditional Tibetan styles. ✉ *15–2 Gongti Beilu* ☏ *010/6415–9442* Ⓜ *Dongsishitiao* ✉ *Holiday Inn Lido, 6 Fangyuan Xilu* ☏ *010/6437–6854.*

The Red Phoenix 红凤凰服装工作室. In this cramped-but-charming Sanlitun showroom, fashion diva Gu Lin designs embroidered satin qipaos, cropped jackets, and men's clothing for stylish foreigners and China's *xin xin ren lei* (literally the "new, new human being," referring to the country's latest flock of successful young professionals). ✉ *30 Sanlitun Bei Jie, Chaoyang District* ☏ *010/6416–4423* Ⓜ *Nongzhanguan.*

Tailor Ma 裁缝妈. Beijing is a great place to indulge in tailor-made clothes, but buyer beware: it's best to give the tailor something to copy, and you should allow plenty of time for fittings. Tailor Ma gets high praise and though he may be more expensive than his neighbors, the quality is much higher. A suit will cost around Y1500. ✉ *3/F, Yaxiu Market, 58 Gongti Beilu, Chaoyang District* ☏ *139/1009–5718* Ⓜ *Tuanjiehu.*

JEWELRY

Shard Box Store 慎 德阁. The signature collection here includes small to midsize jewelry boxes fashioned from the broken shards of antique porcelain. Supposedly the shards were collected during the Cultural Revolution, when scores of antique porcelain pieces were smashed in accordance with the law. Birds, trees, pining lovers, and dragons decorate these affordable ceramic-and-metal containers, which range from Y20 to Y200. ✉ *1 Ritan Beilu,Chaoyang District* ☏ *010/8561–3712* ✉ *2 Jiangtai Lu,near the Holiday Inn Lido* ☏ *010/5135–7638.*

Treasure House 宝月斋. In the Sanlitun embassy district, Treasure House has a modest but slick collection, including silver cuff links and charms inscribed with the Chinese symbols for happiness and longevity. ✉ *1 Sanlitun Beixiaojie* ☏ *010/8451–6096 or 139/1055–5372* Ⓜ *Nongzhanguan.*

MALLS AND DEPARTMENT STORES

Nali Patio 那里花园. You can't miss this bright white Spanish hacienda style minimall—perfect for shoppers who want a selection of stores without the mania of a market or huge megamall. On these four floors you'll find chain stores like Pantry Magic and American Apparel, as well as boutiques like Yiwen Studio, which is run by an up-and-coming local designer. The excellent shoe store Long.com has a good selection of shoes for larger, foreign feet. ■ TIP→ If the mood strikes, head to Apothecary on the 3rd floor for a reviving and beautifully made cocktail. ✉ *81 Sanlitun Beilu, Chaoyang District* ☏ *010/6413–1002* Ⓜ *Tuanjiehu.*

The Place 世贸天阶. With the recent glut of new malls in Beijing, this is probably your most midmarket option; you can't miss it thanks to the huge central LED sky screen (something of a tourist attraction in itself). Here you'll find a large Zara, a collection of inexpensive and decent restaurants, and in the basement there's a good English language bookstore called Chaterhouse. ✉ *Dongdaqiao Lu, 50 m north of Guanghua Lu junction, Chaoyang District* ☏ *010/6587–1188* Ⓜ *Jintaixizhao* ⊕ *www.theplace.cn.*

Sanlitun Village 三里屯 Village. This fashionable complex, split into two zones, is the place to shop thanks to its great range of stores at all price points, cool architecture, and fun people-watching. Village South houses the biggest Adidas store in the world, as well as boutiques for Uniqlo, Reiss, and Steve Madden. The newer and more exclusive Village North has high-end designer stores such as Balenciaga and Emporio Armani. There's also a good cinema and great restaurants. ⊠ *19 Sanlitun Jie, Chaoyang District* ☎ *010/6417–6110* ⊕ *www.sanlitunvillage. com* Ⓜ *Tuanjiehu.*

Shin Kong Place 新光天地. Just east of the CBD, this sophisticated mall is a quiet, refined refuge—probably because the goods are too expensive for the masses—with brands like Bottega Veneta and Gucci. They also carry some midrange names like Club Monaco and Agnes B. If you get peckish, there's an excellent dumpling eatery called Din Tai Fung. ⊠ *87 Jianguo Lu, Chaoyang District* ☎ *010/6530–5888* Ⓜ *Dawang Lu* ⊕ *www.shinkong-place.com.*

MARKETS

Beijing Curio City 北京古玩城. This complex has four stories of kitsch and curio shops and a few furniture vendors, some of whom may be selling authentic antiques. Prices are high (driven up by free-spending tour groups), so don't be afraid to lowball your offer. Ignore the overpriced Duty Free shop at the entrance. ⊠ *Dongsanhuan Nan lu, Exit Third Ring Rd. at Panjiayuan Bridge, Chaoyang District* ☎ *010/6774–7711* Ⓜ *Jinsong.*

Fodor's Choice
★

Panjiayuan Antiques Market 潘家园市场. Every day the sun rises over thousands of pilgrims rummaging in search of antiques and the most curious of curios, though the biggest numbers of buyers and sellers is at the weekends. With over 3,000 vendors crowding an area of 48,500 square meters, not every jade bracelet, oracle bone, porcelain vase, and ancient screen is authentic, but most people are here for the reproductions anyway. Behold the bounty: watercolors, scrolls, calligraphy, Buddhist statues, opera costumes, old Russian SLR cameras, curio cabinets, Tibetan jewelry, tiny satin lotus-flower shoes, rotary telephones, jade dragons, antique mirrors, infinite displays of "Maomorabilia." If you're buying jade, first observe the Chinese customers, how they hold a flashlight to the milky-green stone to test its authenticity. As with all Chinese markets, bargain with a vengeance, as many vendors inflate their prices astronomically for *waiguoren* ("outside country people"). A strip of enclosed stores forms a perimeter around the surprisingly orderly rows of open-air stalls. The friendly owner of the eponymous **Li Shu Lan** decorates her shop (No. 24-D) with antiques from her *laojia*, or countryside hometown. Stop by the **Bei Zhong Bao Pearl Shop** (No. 7-A) for medium-quality freshwater pearls cultivated by the Hu family. Also here are a sculpture zoo, a book

EARLY-BIRD CATCHES

A common superstition in Chinese markets is that if you don't make a sale with your very first customer of the day, the rest of the day will go badly. So set out early, and if you know you're the first customer of the day, bargain relentlessly.

Inspecting the goods at the Panjiayuan Antiques Market

bazaar, reproduction-furniture shops, and a two-story market stashing propaganda posters and Communist literature. Show the taxi driver the Chinese characters for Panjiayuan Shichang. ⊠ *Third Ring Rd. at Panjiayuan Bridge, Chaoyang District* Ⓜ *Jinsong.*

Ritan Office Building Market 日坛商务楼. Don't let the gray-brick and red-trim exterior fool you: the offices inside the Ritan Building are strung with racks of brand-name dresses and funky-fab accessories. Unlike the tacky variations made on knockoff labels and sold in less expensive markets, the collections here, for the most part, retain their integrity—perhaps because many of these dresses are actually designer labels. They're also more expensive, and bargaining is discouraged. The **Ruby Cashmere Shop** (No. 1009) sells genuine cashmere sweaters and scarves at reduced prices. Upstairs, the burning incense and bright red walls of **You Gi** (No. 2006) provide a welcome atmosphere for perusing an overpriced but eccentric collection of Nepalese and Indian clothing and jewelry. ⊠ *15A Guanghua Lu, just east of the south entrance to Ritan Park, opposite the Vietnam Embassy, Chaoyang District* ☎ *010/6502–1528* Ⓜ *Yonganli.*

Fodor's Choice
★ **Silk Alley Market** 秀水市场. Once a delightfully chaotic sprawl of hundreds of outdoor stalls, the Silk Alley Market is now corralled inside a huge shopping center. The government has been cracking down on an increasing number of certain copycat items, so if you don't see that knockoff Louis Vuitton purse or Chanel jacket, just ask; it might magically appear from a stack of plastic storage bins. You will face no dearth, however, of knockoff Pumas and Nikes or Paul Smith polos. Chinese handicrafts and children's clothes are on the top floors. Bargain relentlessly,

check carefully the quality of each intended purchase, and guard your wallet against pickpockets. ⊠ *8 Xiushui Dong Jie, Chaoyang District* ☎ *010/5169–9003* ⊕ *www. xiushui.com.cn* Ⓜ *Yonganli.*

★ **Yaxiu Market** *(Yashow Market)* 雅秀市场. Especially popular among younger Western shoppers, Yaxiu is yet another indoor arena stuffed to the gills with low-quality knockoff clothing and shoes. Prices are slightly cheaper than Silk Alley, but the haggling no less cruel. Don't be alarmed if you see someone sniffing sneakers or suede jackets: they're simply testing if the leather is real. The giant sign outside this bustling clothes market near Sanlitun reads "Yashow," but it's written "YAXIU" in pinyin. ■ **TIP**→ The beauty salons on the 4th floor offer inexpensive manicures and foot rubs if you need a break. ⊠ *58 Gongti Beilu,Chaoyang District* ☎ *010/6416–8699* Ⓜ *Tuanjiehu.*

Zhaojia Chaowai Market. Beijing's best-known venue for affordable antiques and reproduction furniture houses scores of independent vendors who sell everything from authentic Qing Dynasty–era chests to traditional baskets, ceramics, carpets, and curios. Be sure to bargain; vendors routinely sell items for less than half their starting price. ⊠ *43 Huawei Bei Li, Chaoyang District* ☎ *010/6770–6402* Ⓜ *Jinsong.*

SHOES

Long.com 龙店. Stop here to refresh your footwear before a night out in Sanlitun with Reef, Puma, Steve Madden, and Nine West sold at discount prices. ⊠ *81 Sanlitun Beilu, Chaoyang District* ☎ *010/8643–2880* Ⓜ *Tuanjiehu.*

HAIDIAN DISTRICT 海淀区

Travelers usually frequent the northwestern quadrant of Beijing to visit the Summer Palace or the Beijing Zoo, though because Haidian has several universities, cheap and cheerful boutiques aimed at students are commonplace. For something more refined, collectors of antiques can spend hours perusing the quiet halls of **Ai Jia Gu Dong Market** 爱家红木大楼 (⊠ *Chengshousi Lu, Beisanhuan Xilu, Haidian District* ☎ *010/6765–7187* Ⓜ *Zhichunlu*), a large antiques and jade market, hidden just under the South Fourth Ring Road beside the Big Bell Museum. It's open daily, but shops close early on weekdays.

ENGLISH NAME	PINYIN	CHINESE
Ai Jia Gu Dong Market	Àijiā hóngmù dàgúanlóu	爱家红木大楼
Bainaohui Computer Shopping Mall	Bǎinǎohuìdiànnǎo guǎngchǎng	百脑会电脑广场
Bannerman Tang's	Běijīng chéng táng xuān chuántǒng mínjiān wánjùkāifā zhōngxīn	北京盛唐轩传统民间玩具开发中心
Baoguosi Antiques Market	Bàoguósì shōucángpǐn shìchǎng	报国寺收藏品市场
Beijing Curio City	Běijīng gǔwán chéng	北京古玩城
Beijing Silk Shop	Běijīng qiānxiángyì sīchóu shāngdiàn	北京谦祥益丝绸商店
Candy & Caviar	Candy & Caviar	n/a
Daxin Textiles Co.	Dàxīn fǎngzhī	大新纺织
Long.com	Lóng diàn	龙店
Fang Si	Fàng sì	放肆
Fei Space	Fēi	飞
Grifted	Grifted	n/a
Heyan'er	Héyán fúzhuāng diàn	何燕服装店
Hongqiao Market	Hóngqiáo shìchǎng	红桥市场
Lost & Found	Shīwù zhāolǐng	失物招领
Malls at Oriental Plaza	Dōngfāng guǎngchǎng	东方广场购物中心
Nali Patio	Nàli huāyuán	那里花园
Panjiayuan Antique Market	Pānjiāyuán shìchǎng	潘家园市场
Pi'erman Maoyi	Pí'ěrmàn màoyì gōngsī	皮尔曼贸易公司
Plastered T-Shirts	n/a	n/a
Ritan Office Building Market	Rìtán shāngwù lóu	日坛商务楼
Sanlitun	Sānlìtùn	三里屯
Sanlitun Village	Sānlìtùn Village	三里屯 Village
Shard Box Store	Shèndégé	慎 德阁
Sattva	Sattva	n/a
Seasons Place	Jīnróngjiē gòuwùzhōngxīn	金融街购物中心
Shin Kong Place	Xīn guāng tiān dì	新光天地
Silk Alley Market	Xiùshuǐ shìchǎng	秀水市场
Spin	Xuán	旋
Tailor Ma	Cáiféng Mǎ	裁缝妈
Tea Street	Mǎliándǎo cháyè chéng	马连道茶叶批发市场

ENGLISH NAME	PINYIN	CHINESE
The Bookworm	Shūchóng	书虫
The Place	Shìmào tiān jiē	世贸天阶
The Red Phoenix	Hóngfènghuáng fúzhuāng	红凤凰服装工作室
Three Stones Kite Store	Sān dàn zhāifēng zhēngdiàn	三石斋风筝店
Tom Shop	Tom Shop	Tom Shop
Tongrentang	Tóngréntáng	同仁堂
Treasure House	Baǒyuèzāi	宝月斋
Wonderful Electronic Shopping Mall	Lándaǒ dàshà	蓝岛大厦
Woo	Wǔ	妩
Yaxiu Market	Yǎxiù shìchǎng	雅秀市场
Zhaojia Chaowai Antique Market	Zhaòjiā Cháowài gǔdiǎnjiājù shìchǎng	n/a

Arts and Nightlife

WORD OF MOUTH

"The Laoshe teahouse was fun with elaborate teas—my tea looked like a flower unfolding in my glass. And they had a band playing live music on unusual old instruments."

—Magster2005

Updated by
Helena Iveson

No longer Shanghai's staid sister, Beijing is reinventing herself as a party town with just a smattering of the pretensions of her southern sibling. There's now a venue for every breed of boozer, from beer-stained pub to designer cocktail lounge and everything in between. There are also more dance clubs than you can count. An emerging middle class means that you'll find most bars have a mixed crowd and aren't just swamps of expatriates, but there will be spots where one or the other set will dominate.

Bars aside, Beijing has an active, if not international-standard, stage scene. There's not much to see in English, although the opening of the Egg, properly known as the National Center for the Performing Arts, has changed that somewhat. Music and dance transcend language boundaries, and Beijing attracts some fine international composers and ballet troupes for the crowds. For a fun night on the town that you can enjoy no other place in the world, Beijing opera, acrobatics, and kung fu performances remain the best bets.

PLANNING

CITY LISTINGS

The best way to find out what's on or where to party is to pick up one of the free listing magazines found at many bars and restaurants. The best ones are the monthly *The Beijinger, Time Out Beijing*, and *Beijing Talk*, as well as the biweekly *City Weekend*. *The Beijinger* has the most extensive listings, and *City Weekend* and *Beijing Talk* have maps of central Beijing with restaurants and bars. All give bilingual addresses in their listings.

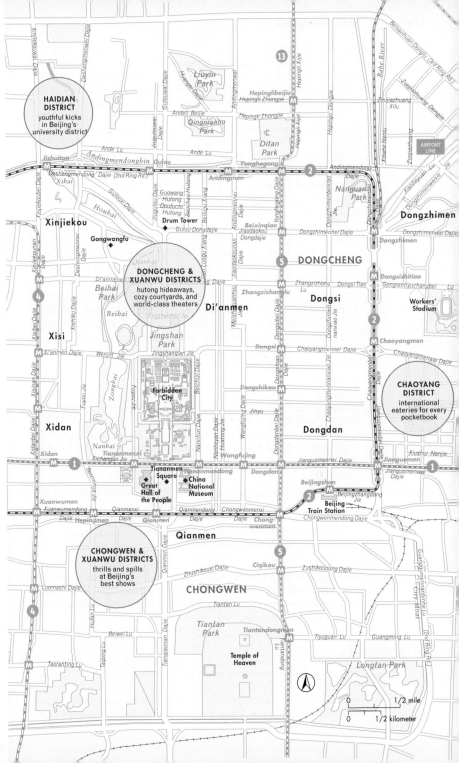

WHAT TO WEAR

The only dress code for Beijing is that there is no dress code. The city's nightlife is such a melting pot that you can find flip-flop-wearing customers in snug jeans sipping extra dirty Grey Goose martinis in the classiest cocktail lounges, and girls done up in their finest finery in piña colada-and-peanut joints. That said, as a general rule people underdress rather than overdress. Remember that Beijing is seriously chilly in the winter (December to March), and you'll need to bundle up. Oh, and many a nice pair of heels has been ruined by the dusty streets and uneven sidewalks around Sanlitun.

GETTING AROUND SAFELY

Most of the bars and clubs are clumped together in districts, so you can amble from pub to wine bar to cocktail lounge on foot. Your best bet is to rely on taxis to get back to your hotel—make sure you pick up a business card from your hotel to show the driver. Nearly all the taxis you see on the roads are licensed. Unless it's raining cats and dogs, you should have no problem hailing a cab, even in the early hours of the morning. After 10:30 PM there's no public transport, so you will have to hail a taxi. Remember that prices rise by 20 percent after 11 PM.

Compared to other international cities, Beijing is generally safe after dark; alcohol-fueled street brawls are rare. The small amount of trouble that occurs mainly involves heavy-handed security guards getting tough with obnoxious expat youths. Stick to well-lit areas, keep your wits about you, and you will be fine.

LAST CALL

While there are pockets of late-night partying, Beijing is no New York when it comes to 24-hour carousing. The more inexpensive bars in the popular Sanlitun district will generally close only when the last punter stumbles out, while hotel bars will have set hours—closing time is usually about 1 AM. The best bets for hard-core night owls are DJ bars like Punk in The Opposite House, or D.Lounge.

SMOKING

Unfortunately, smoking inside bars and clubs is still de rigueur in Beijing. There are a handful of nonsmoking bars such as 12sqm in Nanluoguxiang and on the same street, Passby Bar, which has a nonsmoking section, but partygoers should be prepared to swallow a good dose of nicotine along with their drinks.

COVERS

Happily, next to no bars have a cover charge, except for bars with live music like East Shore Jazz Club and Yugong Yishan and gay-friendly bars like Destination. Even then, the charge will be minimal and often include at least one drink.

THE ARTS

The arts in China took a long time to recover from the Cultural Revolution (1966–76), and political works are still generally avoided. Film and theater reflect an interesting mix of modern and avant-garde Chinese and Western influences. On any given night in Beijing, you can see a drama by the revered playwright Lao She, a satire by a contemporary Taiwanese playwright, or a stage version of *Animal Farm*.

As most of the stage is inaccessible to non-Chinese speakers, visitors to Beijing are more likely to hunt out the big visual spectacles, such as Beijing opera or kung fu displays. These long-running shows are tailored for travelers: your hotel will be able to recommend performances and venues and will likely be able to help you book tickets.

ACROBATICS AND KUNG FU

Chaoyang Theater 朝阳剧场. This space is the queen bee of acrobatics venues, especially designed to unleash oohs and ahhs. Spectacular individual and team acrobatic displays involving bicycles, seesaws, catapults, swings, and barrels are performed here nightly. It's touristy but fun. ⊠ *36 Dongsanhuan Beilu, Chaoyang District* ☎ *010/6507–2421* Ⓜ *Hujialou.*

Fodor's Choice ★ **The Red Theatre** 红剧场. If it's Vegas-style stage antics you're after, the *Legend of Kung Fu* show is what you want. Extravagant martial arts—performed by dancers, not martial artists—are complemented by neon, fog, and heavy-handed sound effects. Shows are garish but also sometimes glorious. ⊠ *44 Xingfu Dajie, Chongwen District* ☎ *010/6710–3671* ⊕ *www.redtheatre.cn* Ⓜ *Tiantan Dong Men.*

Tianqiao Acrobatic Theater 天桥乐茶馆. The Beijing Acrobatics Troupe of China is famous for weird, wonderful shows. Content includes a flashy show of offbeat contortions and tricks, with a lot of high-wire action. Shows are at 7:15 PM every night. ⊠ *30 Beiwei Lu, Xuanwu District* ☎ *010/8315–6300.*

ART GALLERIES

Artist Village Gallery. If you'd like a real change of pace from the city art scene, hire a driver or join a tour to visit the Artist Village in the eastern suburbs of Beijing. More than 500 artists live and work in studio spaces, peasant homes, and old buildings in and around the central village of Songzhuang. Though a trip out to the Artist Village can take a chunk out of your day, it's worth it. The countryside is a stark contrast to the city, and the art is of excellent quality. The gallery itself displays local works in a modern, well-appointed building. Visits are by appointment only, so talk with your hotel concierge before booking a car, or book online. ⊠ *1 Chunbei, Ren Zhuang, Tongxian Songzhuang* ☎ *139/0124–4283 or 010/6959–8343* ⊕ *www.artistvillagegallery.com.*

The CourtYard Gallery Lounge. Although the space here is minuscule—it's in the basement of the CourtYard Restaurant—this gallery still manages to attract some of the most sought-after names in contemporary Chinese art, such as Wang Qingsong, Zhang Dali, and the Gao Brothers. Plus you can have a well-made drink as you peruse the work. ⊠ *95 Donghuamen Dajie, Dongcheng District* ☎ *010/6526–8882* ⊕ *www.courtyard-gallery.com* Ⓜ *Tiananmen East.*

Long March Studio. The Long March Project organizes teams of artists, curators, and scholars to travel to various regions in China, where they create projects with the local community. While you are in the neighborhood, do be sure to explore this area, Beijing's art district, with its warren of galleries, shops, and cafes. ⊠ *4 Jiuxianqiao Rd., Dashanzi, Chaoyang District* ☎ *010/6438–7107* ⊕ *www.longmarchspace.com.*

Red Gate Gallery. This gallery, one of the first to open in Beijing, displays and sells contemporary Chinese paintings and sculpture in the extraordinary space of the old Dongbianmen Watchtower, a centuries-old landmark. The venue is worth a visit even if you're not interested in the art. Be aware that the subway stop listed here is about a 25-minute walk from the gallery. ⊠ *Dongbianmen Watchtower, Chongwenmen Dongjie, Chongwen District* ☎ *010/6525–1005* ⊕ *www.redgategallery. com* Ⓜ *Jianguomen.*

BEIJING OPERA

★ **Chang'an Grand Theater** *(Chang'an Da Xiyuan)* 长安大戏院. At this contemporary theater, as at a cabaret, you sit at tables and can eat and drink while watching lively, colorful performances of Beijing opera. There's also a small museum where you can see costumes and masks from the past. ■ TIP→ A great perk. English subtitles appear above the stage. ⊠ *7 Jianguomennei Dajie, Dongcheng District* ☎ *010/6510–1309.*

Huguang Guildhall *(Huguang Huiguan)* 湖广会馆. The city's oldest Beijing opera theater, the Guildhall, has staged performances since 1807. The hall has been restored to display its original architecture and appearance, and it's one of the most atmospheric places to take in an opera. Even if you don't want to see a whole performance, the museum and gift shop are worth a browse. ⊠ *3 Hufangqiao, Xuanwu District* ☎ *010/6351–8284* ⊕ *www.beijinghuguang.com.*

Lao She Teahouse *(Lao She Chaguan)* 老舍茶馆. This wooden teahouse is named after Lao She, a playwright and novelist who was terribly mistreated during the Cultural Revolution and, according to official records, killed himself in 1966. Now officially rehabilitated, his works are staged here every night. You can order a wide range of traditional snacks to munch on during the performance. ⊠ *3 Qianmenxi Dajie, 3rd floor, Xuanwu District* ☎ *010/6303–6830* ⊕ *www.laosheteahouse.com.*

Fodor's Choice **Liyuan Theater** *(Liyuan Juchang)* 梨园剧场. Though it's unashamedly
★ touristy, it's our top pick. You can watch performers put on makeup before the show (come early) and then graze on snacks and sip tea while watching English-subtitled shows. Glossy brochures complement the crooning. ⊠ *Qianmen Hotel, 175 Yongan Lu, Xuanwu District* ☎ *010/6301–6688 Ext. 8860* ⊕ *www.qianmenhotel.com.*

Tianqiao Happy Teahouse *(Tianqiao Le Chaguan)* 天桥乐茶馆. The spirit of old Beijing lingers in this traditional theater that hosts Beijing operas as well as acrobatics, jugglers, illusionists, and contortionists. ⊠ *113 Tianqiao Shichang, Xuanwu District* ☎ *010/6303–9013.*

MUSIC

Beijing Concert Hall. Beijing's main venue for Chinese and Western classical-music concerts also hosts folk dancing and singing, and many celebratory events throughout the year. The 1,000-seat venue is the

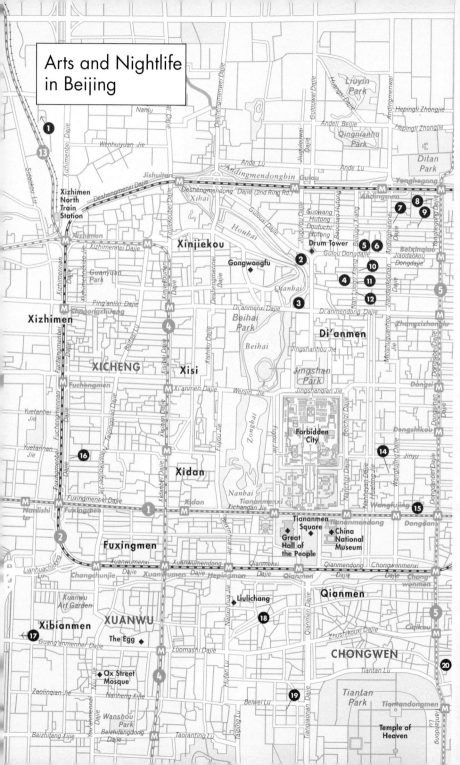

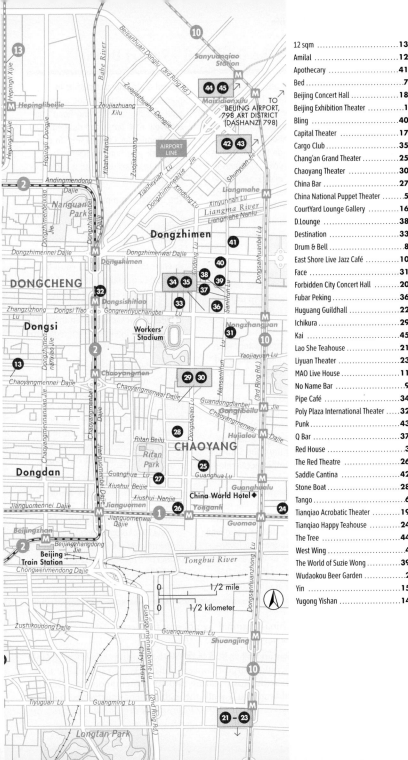

Fringe Art: The Dashanzi 798 Art District

If you are keen to see what the city's art scene has to offer beyond calligraphy, check out the **Dashanzi 798 Art District**. Just as the city is coming of age in the international, political, and economic arenas, so too are Chinese artists. Exploration of social taboos, the use of digital media, and clever installations are juxtaposed against more orthodox forms of canvas paintings and photography. Some efforts may seem like trite knockoffs of American pop art, and Mao references run rampant, but keep in mind this level of expression is still evolving for the public arena. Complete freedom of expression is not tolerated and governmental closings, though rare, are not unheard of.

Built in the 1950s, the factory was a major industrial project designed by East German architects backed by Soviet aid. The factory's decline started in the 1980s, just as Beijing's contemporary art scene began to emerge. The massive relocation of pollutant factories outside the city in preparation for the 2008 Summer Olympic Games further accelerated the decline of the area's manufacturing roots and allowed for the incubation of modern art. The recent government declaration of Dashanzi as a protected arts district has paved the way for a resurgence of inventive local galleries, as well as design studios, restaurants, cafés, and bars. Many of the original artists have moved on to cheaper studios in places such as Caochangdi, a small area outside the Fifth Ring Road that the New York Times had dubbed "a new frontier for Chinese art." To get here, ask your hotel concierge to explain to a taxi driver, as it can be difficult to find.

The Dashanzi compound is more accessible, however, and is immensely walkable; keep in mind this is solely a pedestrian affair unless you arrive by private car. Cabs are not allowed to enter the compound so you'll be required to disembark at any of the entrance gates. Though it's open on weekdays (except Monday), most people visit on weekends, when throngs of locals and foreigners congregate to see what's on display.

To get a feel for what sells abroad, drop by internationally owned galleries such as 798 Photo Gallery or the Ullens Center for Contemporary Art. These established galleries are perennially popular. Also, check out Time-Zone 8 Book Shop, an avant-garde bookshop in the heart of Dashanzi.

UCCA (☎ 010/ 6438–6675 ⊕ www.ucca.org.cn). **Time-Zone 8 Book Shop** (☎ 010/6456–0336). **798 Photo Gallery** (☎ 010/6438–1784 ⊕ www.798photogallery.cn). ⊠ 4 Jiuxianqiao Rd., Dashanzi,Chaoyang District ☎ 010/6438–4862 or 010/6437–6248 ⊕ www.798space.com.

home of the China National Symphony Orchestra. ⊠ 1 Bei Xinhua Jie,Xicheng District ☎ 010/6605–7006.

Fodor's Choice ★ **Forbidden City Concert Hall** 北京音乐厅. With a seating capacity of 1,400, this is one of Beijing's largest concert halls. It is also one of the most well-appointed, with plush seating and top-notch acoustics. Despite the modern building, you'll walk through ancient courtyards to get to the hall—highly romantic. ⊠ In Zhongshan Park, Xichangan Jie, on *the west side of Tiananmen Square, Xicheng District* ☎ *010/6559–8285* Ⓜ *Tiananmen West.*

MAO Live House. This is the place to come for a glimpse into Beijing's cutting-edge music scene. The seedy little space is managed by a Japanese music label that prides itself on seeking out interesting new bands. The sound system is excellent and so are the prices of drinks. ✉ *111 Gulou Dongdajie, Dongcheng District* ☎ *010/6402–5080* ⊕ *www.maolive.com* Ⓜ *Beixin Qiao.*

Poly Plaza International Theater 保利剧院. This is a modern shopping-center-like complex on top of Dongsi Shitiao subway station. One of Beijing's better-known theaters, the Poly hosts Chinese and international concerts, ballets, and musicals. ■ **TIP→** If you're seeking a performance in English, this is your best bet. ✉ *1/F Poly Plaza, 14 Dongzhimen Nandajie, Dongcheng District* ☎ *010/6408–2666* Ⓜ *Dongsi Shitiao.*

THEATER

Beijing Exhibition Theater 北京展览馆剧场. Chinese plays, Western and Chinese operas, and ballet performances are staged in this Soviet-style building that's part of the exhibition center complex. Talk about a wide range of shows: in 2010 the Michael Jackson musical *Thriller* was staged, followed closely by some traditional folk art performances. ✉ *135 Xizhimenwai Dajie, Xicheng District* ☎ *010/6835–4455.*

Capital Theater 首都剧场. This is a busy, modern theater near the Wangfujing shopping street. It often has performances by the respected Beijing People's Art Theatre and various international acts such as British troupe TNT. ✉ *22 Wangfujing Dajie, Dongcheng District* ☎ *010/6525–0996* ⊕ *www.bjry.com* Ⓜ *Wangfujing.*

☺ **China National Puppet Theater** 中国国家木偶剧院. Shadow and hand-puppet shows convey traditional stories—it's lively entertainment for children and adults alike. This venue also attracts overseas performers, including the Moscow Puppet Theater. ✉ *1 Anhuaxili, Chaoyang District* ☎ *010/6425–4847.*

Fodor's Choice ★ **National Centre for Performing Arts** 国家大剧院. Architecturally, the giant silver dome of this performing arts complex is stunning, and its interior holds a state-of-the-art opera house, a music hall, and a theater. The "Egg" offers a world-class stage for national and international performers. If you don't wish to see a show, you can tour the inside of the building by paying for an entrance ticket. ✉ *2 Xi Chang'an Jie, Xicheng District* ☎ *010/6655–0000* ⊕ *www.chncpa.org* Ⓜ *Tiananmen West.*

NIGHTLIFE

Beijing has spent the last decade shaking off its grim Communist image and putting the neon into its nightlife. There are a plethora of cocktail lounges, sports pubs, dance spots, beer halls, and strip bars. The city is changing at a fever pitch, which means that many bars and even bar streets are short-lived, as construction companies aggressively bulldoze

The National Centre for Performing Arts

the old to make way for swanky new developments. Many establishments are knocked together, seemingly overnight, and are of dubious quality.

Sanlitun—the heart of Beijing's nightlife—has spread its party presence around Gongti. Sanlitun Jiuba Jie, or "Bar Street," offers mainly crass live-music pubs; it's quite popular with locals. On Gongti West Gate, a stream of pumping dance clubs have attracted some big-name DJs—Tiesto, Felix Da Housecat, and Paul Oakenfold, among others. The city's main gay club, Destination, is also here.

Houhai, once a quiet lakeside neighborhood home to Beijing's *laobaixing* (ordinary folk), has exploded into a bumping bar scene. This is a great place to come for a drink at dusk: park yourself on an outdoor seat and enjoy. There are a few hidden gems here, but most of the bars are bland and expensive, with disappointingly weak drinks. Stick to the bottled beer to get your money's worth. The hutong, or mazelike neighborhoods, around the lake also hide some cute courtyard bars.

OFF THE BEATEN PATH

There are a couple of smaller pockets with notable watering holes, such as Chaoyang West Gate, which has a predominately expat feel; Dashanzi 798, an artsy warehouse area with wine bars; and Wudaokou, a student district in Haidian with cheap drinks aplenty.

BARS

DONGCHENG AND XICHENG DISTRICTS (INCLUDING HOUHAI)

12sqm 平米. While it's no longer Beijing's smallest bar—it's expanded to a princely 45 sq m—the friendly neighborhood vibe remains the same. The Aussie owner will go out of his way to make you feel welcome as you enjoy some prime people-watching on the street outside. ⊠ *1 Fuxiang Hutong, Nanluoguxiang, Dongcheng District* ☎ *010/6402–1554* ⊕ *www.12sqm.com.*

Fodor'sChoice
★ **Amilal** 按一拉尔. If you have the patience to track this cozy courtyard bar down a tiny alley, you'll be rewarded with one of the city's hidden gems. Grab a seat at one of the rough wooden tables, listen to the low-key live music that's often playing, and enjoy the laidback hutong vibe that's so unique to Beijing. ⊠ *48 Shoubi Hutong, off Gulou Dongdajie, Dongcheng District* ☎ *No phone.*

Bed. Bed earned its place as a trendy bar through its clever name, and built-in pickup line, "Do you want to go to Bed with me?" Although this courtyard bar has cute nooks and crannies and a relaxed feel, it's a bit cold in both senses of the word. The beds are all sharp concrete and the shadows are chilly. We'll admit it's worth a one-night stand if you're new to the city. ⊠ *17 Zhangwang Hutong, Xicheng District* ☎ *010/8400–1554* Ⓜ *Gulou.*

★ **Drum & Bell** 鼓钟咖啡馆. This bar has a perfect location—right between the Drum and Bell towers. The terrace is a comfy perch for a summer afternoon drink, where you scan the surrounding hutong rooftops. Don't get too plastered, though, because the staircase down is very steep. On the ground floor there are jumbles of scruffy sofas tossed with Cultural Revolution memorabilia. ⊠ *41 Zhonglouwan Hutong, Dongcheng District* ☎ *010/8403–3600* Ⓜ *Gulou.*

★ **East Shore Live Jazz Café** 东岸咖啡. The closest thing Beijing has to New Orleans is this bar. Expect cigar smoke, velvet drapes, sepia photographs of jazz greats, and plenty of vintage instruments on display. The owner, local jazz legend Liu Yuan, says he wants to use the bar to promote homegrown jazz talents. On top of the live swing and jazz, the bar boasts the best views of Houhai, either through the floor-to-ceiling windows (complete with telescope) in the bar, or from the small, sparsely furnished rooftop. ■ **TIP**➜ There are no guardrails on the roof, so drink and step with extreme care. ⊠ *Qianhai Nanyan Lu, 2nd fl., next to the Post Office, Xicheng District* ☎ *010/8403–2131.*

Fodor'sChoice
★ **No Name Bar** 无名酒吧. The first bar to open in Houhai is still around, even though its neighbors have already been torn down. It's very relaxed: many expats still list No Name as their favorite bar in the city. The service is refreshingly low-key—a nice change from the sycophantic staff at neighboring venues—and it's all tumbledown elegance with rattan and potted plants. Locals refer to it by the owner's name: Bai Feng. Anyone from tourists to old China hands can be found here. ⊠ *3 Qianhai East Bank, Xicheng District* ☎ *010/6401–8541.*

6

CLOSE UP

7 Nights in the City

Beijing's blossoming nightlife means there's something new every night of the week.

MONDAY

The yellow-silk-clad Shaolin monks at **The Red Theatre** mix dance, acrobatics, and martial arts every night at 7:30 PM for full house after full house.

TUESDAY

It's not easy to borrow or buy English-language books in Beijing. **The Bookworm** (⊠ Building 4, Sanlitun Nanlu, Chaoyang District ☎ 010/6586–9507 ⊕ www.beijingbookworm.com), a restaurant/bar/bookshop/library, is one of the city's few places that offers a literary outlet for English-reading folk. The Bookworm usually hosts a speaker at some point during the week, usually Tuesdays—check the Web site. Other nights you can enjoy live piano music, quiz nights, and wine tasting.

WEDNESDAY

If only to check out what all the fuss is about, you should reserve one night for cocktails at **China Bar** on the 65th floor of the Park Hyatt. Nicely soused, you can then hop in a cab to one of the theaters that play host to **Beijing opera**—try the beautifully restored **Liyuan Theater** for some monkey magic with your classical Chinese music.

THURSDAY

This is usually a good night for the ladies. To celebrate the approach of the weekend, several bars offer free drinks for women, and although this is in the hope of attracting guys on the prowl, it still boils down to . . . free drinks for women. The Hilton's **Zeta Bar** offers free drinks and free entry for girls, as well as a "ladies only" area where boys are banned.

FRIDAY

This would be the night to go clubbing. Check out **Cargo** or **Tango** for mainstream house, or **Punk** for something a bit more intimate and cooler. If there is a famous DJ on the tables, there may be a cover charge to get in.

SATURDAY

This is the ideal night for a romantic evening on **Houhai**—the bar-packed lake north of the Forbidden City. If you are into jazz and blues, head to the excellent **East Shore Live Jazz Café**. Come before 9 PM to get a seat and enjoy the music and some of the best views of the lake, which churns with boats in the summer and ice-skaters in the winter.

SUNDAY

Grabbing a drink in one of **Beijing's hutong**—before they all disappear—is a lovely way to enjoy a city caught between the past and future. Try **Pass By** (⊠ 108 Nanluoguxiang, Dongcheng District ☎ 010/8403–8004).

★ **Yugong Yishan** 愚公移山. This Beijing institution, in its second location, is a chilled-out bar run by two local music fans. It plays host to a range of live bands playing everything from blues to jazz to Afro-Caribbean beats, and attracts an equally diverse crowd. It occasionally charges an entrance fee, depending on the entertainment. Don't bother with the cocktails—instead, nod your head along to the music while sipping a good old Tsingtao beer. ⊠ 3-2 Zhangzizhong Lu, Dongcheng District ☎ 010/8402–8477 ⊕ www.yugongyishan.com Ⓜ Zhang Zizhong Lu.

One of the many drinking establishments on the Sanlitun

CHAOYANG DISTRICT

Apothecary 药剂员. Like an old fashioned pharmacist doling out carefully concocted medicinals, the mixologists at this low-key venue artfully blend all of your favorite ingredients into cocktails that will soothe the soul. Mixologist-in-chief Leon Lee is something of a local celebrity for good reason. The location, in the trendy Nali Patio complex, and the New Orleans-style bar food are bonuses. ⊠ *3/F, Nali Patio, 81 Sanlitun Beilu, Chaoyang District* ☎ *010/5208–6040* ⊕ *apothecarybj. com* Ⓜ *Tuanjie Hu*

China Bar 北京亮酒吧. Perched atop the 65-story Park Hyatt, this upmarket cocktail bar offers bird's-eye views of the city, smog and all! Dark and sultry, the modern Asian decor is minimalist so as not to distract from the views, or the drinks. Cocktails are expertly mixed and Scotch purists can choose from a list of 23 single malts. ⊠ *65th Floor, Park Hyatt Beijing, 2 Jianguomenwai Dajie, Chaoyang District* ☎ *010/8567–1234*

The Den. This old-school dive's attraction is sports on wide-screen TVs. The owner runs the city's amateur rugby club, so you'll find players and their supporters drinking rowdily. Open 24 hours a day, it's guaranteed to be buzzing every night, especially during happy hour, when you can grab half-price drinks and pizza until 10 PM. ⊠ *4 Gongti Donglu, next to the City Hotel, Chaoyang District* ☎ *010/6592–6290* Ⓜ *Tuanjie Hu.*

Fodor's Choice ★ **D.Lounge.** Raising the bar for bars in Beijing, this New York–style lounge is swank, spacious, and has an innovative drink list. At the moment, it's the place to rub elbows with the city's *it* crowd, and occasionally the doormen restrict entry to the more dapperly dressed. It's a bit tricky

GAY AND LESBIAN NIGHTLIFE

(✉ *Solana Mall, 6 Chaoyang Gongyuan Lu, Chaoyang District* ☎ *010/5905–6213*) on Thursdays. Since the scene changes quickly—bars open, close, and reopen at new locations—you should also check online resources. Try ⊕ *www.utopia-asia.com* for updates, or the Facebook page Queer Beijing.

Here are some popular venues:

Destination *(Mudedi)* 目的地. The city's best and most popular gay club has a bouncy dance floor, energetic DJs, and a small lounge area. It gets extremely packed on weekends and attracts a varied crowd of almost all male expats and locals. There's a cover charge at weekends.

✉ *7 Gongti Xilu, Chaoyang District* ☎ *010/6551–5138* Ⓜ *Dongsi Shitiao.*

Pipe Café *(Paipu Jiuba)* 派普酒吧. This bar attracts a crowd of young women dancing to hip-hop on Saturday night. There's a small cover charge. ✉ *Gongti Nanlu, Chaoyang District* ☎ *010/6593–7756.*

West Wing *(Xixiangfang).* This women-oriented teahouse and bar is tucked into the Deshengmen Tower. The quirky bar has karaoke in the courtyard in summer, plus sofas, stools, and board games inside year-round. ✉ *Deshengmen Tower, Xicheng District* ☎ *010/8208–2836* Ⓜ *Deshengmen.*

to find: walk behind Salsa Caribe and head south. ✉ *Sanlitun Nanlu, Chaoyang District* ☎ *010/6593–7710.*

Face 飞色. Stylish without being pretentious, Face is justifiably popular, especially with the mature, well-heeled crowd. The complex has a multitude of restaurants, but the real gem is the bar. Grab a lounge bed surrounded by silky drapes, take advantage of the happy-hour drink specials, and enjoy some premier people-watching. ✉ *26 Dongcaoyuan, Gongti Nanlu, Chaoyang District* ☎ *010/6551–6788.*

Fubar Peking 夫 吧. Beijing's one and only speakeasy isn't as pretentious as you might expect given the rigmarole of finding the place (press a light switch at the back of Stadium Dog and a fake wall slides open). Instead, you'll find a classy joint with some light jazz in the background and well-made Fu-tinis to linger over. ✉ *10-11 Gongti Dong Men, Chaoyang District* ☎ *010/6546-8364.*

Ichikura 一藏. This tiny Japanese bar is the place to go if you're a discerning whiskey drinker. The dimly lit interior, red decor, and hushed conversation give it an air of exclusivity: if James Bond was in Beijing, this is where he'd come. Drinks are taken very seriously here and it shows in both the quality of the alcohol and the professionalism with which it's mixed by the all-Japanese bar staff. ✉ *2/F (entrance via stairs at south wall of Chaoyang Theatre), Chaoyang Theater, 36 Dongsanhuan Beilu, Chaoyang District* ☎ *010/6507–1107* Ⓜ *Hujialou*

Kai 开吧. An often-rowdy club with cheap drinks and a sardine-tin dance floor, Kai attracts hordes of college students and young locals on weekends. On weeknights, however, you can hold a comfortable conversation on the sofas upstairs and admire the surreal art. ⊠ *Sanlitun Beijie, Chaoyang District* ☎ *010/6416–6254* Ⓜ *Tuanjie Hu.*

Punk 朋克. Put aside any fear of a boring hotel bar. Punk, as the name infers, is loud and lively without being pretentious. Located in the basement of the trendy Opposite House Hotel, this DJ bar and club is fun and friendly, and its bar staff mix a mean cocktail. ⊠ *B1, The Opposite House, 11 Sanlitun Beilu, Chaoyang District* ☎ *010 /6410–5222* ⊕ *barpunk.com* Ⓜ *Tuanjie Hu.*

Fodor'sChoice
★
Q Bar. Echo's cocktails—strong, authentic, and not super expensive—are a small legend here in Beijing. This tucked-away lounge off the main Sanlitun drag is an unpretentious option for an evening out. Don't be put off by the fact that it's in a bland, 1980s-styled motel; in the summer the terrace more than makes up for that. ⊠ *Top floor of Eastern Inn Hotel, Sanlitun Nanlu, Chaoyang District* ☎ *010/6595–9239.*

Saddle Cantina. For a touch of Mexico, head to this terra-cotta-colored venue in downtown Beijing. It's packed on summer evenings thanks to its large terrace, perfect for downing one of the brilliant margaritas. The service is friendly, and the house band will have you tapping your feet. Sports fans will appreciate the games on the big screen and everyone loves the half-priced cocktails between 4 and 8. ⊠ *81 Sanlitun Beilu, Chaoyang District* ☎ *010/6400–4330* Ⓜ *Tuanjie Hu.*

★ **Stone Boat** 石舫. This watering hole is a pavilion-style hut on the edge of a pretty lake in Ritan Park. There are dainty ducks, feisty fishermen, and park joggers to observe while you sip chilled white wine. This is one of Beijing's nicest outdoor bars, as long as you don't mind having to use the public toilets opposite the building. ⊠ *Lakeside, southwest corner of Ritan Park, Chaoyang District* ☎ *010/6501–9986* Ⓜ *Jianguomen.*

The Tree. For years now, expats have crowded this bar for its Belgian beer, wood-fired pizza, and quiet murmurs of conversation. It does, however, get a bit smoky; if you're sensitive you may want to give this venue a pass. For pasta instead of pizza, its sister restaurant Nearby the Tree is, well, nearby, at 100 meters to the southeast. ⊠ *43 Sanlitun Beijie,Chaoyang District* ☎ *010/6415–1954* Ⓜ *Tuanjie Hu.*

CHAOYANG WEST GATE

Bling. The name says it all. This is the place to go if you want to see Beijing's young, moneyed, hip-hop crowd dressed up to the nines. A hopping dance floor, the vintage Rolls parked right in the club, and cutting-edge design all add to the club's sexy, fun vibe. If you have the cash, book a VIP table and secure some excellent table service, plus more than a few admiring glances from the girls and guys who haven't made it beyond the barrier. ⊠ *Solana Mall 5-1, No. 6 Chaoyang Park Road, Chaoyang District* ☎ *010/5905–6999.*

The World of Suzie Wong 苏西黄俱乐部. It's no coincidence that this bar is named after a 1957 novel about a Hong Kong prostitute. Come here late at night and you'll find a healthy supply of modern Suzie Wongs and a crowd of expat clients. The sleaze factor is enhanced by its 1930s opium-den design, with China-chic beds overrun with cushions. Suzie Wong's, however, has a reputation for mixing a more-than-decent

BARROOM WITH A VIEW

Drum & Bell 鼓钟咖啡馆. A relaxed rooftop that tempts you to peer through the trees at the Drum Tower in front, the Bell Tower behind, and the rolling tops of hutong 'hoods to the side. ✉ *41 Zhonglouwan Hutong, Dongcheng District* ☎ *010/8403–3600* Ⓜ *Gulou.*

East Shore Live Jazz Café 东岸咖啡. There's no competition: this place has the most fabulous views of Houhai lake, hands-down, and authentic jazz on stage every night. ✉ *Qianhai Nanyan Lu, 2nd fl., next to the Post Office, Xicheng District* ☎ *010/8403-2131.*

Yin 饮 (皇家驿栈. The Emperor Hotel's rooftop terrace bar certainly has the "wow" factor. It overlooks the Forbidden City—perhaps the finest view in all Beijing—and there's even a hot tub if you need to relax. Unsurprisingly, drink prices are high, but it's a fabulous place to show visitors, and befitting the stylishness of the hotel, red lanterns and fashionably outfitted staff add to the classiness of the experience. If only service standards were as high. ✉ *33 Qihelou, Dongcheng District* ☎ *010/6526-5566* Ⓜ *Tiananmen East.*

cocktail and good music. ✉ *1A South Nongzhanguan Lu, Chaoyang West Gate, Chaoyang District* ☎ *010/6593-6049.*

HAIDIAN DISTRICT

The Red House 色家. A simple, no-frills exterior reflects the bar as a whole—bare walls warmed by a roaring fire, friendly bar staff, and a loyal crowd looking for a home away from home to booze in peace. The pizza oven never stops churning out tasty pies, a good accompaniment to the beers on tap. ✉ *Wangzhuang Lu, Wudaokou, Haidian District* ☎ *010/6291-3350* Ⓜ *Wudaokou.*

Wudaokou Beer Garden 五道口啤酒 花 园. Catering to a young and lively crowd who swarm out of the nearby universities, this fun beer garden has cheap drinks and enough good snacks to line your stomach. Stick to beer as the mixed drinks get mixed reports. It's just west of the Wudaokou subway stop. ✉ *Chengfu Lu, Wudaokou, Haidian District* Ⓜ *Wudaokou.*

DANCE CLUBS

DONGCHENG DISTRICT

Tango 糖果. This warehouse-style space is way more interesting than the competition. Without the usual gaudy decor, Tango is roomy enough to take the crowds, and often plays some very loud but good music. One of Beijing's best live music venues, Star Live, is on the second floor. ✉ *79 Hepingli Xijie, South Gate of Ditan Park, Dongcheng District* ☎ *010/6428-2288* Ⓜ *Yonghe Gong.*

CHAOYANG DISTRICT

Cargo Club. Fierce promotions have attracted some top-name international DJs. And in spite of the smallish dance floor, many expats consider Cargo the best club along Gongti Xilu. Perhaps it's the 1980s kitsch. ✉ *6 Gongti Xilu, Chaoyang District* ☎ *010/6551-6898.*

ENGLISH	PINYIN	CHINESE
12sqm	12 píngmǐ	平米
Amilal	àn yī lā'ěr	按一拉尔
Apothecary	Yào jì yuán	药剂员
Bed	n/a	n/a
Beijing Concert Hall	Běijīng yīnyuètīng	北京音乐厅
Beijing Exhibition Theater	Běijīng zhǎnlǎnguǎn jùchǎng	北京展览馆剧场
Bling	n/a	n/a
Capital Theater	Shǒudū jùchǎng	首都剧场
Cargo Club	n/a	n/a
Chang'an Grand Theater	Cháng'ān dàxìyuàn	长安大戏院
Chaoyang Theater	Cháoyáng jùchǎng	朝阳剧场
China Bar	Běijīng liàng jiǔbā	北京亮酒吧
China National Puppet Theater	Zhōngguó guójiā mùǒujùyuà	中国国家木偶剧院
The Den	n/a	n/a
D.Lounge	n/a	n/a
Destination	Mùdìdì	目的地
Drum and Bell	Gǔzhōng kāfēiguǎn	鼓钟咖啡馆
East Shore Live Jazz Café	Dōng'àn kāfēi	东岸咖啡
Face	Fēi sè	飞色
Forbidden City Concert Hall	Zhōngshān gōngyuán yīnyuètáng	中山公园音乐堂
Fubar Peking	Fūbā	夫 吧
Huguang Guildhall	Húguǎng huìguǎn	湖广会馆
Ichikura	Yī cāng	一藏
Kai	Kāi ba	开吧
Lao She Teahouse	Lǎoshě cháguǎn	老舍茶馆
Liyuan Theater	Líyuán jùcháng	梨园剧场
MAO Live House	n/a	n/a
National Centre for Performing Arts	Guójiā dàjùyuàn	国家大剧院
No Name Bar (Bai Feng's)	Wúmíng jiǔbā	无名酒吧
Pipe Café	Pàipǔ jiǔbā	派普酒吧
Poly Plaza International Theater	Bǎolì jùyuàn	保利剧院
Punk	Péng kè	朋克
Q Bar	n/a	n/a

6

ENGLISH	PINYIN	CHINESE
The Red House	Hóng jiā	色家
The Red Theatre	Hóng jùchǎng	红剧场
Saddle Cantina	Mòxīgē cāntīng	n/a
Stone Boat	Shífǎng	石舫
Tango	Tángguǒ	糖果
Tianqiao Acrobatic Theater	n/a	天桥乐茶馆
Tianqiao Happy Teahouse	Tiānqiáolè cháguǎn	天桥乐茶馆
The Tree	n/a	n/a
The World of Suzie Wong	Sūxīhuáng jùlèbù	苏西黄俱乐部
Wudaokou Beer Garden	Wǔdàokǒu píjiǔ huāyuán	五道口啤酒 花 园
Yin (Emperor Hotel)	Yìn (Huángjiā Yìzhàn)	饮（皇家驿栈
Yugong Yishan	Yúgōngyíshān	愚公移山

Best Side Trips

INCLUDING THE GREAT WALL AND THIRTEEN MING TOMBS

WORD OF MOUTH

"Do the important things first! We had a few days in Beijing at the start of last month. It was really hot, and we two old Aussies found we just didn't have the energy to see half the things I had researched. We enjoyed everything we did, but only did half of what I would have liked to."

—Carrabella

WELCOME TO RURAL CHINA

TOP REASONS TO GO

★ **A Great Big Wall:** Postcard views of large sections of the restored Ming Dynasty brick wall rise majestically around you. The sheer scope of this ancient project boggles the mind.

★ **Ming and More:** It's easy to arrange a tour or your own transportation to the Great Wall and the Thirteen Ming Tombs, especially if you go to the Badaling section of the wall.

★ **The Adventure:** There are so many exciting places just within a few hours of Beijing, and for all these places, getting there is half the fun. Traveling through rural China, even for a day trip, is always something of an adventure.

★ **Meet the Locals:** People in rural China can be extremely kind, inviting you to their homes for tea, a meal, or even to stay the night. If you accept an invite, a small gift of fruit or a bottle of *baijiu* (a Chinese spirit distilled from sorghum) is always appreciated.

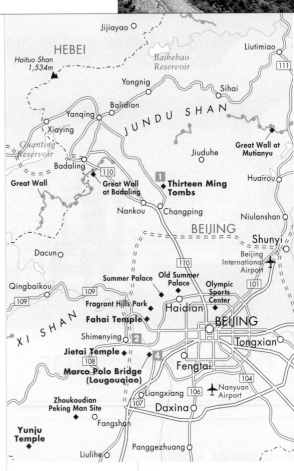

1 Thirteen Ming Tombs. The grandeur of the final resting place for 13 Ming Dynasty emperors gives you an idea of the importance of ancestor worship in ancient China.

2 Fahai Temple and Jietai Temple. Li Tong, a favorite eunuch in Emperor Zhengtong's court built Fahai; its frescos are considered some of the finest examples of Buddhist mural art from the Ming Dynasty. Jietai, China's most ancient Buddhist site, is located just west of Beijing.

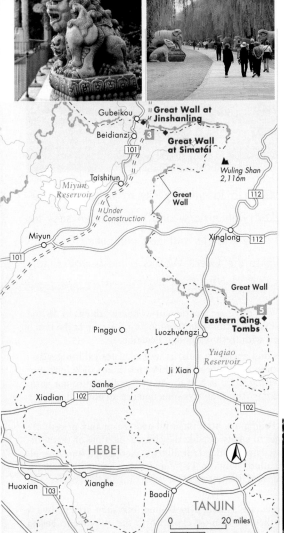

GETTING ORIENTED

If you take a taxi set a price beforehand; the metered fare can add up quickly (generally, rides start at Y10 for the first 3 km, with an additional Y2 for each additional km and another Y2 per every five minutes of waiting time). If you go by train, most hotels will help you buy tickets up to four days in advance for a fee (typically Y5 to Y15 per ticket). There are also small train-ticket windows scattered around the city. Look for the China Railways logo.

7

3 The Great Wall. This awe-inspiring structure is one of the country's most accessible attractions. It's a UNESCO World Heritage Site and the longest man-made structure on earth.

4 Marco Polo Bridge. Beijing's oldest bridge was once part of the Imperial Highway that linked the capital city with central China.

5 Yunju Temple and Eastern Qing Tombs. Don't miss the 14,278 delicately carved Buddhist tablets at Yunju. The Eastern Tombs were modeled after the Thirteen Ming Tombs, but these are even more extravagant and much less touristy.

Updated by
Paul Mooney

Not only is Beijing a fascinating city to visit, but its outskirts are packed with history- and culture-laden sites for the admirer of early empires and their antiquities. First and foremost, a trip to the Great Wall is a must—you simply can't miss it!

After the Great Wall, there are a variety of wonderful things to do and see: you can go horseback riding at Yesanpo, or take a dip at the beach and gorge yourself with fresh seafood in Beidaihe.

Buddhist temples and ancient tombs, as well as historical bridges and anthropological digs, are all located within a few hours of Beijing. For all these sites, getting there is half the fun—traveling through rural China, even for a day trip, is always something of an adventure.

GETTING THERE

Taxis, which in Beijing are both plentiful and reasonably priced, are a good way to get to sights outside the city. At the time of this writing, a Y1 fuel surcharge is added for all trips exceeding 3 km. A small surcharge is also added between 11 PM and 5 AM. As Beijing traffic is getting more congested, the potential for some time stuck in traffic (and the associated cost jump) is high.

Private-car services are available in Beijing, but they aren't always cheap, although they are in most cases worth the investment. **Beijing Limo** (☎ 010/6546–1688 ⊕ *www.beijinglimo.com/english*) has English-speaking drivers, and a variety of cars and buses.

Trains are also a good way to get to your side trips. Some sites, such as Yesanpo, Tianjin, Beidaihe, and Shanhaiguan, are accessible by train. Some trains leave from Beijing Station, in the middle of the city, and others leave from Beijing West Station. Plan to get to the train station at least 30 minutes before your train leaves, as the stations can be confusing for visitors. It's easy to buy train tickets at the station, but if you're on a tight schedule and can't afford a delay, buy a ticket beforehand, especially if you're traveling on peak dates.

TIMING

It'll take you several days to see all the sights outside of Beijing. If you only have time for one, go to the **Great Wall**. If you have two days, head to **Fahai Temple**, about an hour's drive from the center, on the second day. Afterward you can see the **Jietai Temple** and the **Tanzhe Temple** before returning to the city in the afternoon. If you have more time to see the sights outside the city, check out the **Eastern Qing Tombs** on your third day. Wear walking shoes and bring a lunch.

If you have three days or more, and you're looking for a little summertime relaxation, take a day and a night (or, for real relaxation, two days) at **Beidaihe**, to bask on the beach, chow down on seafood, and crash at one of the ubiquitous hotels along the coast.

WHAT TO WEAR

The weather in Beijing and neighboring areas is notoriously fickle, so make sure you dress appropriately. In the summer it's hot; travel with sunglasses, sunscreen, and a wide-brimmed hat. It gets terribly cold in the winter, so dress in layers and pack gloves, a hat, and a scarf. And if you plan to do any hiking, make sure to bring sturdy, comfortable shoes.

Also, checking the weather forecast before an excursion is always a good idea for last-minute wardrobe changes. ■**TIP➔ Don't carry too much cash or expensive jewelry.** Other things to bring along? A camera, a change of clothes if you're staying overnight, and your common sense.

RECOMMENDED TOURS

Every major hotel can arrange guided tours to sites outside Beijing. Among the hotel-based travel agencies are **Beijing Panda Tour** and **China Swan International Tours. China International Travel Service (CITS)**, the official government agency, can also arrange tours.

Contacts Beijing Hikers (⊠ *Room 601, Tower B, Jiuxianqiao Lu Chaoyang District* ☎ *139/1002–5516 or 010/6432–2786* ⊕ *www.beijinghikers.com*) leads hiking tours to assorted locations every weekend.

Beijing Panda Tour (⊠ *Crowne Plaza Beijing, 48 Wangfujing Dajie, Dongcheng District* ☎ *010/5911–9999 Ext. 9277*).

The China Guide (⊕ *www.thechinaguide.com*) is a Beijing-based, American-managed travel agency offering tours that do *not* make shopping detours.

China International Travel Service (⊠ *28 Jianguomenwai Dajie, Chaoyang District* ☎ *010/6515–8565* ☎ *010/6515–8603* ⊕ *www.cits.net*).

China Swan International Tours (⊠ *4 Fl., Longhui Building, 1 Nongguang Nanli, Dongsanhuan, Chaoyang District* ☎ *010/8737–2266* ⊕ *www. china-swan.com.cn*).

Chinese Culture Club/The Beijing Amblers (⊠ *Room 101, Kent Center, 29 Anjialou, LiangmaqiaoLu, Chaoyang District* ☎ *010/6432–9341* ⊕ *www.chinaculturecenter.org*).

Compass Tourist Information. This is a cheap tour service that caters to backpackers. Tours are generally one-half to one-third the price of CITS. ⊠ *15 Guangqumenwai Dajie, Chaoyang District* ☎ *010/6308–3201*.

7

TO MING OR NOT TO MING?

Most visitors to the Ming Tombs visit them as part of a longer excursion, usually to the Great Wall. A leisurely walk down the Sacred Way, inspecting the series of charming bigger-than-life statues of imperial officials and animals, is probably the best way to spend an hour or two. Only three of the Ming Tombs are open to visitors (Changling, Dingling, and Zhaoling), and none of them are much more than a deep concrete bunker with a huge nondescript concrete coffin at the bottom, which you have to buy a ticket to visit. If you're blessed with a little more time, you can pay a more private homage to the spirit of Emperor Zhu Zhaigou at his tomb at Zhaoling, which is at the far end of the valley. It's quainter and much less frequently visited.

Cycle China (☎ 1391/188–6524 ⊕ *www.cyclechina.com*) offers scheduled and personalized cycling tours throughout China.

Stretch-A-Leg Travel Service (✉ *2/F, 34 Lane Ten, Dong Si, Dongcheng District* ☎ *1360/109–4588* ⊕ *www.stretchalegtravel.com*) specializes in small group and personalized tours of Beijing hutongs and off-the-beaten-track sights by expert guides.

Wild China (*Room 801, Oriental Place, 9 Dongfang Dong Lu, Chaoyang District* ☎ *010/6465–6602* ⊕ *www.wildchina.com*) is a premium travel company offers distinctive, ecologically sensitive journeys all over China.

THIRTEEN MING TOMBS 明十三陵

48 km (30 mi) north of Beijing.

A narrow valley just north of Changping is the final resting place for 13 of the Ming Dynasty's 16 emperors (the first Ming emperor was buried in Nanjing; the burial site of the second one is unknown; and the seventh Ming emperor was dethroned and buried in an ordinary tomb in northwestern Beijing). Ming monarchs once journeyed here each year to kowtow before their clan forefathers and make offerings to their memory. The area's vast scale and imperial grandeur convey the importance attached to ancestor worship in ancient China.

The road to the Thirteen Ming Tombs begins beneath an imposing stone portico that stands at the valley entrance. Beyond the entrance, the **Shendao** (✉ *Y30 [Y20 Nov.–Mar.]* ⊗ *Apr.–Oct., daily 8–5:30; Nov.–Mar., daily 8–5*), or Sacred Way, once reserved for imperial travel, passes through an outer pavilion and between rows of stone sculptures—imperial advisers and huge elephants, camels, lions, and horses—on its 7-km (4½-mi) journey to the burial sites. The **spirit way** leads to **Changling** (☎ *010/6076–1888* ✉ *Y45* ⊗ *Apr.–Oct., daily 8–5:30; Nov.–Mar., daily 8–5:00*), the head tomb built for Emperor Yongle in 1427. The designs of Yongle's great masterpiece, the Forbidden City, are echoed in this structure. Changling and a second tomb, **Dingling** (☎ *010/6076–1423* ✉ *Y70 [Y50 Nov.–Mar.]* ⊗ *Apr.–Oct., daily 8:30–6; Nov.–Mar., daily 8:30–5:30*), were rebuilt in the 1980s and opened to the public. Both complexes suffer from overrestoration and overcrowding, but they're worth visiting if only for the tomb relics on display in the small museums at each site. Dingling is particularly worth seeing because this tomb of Emperor Wanli is the only Ming Dynasty tomb that has been excavated. Unfortunately, this was done in 1956 when China's archaeological skills were sadly lacking, resulting in irrecoverable losses. Nonetheless, it is interesting to compare this underground vault with the tomb of Emperor Qianlong at Qingdongling. Allow ample time for a hike or drive northwest from Changling to the six fenced-off **unrestored tombs,** a short distance farther up the valley. Here crumbling walls conceal vast courtyards shaded by pine trees. At each tomb, a stone altar rests beneath a stela tower and burial mound. In some cases the wall that circles the burial chamber is accessible on steep stone stairways that ascend from either side of the altar. At the valley's terminus (about 5 km [3 mi] northwest of Changling), the **Zhaoling Tomb** rests beside a traditional walled village. This thriving hamlet is well worth exploring.

Picnics amid the ruins have been a favorite weekend activity among Beijingers for nearly a century; if you picnic here, be sure to carry out all trash. ⊠ *Changping County* 💲 *Y30 for Zhaoling tomb.*

FAHAI TEMPLE 法海寺

20 km (12 mi) west of Beijing.

The stunning works of Buddhist mural art at Fahai Temple, which underwent extensive renovation and reopened in 2008, are among the most underappreciated sights in Beijing. Li Tong, a favored eunuch in the court of Emperor Zhengtong (1436–49), donated funds to construct Fahai Temple in 1443. The project was highly ambitious: Li Tong invited only celebrated imperial and court painters to decorate the temple. As a result, the murals in the only surviving chamber of that period, Daxiongbaodian (the Mahavira Hall), are considered the finest examples of Buddhist mural art from the Ming Dynasty. Sadly, statues of various Buddhas and one of Li Tong himself were destroyed during China's Cultural Revolution.

The most famous of the nine murals in Mahavira Hall is a large-scale triptych featuring Guanyin (the Bodhisattva of Compassion) and Wenshu (the Bodhisattva of Marvelous Virtue and Gentle Majesty) in the center, and Poxian (the Buddha of Universal Virtue) on either side. The depiction of Guanyin follows the theme of "moon in water," which compares the Buddhist belief in the illusoriness of the material world to the reflection of the moon in the water. Typically painted with Guanyin are her legendary mount Jin Sun and her assistant Shancai Tongzi. Wenshu is often presented with a lion, symbolic of the bodhisattva's wisdom and strength of will, while Poxian is shown near a six-tusked elephant, each tusk representing one of the qualities that leads to enlightenment. On the opposite wall is the *Sovereign Sakra and Brahma* mural, with a panoply of characters from the Buddhist canon.

The murals were painted during the time of the European Renaissance, and though the subject matter is traditional, there are comparable

Continued on page 222

THE GREAT WALL

For some people, the Great Wall is the main reason for a trip to China; for any visitor to Beijing, it's a must-see. Originally intended to keep foreigners out, the world's most famous wall has become the icon of an increasingly open nation. One of the country's most accessible attractions, the Great Wall promises both breathtaking scenery and cultural illumination.

Built by successive dynasties over two millennia, the Great Wall isn't one structure built at one time, but a series of defensive installations that shrank and grew. Especially vulnerable spots were more heavily fortified, while some mountainous regions were left un-walled altogether. The actual length of the wall remains a topic of considerable debate: at its longest, some estimates say the protective cordon spans 6,437 km (4,000 mi)—a distance wider than the United States. Although attacks, age, and pillaging (not to mention today's tourist invasion) have caused the crumbling of up to two-thirds of its length, new sections are being uncovered even today.

As kingdoms scrambled to protect themselves from marauding nomads, portions of wall cropped up, leading to a motley collection of northern borders. It was the first emperor of a unified China, Qin Shi-huang (circa 259–210 BC), founder of the Qin Dynasty, who linked these fortifications into a single network. By some accounts, Qin mustered nearly a million people, or one-fifth of China's workforce, to build this massive barricade, a mobilization that claimed countless lives and gave rise to many tragic folktales.

The Ming Dynasty fortified the wall like never before: for an estimated 5,000 km (3,107 mi), it stood 26 feet tall and 30 feet wide at its base. However, the wall failed to prevent the Manchu invasion that toppled the Ming in 1644. That historical failure hasn't tarnished the Great Wall's image, however. Although China once viewed it as a model of feudal oppression, the Great Wall is now touted as the national symbol. "Love China, Restore the Great Wall," declared Deng Xiaoping in 1984. Since then large sections have been repaired and opened to visitors, turning it also into a symbol of the tension between preservation and restoration in China.

AN ETERNAL WAIT

One legend concerns Lady Meng, whose husband was kidnapped on their wedding night and forced to work on the Great Wall. She traveled to the work site to await his return, believing her determination would bring him back. She waited so long that, in the end, she turned into a rock, which to this day stands at the head of the Great Wall in the beautiful seaside town of Qinhuangdao.

Barnes & Noble Booksellers #2238
7851 L. Tysons Corner Center
McLean, VA 22102
703-506-2937

STR:2238 REG:011 TRN:1793 CSHR:MARTIN P

Fodor's Beijing, 3rd Edition
  9781400005260   T1
  (1 @ 19.99)   19.99

Subtotal   19.99
Sales Tax T1 (6.000%)   1.20
TOTAL   21.19
MASTERCARD   21.19
  Card#: XXXXXXXXXXXX2775
  Expdate: XX/XX
  Auth: 02245P
  Entry Method: Swiped

A MEMBER WOULD HAVE SAVED   2.00

        Thanks for shopping at
           Barnes & Noble

101.31A   03/22/2013 09:47PM

CUSTOMER COPY

returned, and can be exchanged only for the same title and only if defective. NOOKs purchased from other retailers or sellers are returnable only to the retailer or seller from which they are purchased, pursuant to such retailer's or seller's return policy. Magazines, newspapers, eBooks, digital downloads, and used books are not returnable or exchangeable. Defective NOOKs may be exchanged at the store in accordance with the applicable warranty.

Returns or exchanges will not be permitted (i) after 14 days or without receipt or (ii) for product not carried by Barnes & Noble or Barnes & Noble.com.

Policy on receipt may appear in two sections.

Return Policy

With a sales receipt or Barnes & Noble.com packing slip, a full refund in the original form of payment will be issued from any Barnes & Noble Booksellers store for returns of undamaged NOOKs, new and unread books, and unopened and undamaged music CDs, DVDs, and audio books made within 14 days of purchase from a Barnes & Noble Booksellers store or Barnes & Noble.com with the below exceptions:

A store credit for the purchase price will be issued (i) for purchases made by check less than 7 days prior to the date of return, (ii) when a gift receipt is presented within 60 days of purchase, (iii) for textbooks, or (iv) for products purchased at Barnes & Noble College bookstores that are listed for sale in the Barnes & Noble Booksellers inventory management system.

Opened music CDs/DVDs/audio books may not be returned, and can be exchanged only for the same title and only if defective. NOOKs purchased from other retailers or sellers are returnable only to the retailer or seller from which they are purchased, pursuant to such retailer's or seller's return policy. Magazines, newspapers, eBooks, digital downloads, and used books are not returnable or exchangeable. Defective NOOKs may be exchanged at the store in

MATERIALS & TECHNIQUES

■ During the 2nd century BC, the wall was largely composed of packed earth and piled stone.

■ Some sections, like those in the Taklimakan Desert, were fortified with twigs, sand, and even rice (the jury's still out on whether workers' remains were used as well).

■ The more substantial brick-and-mortar ruins that wind across the mountains north of Beijing date from the Ming Dynasty (14th–17th centuries). Some Ming mortar kilns still exist in valleys around Beijing.

YOUR GUIDE TO THE GREAT WALL

As a visitor to Beijing, you simply must set aside a day to visit one of the glorious Great Wall sites just outside the capital. The closest, Badaling, is just an hour from the city's center—in general, the farther you go, the more rugged the terrain. So choose your adventure wisely!

BADALING, the most accessible section of the Great Wall, is where most tours go. This location is rife with Disneylike commercialism, though: from the cable car you'll see both the heavily reconstructed portions of wall and crowds of souvenir stalls.

If you seek the wall less traveled, book a trip to fantastic **MUTIANYU**, which is about the same distance as Badaling from Beijing. You can enjoy much more solitude here, as well as amazing views from the towers and walls.

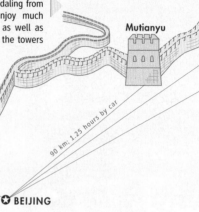

Mutianyu

Badaling

70 km; 1 hour by car

90 km; 1.25 hours by car

✪ BEIJING

TRANSPORTATION

CARS: The easiest and most comfortable way to visit the wall is by private car. Though taxis are occasionally willing to make the trip to more accessible sections like Badaling and Mutianyu, most hotels can arrange a four-passenger car and an English-speaking driver for 8 hours at around Y400–Y600. Settle details in advance, and remember that it's polite to invite your driver to eat meals with you. To ensure your driver doesn't return to Beijing without you, pay after the trip is over.

TOURS: In addition to the tour buses that gather around Tiananmen Square, most hotels and tour companies offer trips (in comfortable, air-conditioned buses or vans) to Badaling, Mutianyu, Simatai, and Jinshanling. ■TIP➔ Smaller, private tours are generally more rewarding than large bus trips. Trips will run between Y100 and Y500 per person, but costs vary depending on the group size, and can sometimes be negotiated. Wherever you're headed, book in advance.

TOUR OPERATORS

OUR TOP PICKS

■ **CITS (China International Tour Service)** runs bus tours to Badaling and private tours to Badaling, Mutianyu, and Simatai. (Y400, Y500, Y600 per person) ✉ 1 Dongdan Bei DAJIE, Dongcheng District ☎ 010/6522–2991 ⊕ www.cits.net

■ **Beijing Service** leads private guided tours by car to Badaling, Mutianyu, and Simatai (Y420–Y560 per person for small groups of 3–4 people). ☎ 010/5166–7026 ✍ travel@beijingservice.com ⊕ www.beijingservice.com

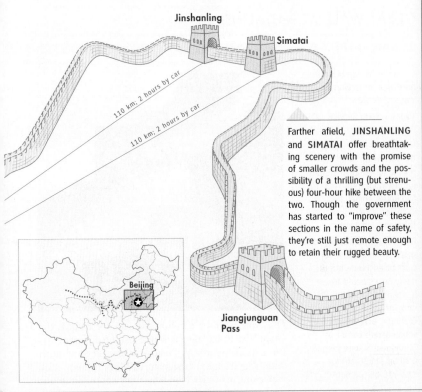

Farther afield, **JINSHANLING** and **SIMATAI** offer breathtaking scenery with the promise of smaller crowds and the possibility of a thrilling (but strenuous) four-hour hike between the two. Though the government has started to "improve" these sections in the name of safety, they're still just remote enough to retain their rugged beauty.

■ **Great Wall Adventure Club** organizes private bus and car trips to Jinshanling–Simatai (Y380–Y650) and Mutianyu (Y160–Y350). ☎138/1154–5162 ✎great-wall@greatwalladventure.com ⊕www.greatwalladventure.com

ADDITIONAL TOURS

■ **Abercrombie & Kent** also offers pricey personalized group tours to the wall. Call for prices. ☎010/6507–7125 ⊕www.abercrombiekent.com

■ **Cycle China** runs good guided hiking tours of the unrestored Wall at Jiankou, as well as personalized tours to Simatai and Mutianyu. (Y550–Y750 for minimum of 5 people). ☎010/6402–5653, ⊕www.cyclechina.com

■ **David Spindler**, a Great Wall expert, runs private tours to various sites. Contact him for prices, schedules, and details through Wild China ☎010/6465–6602 Ext. 314 ✎info@wildchina.com ⊕www.wildchina.com

■ **Dragon Bus Tours**, which picks up at major hotels, has tours to Badaling (with Ming Tombs), Mutianyu, and a bus to Simatai—with an occasional stop at a souvenir factory. (Y280–350; Y350-Y500 for Simatai) ☎010/6515–8565 ✎service@beijinghighlights.com

■ **Gray Line/Panda Tours**, with branches in a dozen high-end hotels in Beijing, runs bus tours to Badaling (and Ming Tombs), Mutianyu, and Simatai—but beware of stops at souvenir factories. (Y280 per person) ⊠4 fl., Shuang'an Dashi, 421 Beisanhuan, haidian ☎010/6525–8372 ⊕www.pandatourchina.cn

GREAT WALL AT BADALING

GETTING THERE

Distance: 70 km (43 mi) northwest of Beijing, in Yanqing County

Tours: Beijing Service, CITS, Dragon Bus Tours, Gray Line/Panda Tours

By Car: A car for four people to Badaling should run no more than Y600 for five hours, sometimes including a stop at the Thirteen Ming Tombs.

By Bus: It's hard to wander south of Tiananmen Square without encountering the many buses going to Badaling. Choose wisely: look for the 1 or 5 bus at Qianmen, across from the southeastern corner of Tiananmen Square (departs 6:30 am–11:30 am for Y12–Y18 per person).

FAST FACTS

Phone: 010/6912–1383
Hours: Daily 6:30 am–7 pm
Admission: Y40 Apr.–Nov.; cable car is an additional Y35 one-way, Y50 round-trip
Web Site: www.badaling. gov.cn

Only one hour by car from downtown Beijing, the Great Wall at Badaling is where visiting dignitaries go for a quick photo-op. Postcard views abound here, with large sections of the restored Ming Dynasty brick wall rising majestically to either side of the fort. In the distance, portions of the early-16th-century Great Wall disintegrate into more romantic but inaccessible ruins.

Badaling is convenient to the Thirteen Ming Tombs and outfitted with tourist-friendly facilities, so it's popular with tour groups and is thus often crowded, especially on weekends. ■TIP→ People with disabilities find access to the wall at Badaling better than elsewhere in the Beijing area. You can either take the cable car to the top, or you can walk up the gently sloping steps, relying on handrails if necessary. On a clear day you can see for miles across leafy, undulating terrain from atop the battlements. The admission price also includes access to the China Great Wall Museum and the Great Wall Circle Vision Theater.

■TIP→ Most tours to Badaling will take you to the Thirteen Ming Tombs, as well. If you don't want a stop at the tombs—or at a tourist-trapping jade factory or herbal medicine center along the way—be sure to confirm the itinerary before booking.

GREAT WALL AT MUTIANYU

GETTING THERE

Distance: 90 km (56 mi) northeast of Beijing, in Huairou County

Tours: CITS, Gray Line/Panda Tours, Great Wall Adventure Tour

By Car: A car to Mutianyu should cost no more than Y600 for the day—it takes about an hour to get there.

By Bus: Take Bus 916/936 from Dongzhimen to Huairou (Y5). From there take a minibus to Mutianyu (Y25–Y30) or hire a taxi to take you there and back to the bus station (about Y50 each way, Y100–Y150 round-trip after bargaining). On weekends and national holidays, the tourist Bus 6 from outside the South Cathedral at Xuanwumen goes directly to Mutianyu (Y50, leaves 6:30–8:30 am).

FAST FACTS

Phone: 010/6162–6873 or 010/6162–6022

Hours: Daily 7:30 am– 5:30 pm

Admission: Y45 (students half-price); chairlift, Y35; cable car, Y45 one-way, Y65 round trip with toboggan descent

★ **Fodor's Choice** Slightly farther from downtown Beijing than Badaling, the Great Wall at Mutianyu is more spectacular and, despite the occasional annoyances of souvenir stands, significantly less crowded. This long section of wall, first built during the Northern Qi Dynasty (6th century) and restored and rebuilt throughout history, can offer a solitary Great Wall experience, with unforgettable views of towers winding across mountains and woodlands. On a clear day, you'll swear you can see the deserts of Mongolia in the distance.

The lowest point on the wall is a strenuous one-hour climb above the parking lot. As an alternative, you can take a cable car on a breathtaking ride to the highest restored section (this is how President Bill Clinton ascended in 1998), from which several hiking trails descend. Take a gorgeous 11/2-hour walk east to reach another cable car that returns to the same parking lot. Mutianyu is also known for its toboggan run.

■ **TIP→** For those taking a car, the road from Huairou, a suburb of Beijing, to Mutianyu follows a river upstream and is lined with restaurants selling fresh trout. In addition, Hongluo Temple is a short drive from the bottom of the mountain.

GREAT WALL AT SIMATAI

GETTING THERE

Distance: At around 110 km (68 mi) northeast of Beijing, Simatai is farther than Badaling and Mutianyu, but is well worth the trip—the road runs through lovely farmland, and few visitors make the trek.

Tours: Most hotels offer tours here, as do CITS, Gray Line/Panda Tours, and Great Wall Adventure Tour.

By Car: A car to Simatai should be no more than Y800 for the day. If you plan to hike from Jinshanling to Simatai, or vice versa, have your car drop you off at one and pick you up at the other.

By Bus: Take the early-morning Bus 916 from the bus station at Dongzhimen (Y20), starting at 6 am. On weekends and holidays, a luxury bus leaves Qianmen at 8:30 am (Y85 round-trip) and leaves Simatai at 3 pm.

FAST FACTS

Phone: 010/6903–5025 or 010/6903–1051

Hours: Daily 8 am–5 pm

Admission: Y40; cable car, Y30 one-way, Y50 round-trip. If you hike to Jinshanling, you will have to buy another Y5 ticket at the border.

★ Remote and largely unrestored, the Great Wall at Simatai is ideal if you're seeking adventure. Near the frontier garrison at Gubeikou, the wall traverses towering peaks and hangs precariously above cliffs. Be prepared for no-handrails hiking, tough climbs, and unparalleled vistas. Several trails lead to the wall from the parking lot.

In summer, a cable car takes you two-thirds of the way up; from there it's a steep 40-minute climb to the summit. Heading east from the Miyun reservoir at a moderate pace will take you to Wangjing Ta, the 12th watchtower, after about 3 hours. For a longer hike, head west over the bridge toward the restored Jinshanling section.

The hike to Jinshanling is a strenuous 9 km (5.6 mi), usually taking around 4 hours up and down sublime sections of the wall. Be aware that crossing to Jinshanling costs Y5. People who wish to hike from one to the other often ask their driver to wait for them at their destination. (Note that hikers usually go from Jinshanling to Simatai, where buses back to Beijing are easier to find.)

GREAT WALL AT JINSHANLING

GETTING THERE

Distance: 110 km (68 mi) northeast from Beijing

Tours: CITS, Cycle China, Gray Line/Panda Tours, Great Wall Adventure Tour

By Car: A car should be no more than Y800; the ride is about two hours. If you plan to hike from Jinshanling to Simatai, as many do, it makes sense to be dropped off at Jinshanling and have your car pick you up at Simatai.

By Train: Take train L671, which departs at 7:25 am from Beijing North Railway Station, to Gubeikou; there switch to a local minibus or taxi to Jinshanling.

By Bus: Take a minibus from Dongzhimen long-distance bus station to Miyun (Y8) and then change to a local bus or taxi. Or take a Chengde-bound bus from Dongzhimen and get off at Jinshanling; a cab can bring you to the entrance for Y10.

★ Though it lacks the rugged adventure of Simatai, Jinshanling is perhaps the least restored of the major Great Wall sections near Beijing, as well as the least visited. Besides being the starting point for a fantastic four-hour hike to Simatai, Jinshanling also serves as one of the few sections of the Great Wall on which you can camp overnight.

A starry night here is gorgeous and unforgettable—go with a tour group such as Cycle China. Don't forget to pack a piece of charcoal and paper to make rubbings of bricks that still bear the stamp of the date they were made.

FAST FACTS

Phone: 031/4883-0222 or 138/3144-8986

Hours: Daily 8 am–5 pm

Admission: Y50; Y398, Y498, Y598 for overnight stays. If you hike to Simatai, you will have to buy another Y5 ticket at the border

GREAT WALL MARATHON

Not for the faint of heart, the Great Wall Marathon (and half marathon) takes place each May. The marathon covers approximately 6.5 km (4 mi) of the Great Wall, with the rest of the course running through lovely valleys in rural Tianjin.

⊕ www.great-wall-marathon.com

experiments in perspective taking place in the depiction of the figures, as compared with examples from earlier dynasties. Also of note is a highly unusual decorative technique; many contours in the hall's murals, particularly on jewelry, armor, and weapons, have been set in bold relief by the application of fine gold threads.

The temple grounds are also beautiful, but of overriding interest are the murals themselves. Visitors stumble through the dark temple with rented flashlights (free with your ticket). Viewing the murals in this way, it's easy to imagine oneself as a sort of modern-day Indiana Jones unraveling a story of the Buddha as depicted in ancient murals of unrivaled beauty. Fahai Temple is only a short taxi ride from Beijing's Pingguoyuan subway station. ⊠ *Moshikou Lu, take an approximate Y12 taxi ride from Pinguoyuan subway station directly to the temple, Shijingshan District, Beijing* ☎ *010/8871–5776* 🖭 *Y100 plus Y20 for entrance to the temple complex* ⊗ *Daily 9–4.*

Eunuchs have played an important role throughout Chinese history, often holding great influence over affairs of state, yet surprisingly little is known about them. The **Beijing Eunuch Culture Exhibition Hall** 北京宦官文化陈列馆 near the magnificent **Tian Yi Mu** 田义幕 begins to redress this lack of information. Tian Yi (1534–1605) was only nine when he was castrated and sent into the service of the Ming emperor Jiajing. He spent the next 63 years of his life serving three emperors and rose to one of the highest ranks in the land, the Director of Ceremonies. His tomb, though not as magnificent as the Thirteen Ming Tombs, nonetheless befits a man of such high social status. Particularly noteworthy in the tomb complex are the stone carvings around the base of the central mound depicting ancient anecdotes. The four smaller tombs on either side belong to other eunuchs who wished to pay tribute to Tian Yi by being buried in the same compound with him.

The small exhibition hall at the front of the tomb complex contains limited background information, most of it in Chinese, about famous eunuchs. Keep an eye out for the ancient Chinese character meaning "to castrate," which resembles two knives, one inverted, side by side. Also here is a list of all the temples in Beijing that were founded by eunuchs. The hall and tomb are a five-minute walk from Fahai Temple; just ask people the way to Tian Yi Mu. ⊠ *80 Moshikou Lu, Shijingshan District, Beijing* ☎ *010/8872–4148* 🖭 *Y8* ⊗ *Daily 9–5.*

JIETAI TEMPLE 戒台寺

★ *35 km (22 mi) west of Beijing.*

On a wooded hill west of Beijing, Jietai Temple is one of China's most famous ancient Buddhist sites. Its four main halls occupy terraces on a gentle slope up to Ma'an Shan (Saddle Hill). Originally built in AD 622, it's been used for the ordination of Buddhist novices since the Liao Dynasty. The temple complex expanded over the centuries and grew to its current scale in a major renovation conducted by devotees during the Qing Dynasty (1644–1912). The temple buildings, plus three magnificent bronze Buddhas in the Mahavira Hall, date from this period.

YESANPO & BEIDAIHE

Yesanpo 野三坡 (150 km [90 mi] northeast of Beijing) is a sleepy village between Beijing and neighboring Hebei province. Go here if you're craving a slower-paced scene and some outdoor fun. The accommodations aren't first class, but there are plenty of great things to do. Leave Beijing from Beijing West Station for the two-hour ride. Traditionally, locals have houses with extra rooms for guests, and owners will strive to make your stay as comfortable as possible. A clean room with two beds and an air conditioner should run you no more than Y150. There are also a few hotels on the main street by the train station with rooms running approximately Y200. This scenic town is nestled in a valley. The area is best toured on horseback, and horses are available for rent for Y300 per day (with a guide), or Y100 for an hour or so. Yesanpo is also known for its whole barbecued lamb. Train No. 6437 leaves Beijing West Station at 5:44 PM and arrives at 8:29 PM. Return train 6438 leaves at 09:34 AM daily.

Chairman Mao and the party's favorite spot for sand, sun, and seafood, **Beidaihe** 北戴河, (250 km [170 mi] northeast of Beijing) is one of China's few beach resorts (though it's definitely no Bali). This crowded spot is just 2½ hours by train from Beijing Station. Nearly every building in town has been converted to a hotel, and every restaurant has tanks of pick-your-own seafood lining the street.

There is also a huge potbellied Maitreya Buddha carved from the roots of what must have been a truly enormous tree. To the right of this hall, just above twin pagodas, is the Ordination Terrace, a platform built of white marble and topped with a massive bronze statue of Shakyamuni Buddha seated on a lotus flower. Tranquil courtyards, where ornate stelae and well-kept gardens bask beneath the scholar tree and other ancient pines, add to the temple's beauty. Many modern devotees from Beijing visit the temple on weekends. Getting to Jietai and nearby the Tanzhe temple is easy using public transportation. Take subway Line 1 to its westernmost station, Pingguoyuan. From there, take the No.931 public bus to either temple—it leaves every half hour and the ride takes about 70 minutes. A taxi from Pingguoyuan to Jietai Temple should be Y50 to Y60; the bus fare is Y6. ⊠ *Mentougou County* ☏ *010/6980–6611* ⊑ *Y45* ⊙ *Daily 8–5*.

NEARBY

Farther along the road past Jietai Temple, Tanzhe Temple 潭哲寺 **is a Buddhist complex nestled in a grove of** *zhe* **(cudrania) trees. Established around** AD **400 and once home to more than 500 monks, Tanzhe was heavily damaged during the Cultural Revolution. It has since been restored, but if you look closely at some of the huge stone tablets, or** *bei*, **littered around the site you'll see that many of the inscriptions have been destroyed. The complex makes an ideal side trip from Jietai Temple or Marco Polo Bridge.** ⊠ *10 km (6 mi) northeast of Jietai Temple, 45 km (28 mi) west of Beijing, Mentougou County* ☏ *010/6086–2500* ⊑ *Y55* ⊙ *Daily 7:30–5:30.*

MARCO POLO BRIDGE 卢沟桥

16 km (10 mi) southwest of Beijing's Guanganmen Gate.

Built in 1192 and reconstructed after severe flooding during the Qing Dynasty, this impressive span—known as Marco Polo Bridge because it was allegedly praised by the Italian wayfarer—is Beijing's oldest bridge. Its 11 segmented-stone arches cross the Yongding River on what was once the Imperial Highway that linked Beijing with central China. The bridge's marble balustrades support nearly 485 carved-stone lions that decorate elaborate handrails. Note the giant stone slabs that comprise the bridge's original roadbed. Carved imperial stelae at either end of the span commemorate the bridge and surrounding scenery.

The Marco Polo Bridge is best remembered in modern times as the spot where invading Japanese armies clashed with Chinese soldiers on June 7, 1937. The assault began Japan's brutal eight-year occupation of eastern China, which ended with Tokyo's surrender at the end of World War II. The bridge has become a popular field-trip destination for Beijing students. On the Beijing side of the span is the **Memorial Hall of the War of Resistance Against Japan.** Below the bridge on the opposite shore, local entrepreneurs rent horses (the asking price is Y120 per hour, but you should bargain) and lead tours of the often-dry grassy riverbed. ⊠ *Near Xidaokou, Fengtai District, Beijing* ☎ *010/8389–4614* 🎫 *Y20* 🕓 *Daily 7 AM–8 PM.*

ZHOUKOUDIAN PEKING MAN SITE 周口店北京人现场

48 km (30 mi) southwest of Beijing.

This area of lime mines and craggy foothills ranks among the world's great paleontological sites (and served as the setting for Amy Tan's *The Bonesetter's Daughter*). In 1929 anthropologists, drawn to Zhoukoudian by apparently human "dragon bones" found in a Beijing apothecary, unearthed a complete cranium and other fossils dubbed *Homo erectus pekinensis*, or Peking Man. These early remains, believed to be nearly 700,000 years old, suggest (as do similar *Homo erectus* discoveries in Indonesia) that humankind's most recent ancestor originated in Asia, not Europe (though today some scientists posit that humans evolved in Africa first and migrated to Asia). A large-scale excavation in the early 1930s further unearthed six skullcaps and other hominid remains, stone tools, evidence of fire, plus a multitude of animal bones, many at the bottom of a large sinkhole believed to be a trap for woolly rhinos and other large game. Sadly, the Peking Man fossils disappeared under mysterious circumstances during World War II, leaving researchers only plaster casts to contemplate. Subsequent digs at Zhoukoudian have yielded nothing equivalent to Peking Man, although archaeologists haven't yet abandoned the search. Trails lead to several hillside excavation sites. A small museum showcases a few (dusty) Peking Man statues, a collection of Paleolithic artifacts, two mummies, and some fine animal fossils, including a bear skeleton and a saber-toothed tiger skull.

Four hundred eighty-five carved stone lions decorate the Marco Polo Bridge.

Because of the importance of Peking Man and the potential for other finds in the area, Zhoukoudian is a UNESCO World Heritage Site, but it may not be of much interest to those without a particular inclination for the subject. If you should find yourself here with little to do after your museum visit and the few dig locations, consider a little hike into the surrounding hills, which are named the Dragon Bone Mountains. ✉ *Zhoukoudian* ☎ *010/6930–1278* 🖃 *Y30* ◷ *Daily 8:30–4:30.*

YUNJU TEMPLE 云居寺

75 km (47 mi) southwest of Beijing.

Yunju Temple is best known for its mind-boggling collection of 14,278 minutely carved Buddhist tablets. To protect the Buddhist canon from destruction by Taoist emperors, the devout Tang-era monk Jing Wan carved Buddhist scriptures into stone slabs that he hid in sealed caves in the cliffs of a mountain. Jing Wan spent 30 years creating these tablets until his death in AD 637; his disciples continued his work for the next millennium into the 17th century, thereby compiling one of the most extensive Buddhist libraries in the world. A small pagoda at the center of the temple complex commemorates the remarkable monk. Although the tablets were originally stored inside Shijing Mountain behind the temple, they are now housed in rooms built along the temple's southern perimeter.

Four central prayer halls, arranged along the hillside above the main gate, contain impressive Ming-era bronze Buddhas. The last in this row, the Dabei Hall, displays the spectacular *Thousand-Armed*

The Eastern Qing Tombs are the most expansive burial grounds in China.

Avalokiteshvara. This 13-foot-tall bronze sculpture—which actually has 24 arms and five heads and stands in a giant lotus flower—is believed to embody boundless compassion. A group of pagodas, led by the 98-foot-tall Northern Pagoda, is all that remains of the original Tang complex. These pagodas are remarkable for their Buddhist reliefs and ornamental patterns. Heavily damaged during the Japanese occupation and again by Maoist radicals in the 1960s, the temple complex remains under renovation. ✉ *Off Fangshan Lu, Nanshangle Xiang, Fangshan County* ☎ *010/6138–9612* 🎫 *Y40* ⏲ *Daily 8:30–5 summer, 8:30–4:30 winter.*

EASTERN QING TOMBS 清东陵

Fodor's Choice ★ *125 km (78 mi) east of Beijing.*

Modeled on the Thirteen Ming Tombs, the Eastern Qing Tombs replicate the Ming spirit ways, walled tomb complexes, and subterranean burial chambers. But they're even more extravagant in their scale and grandeur, and far less touristy. The ruins contain the remains of five emperors, 14 empresses, and 136 imperial concubines, all laid to rest in a broad valley chosen by Emperor Shunzhi (1638–61) while on a hunting expedition. By the Qing's collapse in 1911, the tomb complex covered some 18 square mi (46 square km) of farmland and forested hillside, making it the most expansive burial ground in all China.

The Eastern Qing Tombs are in much better repair than their older Ming counterparts. Although several of the tomb complexes have undergone extensive renovation, none is overdone. Peeling paint, grassy courtyards, and numerous stone bridges and pathways convey a sense of the area's original grandeur. Often visitors are so few that you may feel as if you've stumbled upon an ancient ruin unknown beyond the valley's farming villages.

Of the nine tombs open to the public, two are not to be missed. The first is **Yuling,** the resting place of the Qing Dynasty's most powerful sovereign, Emperor Qianlong (1711–99), who ruled China for 59 years. Beyond the outer courtyards, Qianlong's burial chamber is accessible from inside Stela Hall, where an entry tunnel descends some 65 feet (20 m) into the ground and ends at the first of three elaborately carved marble gates. Beyond, exquisite carvings of Buddhist images and sutras rendered in Tibetan adorn the tomb's walls and ceiling. Qianlong was laid to rest, along with his empress and two concubines, in the third and final marble vault, amid priceless offerings looted by warlords early in the 20th century.

THE LOCALS

The attention foreign travelers receive in rural China may seem overwhelming, but it is usually good-natured and best responded to with politeness. Locals can be extremely kind, inviting you to their homes for tea, a meal, or even to stay the night. If you wish to turn them down, do so politely. However, taking them up on their hospitality can be extremely rewarding. Those who invite you to their homes are doing it out of kindness (Confucius said, "To have friends come from afar, isn't that happiness?"). A gift of a small quantity of fruit or a bottle of *baijiu* (a Chinese spirit distilled from sorghum) is always appreciated.

Dingdongling was built for the infamous Empress Dowager Cixi (1835–1908). Known for her failure to halt Western-imperialist encroachment, Cixi once spent funds allotted to strengthen China's navy on a traditional stone boat for the lake at the Summer Palace. Her burial compound, reputed to have cost 72 tons of silver, is the most elaborate (if not the largest) at the Eastern Qing Tombs. Many of its stone carvings are considered significant because the phoenix, which symbolized the female, is level with, or even above, the imperial (male) dragon—a feature, ordered, no doubt, by the empress herself. A peripheral hall paneled in gold leaf displays some of the luxuries amassed by Cixi and her entourage, including embroidered gowns, jewelry, imported cigarettes, and even a coat for one of her dogs. In a bow to tourist kitsch, the compound's main hall contains a wax statue of Cixi sitting Buddha-like on a lotus petal flanked by a chambermaid and a eunuch.

The Eastern Qing Tombs are a two- to three-hour drive from the capital. The rural scenery is dramatic, and the trip is one of the best full-day excursions outside Beijing. Consider bringing a bed sheet, a bottle of wine, and boxed lunches, as the grounds are ideal for a picnic. ⊠ *Near Malanguan, Hebei province, Zunhua County* ☎ *0315/694–4467* 🖃 *Y120* ⊙ *Daily 8:30–5*

ENGLISH	PINYIN	CHINESE
Beidaihe	Biidàihé	北戴河
Beijing Eunuch Culture Exhibition Hall	Běijīng huànguān wénhuà chénlièguǎn	北京宦官文化陈列馆
Changling	Chánglíng	长陵
Dingling	Dìnglíng	定陵
Eastern Qing Tombs	Qīngdōnglíng	清东陵
Fahai Temple	Fǎhǎi sì	法海寺
The Great Wall	Chángchéng	长城
Huanghua Cheng	Huanghua cheng	黄花城
Jietai Temple	Jiètái sì	戒台寺
Marco Polo Bridge	Lúgōu qiáo	卢沟桥
The Spirit Way	Shén lù	神路
Tanzhe Temple	Tánzhè sì	潭柘寺
Thirteen Ming Tombs	Míng Shísānlíng	明十三陵
Tianjin	Tiānjīn	天津
Tian Yi Mu	Tiányì mù	田义幕
Yesanpo	Yěsān pō	野三坡
Yunju Temple	Yúnjū sì	云居寺
Zhaoling Tomb	Zhāo líng	n/a
Zhoukoudian Peking Man Site	Zhōukǒudiàn Běijīngrén xiànchǎng	周口店北京人现场

CHINESE VOCABULARY

	CHINESE	ENGLISH EQUIVALENT	CHINESE	ENGLISH EQUIVALENT
CONSONANTS				
	b	**b**oat	p	**p**ass
	m	**m**ouse	f	**f**lag
	d	**d**ock	t	**t**ongue
	n	**n**est	l	**l**ife
	g	**g**oat	k	**k**eep
	h	**h**ouse	j	and **y**et
	q	**ch**icken	x	**sh**ort
	zh	ju**dge**	ch	chur**ch**
	sh	**sh**eep	r*	**r**ead
	z	see**ds**	c	do**ts**
	s	**s**eed		
VOWELS				
	ü	**you**	ia	**y**ard
	üe	**you** + e	ian	**y**en
	a	f**a**ther	iang	**young**
	ai	k**i**te	ie	**ye**t
	ao	n**ow**	o	**a**ll
	e	**ea**rn	ou	g**o**
	ei	d**ay**	u	w**oo**d
	er	c**u**rve	ua	w**a**ft
	i	**yi**eld	uo	w**a**ll
	i (after z, c, s, zh, ch, sh)	th**u**nder		

WORD ORDER

The basic Chinese sentence structure is the same as in English, following the pattern of subject-verb-object:

He took my pen.   Tā ná le wǒ de bě.

S   V   O   S   V   O

NOUNS

There are no articles in Chinese, although there are many "counters," which are used when a certain number of a given noun is specified. Various attributes of a noun—such as size, shape, or use—determine which counter is used with that noun. Chinese does not distinguish between singular and plural.

a pen   yìzhī bǐ
a book   yìběn shū

VERBS

Chinese verbs are not conjugated, and they do not have tenses. Instead, a system of word order, word repetition, and the addition of a number of adverbs serves to indicate the tense of a verb, whether the verb is a suggestion or an order, or even whether the verb is part of a question. Tāzaì ná wǒ de bǐ. (He is taking my pen.) Tā ná le wǒ de bǐ. (He took my pen.) Tā you méi you ná wǒ de bǐ? (Did he take my pen?) Tā yào ná wǒ de bǐ. (He will take my pen.)

TONES

In English, intonation patterns can indicate whether a sentence is a statement (He's hungry.), a question (He's hungry?), or an exclamation (He's hungry!). In Chinese, words have a particular tone value, and these tones are important in determining the meaning of a word. Observe the meanings of the following examples, each said with one of the four tones found in standard Chinese: mā (high, steady tone): mother; má (rising tone, like a question): fiber; mǎ (dipping tone): horse; and mà (dropping tone): swear.

PHRASES

You don't need to master the entire Chinese language to spend a week in China, but taking charge of a few key phrases in the language can aid you in just getting by.

COMMON GREETINGS

Hello/Good morning	Nǐ hǎo/Zǎoshàng hǎo
Good evening	Wǎnshàng hǎo
Good-bye	Zàijiàn
Title for a married woman or an older unmarried woman	Tàitai/Fūrén
Title for a young and unmarried woman	Xiǎojiě
Title for a man	Xiēnshēng
How are you?	Nǐ hǎo ma?
Fine, thanks. And you?	Hěn hǎo. Xièxie. Nǐ ne?
What is your name?	Nǐ jiào shénme míngzi?
My name is . . .	Wǐ jiào . . .
Nice to meet you	Hěn gěoxìng rènshì nǐ
I'll see you later.	Huítóu jiàn.

POLITE EXPRESSIONS

Please	Qǐng.
Thank you	Xièxiè.
Thank you very much.	Fēicháng gǎnxie.
You're welcome.	Bú yòng xiè.
Yes, thank you.	Shì de, xièxiè.
No, thank you.	Bù, xièxiè.
I beg your pardon.	Qǐng yuánliàng.
I'm sorry.	Hěn baòqiàn.
Pardon me.	Dùibùqǐ.
That's okay.	Méi shénme.
It doesn't matter.	Méi guěnxi.
Do you speak English?	Nǐ shuō Yīngyǔ ma?
Yes.	Shì de.
No.	Bù.
Maybe.	Huòxǔ.
I can speak a little.	Wǐ néng shūo yī diǎnr.
I understand a little.	Wǐ dǐng yì diǎnr.
I don't understand.	Wǐ bù dǐng.
I don't speak Chinese very well.	Wǐ Zhōngwén shūo de bù haǐ.
Would you repeat that, please?	Qǐng zài shūo yíbiàn?
I don't know.	Wǐ bù zhīdaò.
No problem.	Méi wèntí.
It's my pleasure.	Lèyì er wéi.

NEEDS AND QUESTION WORDS

I'd like . . .	Wǐ xiǎng . . .
I need . . .	Wǐ xūyào . . .
What would you like?	Nǐ yaò shénme?
Please bring me . . .	Qǐng gěi wǐ . . .
I'm looking for . . .	Wǐ zài zhǎo . . .
I'm hungry.	Wǐ è le.

I'm thirsty.	Wǐ kǐukě.
It's important.	Hěn zhòngyào.
It's urgent.	Hěn jǐnjí.
How?	Zěnmeyàng?
How much?	Duōshǎo?
How many?	Duōshǎo gè?
Which?	Nǎ yí gè?
What?	Shénme?
What kind of?	Shénme yàng de?
Who?	Shuí?
Where?	Nǎli?
When?	Shénme shíhòu?
What does this mean?	Zhè shì shénme yìsi?
What does that mean?	Nà shì shénme yìsi?
How do you say . . . in Chinese?	. . . yòng Zhōngwén zěnme shūo?

AT THE AIRPORT

Where is . . .	. . . zài nǎr?
customs?	Hǎigūan
passport control?	Hùzhào jiǎnyàn
the information booth?	Wènxùntái
the ticketing counter?	Shòupiàochù
the baggage claim?	Xínglǐchù
the ground transportation?	Dìmìan jiěotōng
Is there a bus service	Yǐu qù chéng lǐ de gōnggòng
to the city?	qìchē ma?
Where are . . .	. . . zài nǎr?
the international departures?	Guójì hángběn chūfě diǎn
the international arrivals?	Guójì hángběn dàodá diǎn
What is your nationality?	Nǐ shì něi guó rén?
I am an American.	Wǐ shì Měiguó rén.
I am Canadian.	Wǐ shì Jiěnádà rén.

AT THE HOTEL, RESERVING A ROOM

I would like a room . . .	Wǐ yào yí ge fángjiěn.
for one person	děnrén fáng
for two people	shuěngrén fěng
for tonight	jīntīan wǎnshàng
for two nights	liǎng gè wǎnshàng
for a week	yí ge xīngqī
Do you have a different room?	Nǐ hái yǐu bié de fángjiěn ma?
with a bath	dài yùshì de fángjiěn
with a shower	dài línyù de fángjiěn
with a toilet	dài cèsuǐ de fángjiěn
with air-conditioning	yǐu kōngtiáo de fángjiěn
How much is it?	Duōshǎo qián?
My bill, please.	Qǐng jiézhàng.

AT THE RESTAURANT

Where can we find a good restaurant?	Zài nǎr kěyǐ zhǎodào yìjiě hǎo cěnguǎn?
We'd like a(n) . . . restaurant.	Wǐmen xiǎng qù yì gè . . . cěnguǎn.
elegant	gěo jí
fast-food	kuàicěn
inexpensive	piányì de
seafood	hǎixiěn
vegetarian	sùshí
Café	Kěfeī diàn
A table for two	Liǎng wèi
Waiter, a menu please.	Fúwùyuán, qǐng gěi wǐmen càiděn.
The wine list, please.	Qǐng gěi wǐmen jǐuděn.
Appetizers	Kěiwèi shíwù
Main course	Zhǔ cài
Dessert	Tiándiǎn
What would you like?	Nǐ yào shénme cài?
What would you like to drink?	Nǐ yào hē shénme yǐnliào?

Can you recommend a good wine?	Nǐ néng tūijiàn yí ge hǎo jǐu ma?
Wine, please.	Qǐng lǎi diǎn jǐu.
Beer, please.	Qǐng lǎi diǎn píjiǔ.
I didn't order this.	Wǐ méiyǐu diǎn zhè gè.
That's all, thanks.	Jiù zhèxie, xièxiè.
The check, please.	Qǐng jiézhàng.
Cheers!/Bottoms Up!	Gēnbēi! Zhù nǐ shēntì
To your health!	jiànkěng.

OUT ON THE TOWN

Where can I find . . .	Nǎr yǐu . . .
an art museum?	yìshù bówùguǎn?
a museum of natural history?	zìránlìshǐ bówùguǎn?
a history museum?	lìshǐ bówugǔan?
a gallery?	huàláng?
interesting architecture?	yǐuqù de jiànzhùwù?
a church?	jiàotáng?
the zoo?	dòngwùyuán?
I'd like . . .	Wǐ xiǎng . . .
to see a play.	kàn xì.
to see a movie.	kàn diànyǐng.
to see a concert.	qù yīnyuèhuì.
to see the opera.	kàn gējù.
to go sightseeing.	qù guěnguěng.
to go on a bike ride.	qí děnchē.

SHOPPING

Where is the best place to go shopping for . . .	Mǎi . . . zuì hǎo qù nǎr?
clothes?	yīfu
food?	shíwù
souvenirs?	jìniànpǐn
furniture?	jīajù
fabric?	bùliào

antiques?	gǔdǐng
books?	shūjí
sporting goods?	yùndòng wùpǐn
electronics?	diànqì
computers?	diànnǎo

DIRECTIONS

Excuse me. Where is . . .	Duìbùqǐ . . . zài nǎr?
the bus stop?	Qìchēzhàn
the subway station?	Dìtiězhàn
the rest room?	Xǐshǐujiěn
the taxi stand?	Chūzū chēzhàn
the nearest bank?	Zùijìn de yínháng
the hotel?	Lü˘guǎn
To the right	Zài yòubiěn.
To the left.	Zài zuǐbiěn.
Straight ahead.	Wǎng qián zhízǐu.
It's near here.	Jiuzài zhè fùjìn.
Go back.	Wǎng húi zǐu.
Next to . . .	Jǐnkào . . .

TIME

What time is it?	Xiànzài shénme shíjiěn?
It is noon.	Zhōngwǔ.
It is midnight.	Bànyè.
It is 9:00 a.m.	Shàngwǔ jǐu diǎn.
It is 1:00 p.m.	Xiàwǔ yì diǎn.
It is 3 o'clock.	Sěn diǎn (zhōng).
5:15	Wǔ diǎn shíwǔ fēn.
7:30	Qī diǎn sěnshí (bàn).
9:45	Jǐu diǎn sìshíwǔ.
Now	Xiànzài
Later	Wǎn yì diǎnr

Immediately	Mǎshàng
Soon	Hěn kuài

DAYS OF THE WEEK

Monday	Xīngqī yī
Tuesday	Xīngqī èr
Wednesday	Xīngqī sěn
Thursday	Xīngqī sì
Friday	Xīngqī wǔ
Saturday	Xīngqī liu
Sunday	Xīngqī rì (tiěn)

MODERN CONNECTIONS

Where can I find . . .	Zài nǎr kěyǐ shǐ yòng . . .
a telephone?	dianhuà?
a fax machine?	chuánzhēnjī?
an Internet connection?	guójì wǎnglù?
How do I call the United States?	Gěi Měiguó dǎ diànhuà zěnme dǎ?
I need . . .	Wǐ xūyào . . .
a fax sent.	fě chuánzhēn.
a hookup to the Internet.	yǔ guójì wǎnglù liánjiē.
a computer.	diànnǎo.
a package sent overnight.	liányè bǎ běoguǐ jìchū.
some copies made.	fùyìn yìxiē wénjiàn.
a VCR and monitor.	lùyǐngjī he xiānshiqì.
an overhead projector and markers.	huàndēngjī he biěoshìqì.

EMERGENCIES AND SAFETY

Help!	Jiumìng a!
Fire!	Jiuhuǐ a!
I need a doctor.	Wǐ yào kàn yīshēng.
Call an ambulance!	Mǎshàng jiào jiuhùchē!
What happened?	Fěshēng le shénme shì?
I am/My wife is/My husband is/	Wǐ/Wǐ qīzi/Wǐ Zhàngfu/

My friend is/Someone is . . . very sick.	Wǒ péngyǒu/Yǒu rén . . .
having a heart attack.	bìng de hěn lìhài.
choking.	yēzhù le.
losing consciousness.	yūndǎo le.
about to vomit.	yào ǒutù le.
having a seizure.	yòu fēbìng le.
stuck.	bèi kǎ zhù le.
I can't breathe.	Wǒ bù néng hūxī.
I tripped and fell.	Wǒ bàn dǎo le.
I cut myself.	Wǒ gē shāng le.
I drank too much.	Wǒ jiǔ hē de tài duō le.
I don't know.	Wǒ bù zhīdào.
I've injured my . . .	Wǒ de . . . shòushāng le.
head	tóu
neck	bózi
back	Bèi
arm	shǒubèi
leg	tuǐ
foot	jiǎo
eye(s)	yǎnjīng
I've been robbed.	Wǒ bèi qiǎng le.

NUMBERS

0	Líng
1	Yī
2	Er
3	Sān
4	Sì
5	Wǔ
6	Lìu
7	Qī
8	Bā

9	Jǐu
10	Shí
11	Shíyī
12	Shí'èr
13	Shísĕn
14	Shísì
15	Shíwǔ
16	Shílìu
17	Shíqī
18	Shíbĕ
19	Shíjĭu
20	Ershí
21	Ershíyī
22	Ershí'èr
23	Eshísĕn
30	Sĕnshí
40	Sìshí
50	Wǔshí
60	Lìushí
70	Qīshí
80	Bĕshí
90	Jĭushí
100	Yìbǎi
1,000	Yìqiĕn
1,100	Yìqiĕn yìbǎi
2,000	Liǎngqiĕn
10,000	Yíwàn
100,000	Shíwàn
1,000,000	Bǎiwàn

Travel Smart Beijing

WORD OF MOUTH

"Getting a taxi to take you anywhere within reason at short notice is no problem at all in Beijing. As your chance of getting an English-speaking driver will be on par with winning the lottery, I'd ask your hotel concierge or front desk to make the arrangements."

—Neil_Oz

GETTING HERE AND AROUND

Beijing has exploded over the past three decades thanks to China's impressive economic boom. For the last few years that growth went into overdrive as the city prepared to host the 2008 Olympics. They invested around $20 billion on infrastructure, adding impressive modernistic architecture to its skyline in the process. The constant music of machinery—and a steady by-product of dust—filled the air as Beijing erected new expressways, subways, and buildings. Whole neighborhoods were demolished, constructed, or renovated. Some, such as the quaint Gulou neighborhood near the Drum and Bell towers in north-central Beijing, are preparing for the bulldozers as prime property areas become scarcer. Old-timers can hardly recognize many sections of the city, and maps go out of date almost overnight. It's a good idea to get the latest bilingual version on arrival.

The city's five concentric ring roads look like a target, with the Forbidden City in the bull's-eye. The Second Ring Road follows the line of the old city walls, and circular subway Line 2 runs below it. Note that, oddly, there is no First Ring Road. The Third Ring Road passes through part of Beijing's Central Business District (CBD) and links up with the Airport Expressway. Traffic in Beijing can be a nightmare, especially at rush hour when the gridlock extends from the center of the city all the way out to the Fourth Ring Road. With two modern subway lines recently added, and several more under construction, taking the subway is becoming a good option. The new Capital Airport Subway Line (20 minutes from the airport to the Dongzhimen subway stop at the northeast of the city center) and Beijing's new electronic subway fare system—where all rides no matter how distant cost a flat Y2, or around $0.30, fare—are transport boons.

The city's wide main streets are laid out on a grid system. Roads run north–south or east–west. These compass points often make up part of the street name, so *bei* (north), *dong* (east), *nan* (south), *xi* (west), and *zhong* (middle) are useful words to know. Networks of ancient lanes and alleys known as *hutong* run between these main streets, though they are fast falling prey to developers and many have suffered the wrath of the wrecking ball.

Beijing's most important thoroughfare runs east–west along the top of Tiananmen Square. Generally known as Chang'an Jie or the "Avenue of Heavenly Peace," it actually changes names several times along its length (as do many other major streets).

The three remaining ring roads have equally unimaginative names (Fourth, Fifth, Sixth). Along the center of the north Fourth Ring Road is Olympic Park, where you'll find the impressive National Stadium ("the Bird's Nest") and the National Aquatics Center ("the Water Cube"). If you're sticking to central Beijing, these roads aren't much use, though fare-hungry taxi drivers would love you to believe otherwise.

▌ BY AIR

Beijing is one of China's three major international hubs, along with Shanghai and Hong Kong. The number of nonstop flights to Beijing has been increasing as China's air-travel industry continues to liberalize. You can catch a nonstop flight here from New York (13¾ hours), Washington, D.C. (13 hours), Chicago (13½ hours), Sydney (11½ hours), Los Angeles (13 hours), Seattle (11 hours), and London (11 hours). As new nonstop flights seem to be added every few months, check travel sites online or with your travel agent for details. Besides state-run stalwart Air China, carriers such as Hainan

Airlines, China Southern, and China Eastern have all added nonstop flights recently. Multiple-stop flights from other cities generally stop in Tokyo, Seoul, Hong Kong, or Vancouver.

Airlines and Airports Airline and Airport Links.com (⊕ *www.airlineandairportlinks.com*) has links to many of the world's airlines and airports.

Airline Security Issues Transportation Security Administration (⊕ *www.tsa.gov*) has answers for almost every question that might come up.

AIRLINE TICKETS

There are a number of Chinese cities included in the One World Alliance Visit Asia Pass. They include major destinations like Beijing, Shanghai, and Hong Kong, as well as interior stops such as Xi'an, Chengdu, Xiamen, Nanjing, Kunming, and Wuhan. Cities are grouped into zones and there is a flat rate for each zone. The pass does not include flights from the United States. Inquire through American Airlines, Cathay Pacific, or any other One World member. It won't be the cheapest way to get around, but you'll be flying on some of the world's best airlines.

If you are flying into Asia on a Sky Team airline (Delta or Continental, for example) you're eligible to purchase their Asia Pass or China Pass. The China Pass allows travel to 106 destinations and prices are based on zone structure. The pass works on a coupon basis; the minimum three coupons cost $600, whereas six come to $1,128.

The Star Alliance China Air Pass is a good choice if you plan to stop in multiple destinations within China. With one ticket you can choose from 71 different locations, though the ticket is only good for three to 10 individual flights on Air China or Shanghai Airlines. The catch? You have to fly into the country on one of their flights. Hong Kong isn't included in the pass, but Shenzhen, just over the border, gets you close enough. Bear in mind that Chinese domestic flight schedules can be changed or canceled at a moment's notice.

Air Pass Info Asia Pass (☎ *800/523–3273 Continental, 800/221–1212 Delta* ⊕ *www. skyteam.com*). **China Air Pass** (☎ *800/241– 6522 United, 800/428–4322 U.S. Airways, Star Alliance members* ⊕ *www.staralliance.com*). **Visit Asia Pass** (☎ *800/233–2742 OneWorld Alliance Cathay Pacific* ⊕ *www.oneworld.com*).

AIRPORTS

The efficient Beijing Capital International Airport (PEK) is 27 km (17 mi) northeast of the city center. There are three terminals, connected by walkways and a tram system. Departures and arrivals operate out of all of them; T1 serves mainly domestic flights, while T2 and T3 serve both domestic and international flights. If you can't find your flight on the departure board when you arrive, check that you're in the correct terminal. The best advice is to check with the airport Web site before you depart from Beijing, as you'll need to let the taxi driver know which terminal you need to be dropped off at.

Beijing's airport tax (enigmatically known as the "airport construction fee") is Y90 for international flights and Y50 for domestic. These taxes are now incorporated into your ticket prices, replacing the antiquated coupon system Beijing had before.

Clearing customs and immigration can take a while depending on how busy the airport is. Make sure you arrive at least two hours before your scheduled flight time. Also be sure to fill out the departure card before getting in line at the immigration check or you'll have to leave the line, fill out the card, and get back in at the end.

Both Chinese and Western-style fast-food outlets are available if you hunt around. Most are open from around 7 AM to 11 PM. Prices for food and drink have been standardized for the most part at the various concessions, but it's still ridiculously expensive.

The airport is open all day. There is an uninspiring transit lounge for T1 and T2 in which to while away the hours. T3's waiting area is a bit more comfortable. If you've got a long stopover and need a rest, consider buying a package from the Plaza Premium Traveler's Lounge, near Gate 11 in the international section of T2, or on the left-hand side as you enter the domestic area, also in T2. It has comfortable armchairs, Internet access, newspapers, and a buffet. Unfortunately, it's closed between midnight and 6 AM. There's another rest area in the basement, with private rooms, that is open 24 hours. The third-floor recreation center has traditional massage facilities and a hairdresser.

While wandering the airport, someone may approach you offering to carry your luggage, or even just to give you directions. Be aware that this "helpful" stranger will almost certainly expect payment.

Airport Information Beijing Capital International Airport (PEK) (☎ 010/6454–1100 ⊕ www.bcia.com.cn).

GROUND TRANSPORTATION

The easiest way to get from the airport to Beijing is by taxi. In addition, most major hotels have representatives at the airport able to arrange a car or minivan. When departing from Beijing by plane, prebook airport transport through your hotel.

When you arrive, head for the clearly labeled taxi line just outside the terminal, beyond a small covered parking area. The (usually long) line moves quickly. Ignore offers from touts trying to coax you away from the line—they're privateers looking to rip you off. At the head of the line, a dispatcher will give you your taxi's number, useful in case of complaints or forgotten luggage. Prices per km are displayed on the side of the cab. Insist that drivers use their meters, and do not negotiate a fare. If the driver is unwilling to comply, feel free to change taxis.

Most of the taxis serving the airport are large-model cars, with a flag-fall of Y10 (good for 3½ km) plus Y2 per additional km. The trip to the center of Beijing costs around Y90, including the Y10 toll for the airport expressway. If you're caught in rush-hour traffic, expect standing surcharges of Y2 per every five minutes. In light traffic it takes about 40 minutes to reach the city center, during rush hour expect a one-hour cab ride. After 11 PM, taxis impose a 20% late-night surcharge.

Another option is the newly built Capital Airport Subway Line which departs from T2 and T3 and goes to Dongzhimen station on the northeast corner of the Second Ring Road, on the edge of central Beijing. The best thing about this: only 20 minutes travel time at a price of Y25. Air-conditioned airport shuttle buses are another cheap way of getting into town. There are six numbered routes, all of which leave from outside the arrivals area. Tickets cost Y16—buy them from the ticket booth just inside the arrival halls. Most services run every 15 to 30 minutes. There's a detailed route map on the airport Web site.

FLIGHTS

Air China is the country's flagship carrier. It operates nonstop flights from Beijing to various North American and European cities. Its safety record has improved dramatically, and it is now part of Star Alliance. China Southern is the major carrier for domestic routes. Like all Chinese carriers, it's a regional subsidiary of the Civil Aviation Administration of China (CAAC).

You can make reservations and buy tickets in the United States directly through airline Web sites or with travel agencies. It's worth contacting a Chinese travel agency like China International Travel Service (CITS) (⇨ *Visitor Information below*) to compare prices, as these can vary substantially. If you're in China and want to book flights to other cities in the country, the Web site ⊕ *www.ctrip.com* is an excellent option. Flights though this Web site are often much cheaper than if you book them through a foreign Web site.

The service on most Chinese airlines is more on par with low-cost American airlines than with big international carriers—be prepared for limited legroom, iffy food, and possibly no personal TV. More important, always arrive at least two hours before departure, as chronic overbooking means latecomers lose their seats.

Airline Contacts Continental Airlines (☎ 800/523–3273 for U.S. and Mexico reservations, 800/231–0856 for international reservations ⊕ www.continental. com). **United Airlines** (☎ 800/864–8331 for U.S. reservations, 800/538–2929 for international reservations ⊕ www.united.com). **Air Canada** (☎ 010/6468–2001 in Beijing ⊕ www.aircanada.com). **British Airways** (☎ 010/6512–4070 ⊕ www.ba.com).

▌ BY BUS

TO BEIJING

China has fabulous luxury long-distance buses with air-conditioning and movies. However, buying tickets on them can be complicated if you don't speak Chinese, and you may end up on a cramped school bus. Taking a train or an internal flight is often much easier. Buses depart from the city's several long-distance bus stations. The main ones are: Dongzhimen (Northeast); Muxiyuan (at Haihutun in the South); Beijiao, also called Dewai (North); and Majuan or Guangqumen (East).

Bus Information Note that information is not usually available in English at any of these phone numbers and sometimes the numbers don't even work. It's best to have your hotel or a travel agent make arrangements.

Beijiao (✉ Huayan Beili, Chaoyang District ☎ 010/8284–7096). **Dongzhimen** (✉ Dongzhimenwaixie Jie, Chaoyang District ☎ 010/6467–4995). **Muxiyuan** (✉ Nanyuan Lu, Fengtai District ☎ 010/6726–7149). **Majuan** (✉ Guangqumenwai Lu, Chaoyang District ☎ 010/6771–7620).

NOT SO LUCKY NUMBER?

Sichuan Airlines bought the number 28/8888–8888 for 2.33 million yuan ($280,723) during an auction of more than 100 telephone numbers in 2003, making it the most expensive telephone number in the world. The number eight (*ba* in Chinese) is considered lucky in China, as it sounds similar to *fa*, the first character in the phrase *facai*, which means "to gain wealth." Nevertheless, many doubt the luck of this number since the deluge of misfortune that struck China in 2008, most important the 8.0 Sichuan earthquake that killed around 70,000 people.

WITHIN BEIJING

Unless you know Beijing well, public buses aren't the best choice for getting around. There are hundreds of routes, which are hot and crowded in summer and cold and crowded in winter. Just getting on and off can be, quite literally, a fight.

The Beijing Public Transportation Corporation is the city's largest bus service provider. Routes 1 to 199 are regular city buses, and cost a flat fare of Y1. Routes 201 through 212 only run at night, costing Y2. Routes numbered 300 or higher are suburban, and fares depend on how far you're going—have your destination written in Chinese, as you have to tell the conductor so they can calculate your fare. If you bought an IC card for the subway, you can use it on buses. Most buses allow you to scan your card as you board. On the suburban buses you'll scan as you board and as you depart, calculating the fare. For buses that go even farther afield, there is a conductor onboard who will take your fare or scan your card. Newer, air-conditioned buses have an 800 route number; prices vary, but start at Y3. They also run more expensive tourist buses going to sights in and around the city—to the Summer Palace and Great Wall, for example. Prices start at Y40.

Contact **Beijing Public Transportation Corporation** (⊕ www.bjbus.com).

▌ BY CAR

In a nutshell, renting a car is not a possibility when vacationing in Beijing: neither U.S. licenses nor IDPs are recognized in China. Nevertheless, this restriction should be cause for relief, as the city traffic is terrible and its drivers manic. A far better idea, if you want to get around by car, is to put yourself in the experienced hands of a local driver and sit back and relax. All the same, consider your itinerary carefully before doing so—the expanded subway system can be far quicker for central areas. Save the cars for excursions outside the city.

The quickest way to hire a car and driver is to flag down a taxi and hire it for the day. After some negotiating, expect to pay between Y350 and Y600, depending on the type of car. Most hotels can make arrangements for you, though they often charge you double that rate—you can probably guess whose pocket the difference goes into. Most drivers do not speak English, so it's a good idea to have your destination and hotel names written down in Chinese, as well as a few sentences telling them you'd like to rent their service for the day.

Another alternative is American car-rental agency Avis, which includes mandatory chauffeurs as part of all rental packages. A car and driver usually cost Y740 to Y850 per day for an economy vehicle.

Contacts **Avis** (☎ 400/882–1119 ⊕ www. avischina.com).

▌ BY SUBWAY

With street-level traffic getting more crazed by the minute, Beijing's quick and efficient subway system is an excellent way to get about town. After operating for years with only two lines, the network is growing exponentially—there are now eight either fully or partly operating lines.

Extensions on some of these, as well as brand new lines, are in the construction or planning phase.

At this writing, there are nine lines open. Line 1 (red) runs east–west under Chang'an Jie, crossing through the heart of the city. The circle line, or Line 2 (blue), runs roughly under the Second Ring Road. There are interchange stations between lines 1 and 2 at Fuxingmen and Jianguomen. The first north–south line, Line 5, gives access to the Lama Temple, the Temple of Heaven, and the Temple of Earth. Part of Line 10 is now open around the Olympic Village and the Olympic Branch Line extends north from there. The newest, the Hong Kong–operated Line 4, runs from the city's university district in Haidian in the northwest and skirts southeast through the western part of central Beijing. The Airport Line connects the Dongzhimen interchange with the airport—now a 20-minute jaunt at about Y25. The two remaining lines are mainly used by commuters and are less useful for sightseeing. The Batong Line extends Line 1 eastward, whereas Line 13 loops north off Line 2.

Subway stations are marked by blue signs with a "D" (for *di tie*, or subway) in a circle. Signs are not always obvious, so be prepared to hunt around for entrances or ask directions; *Di tie zhan zai nar?* (Where's the subway station?) is a useful phrase to remember. But sometimes simply saying *di tie* with an inquiring look may get you better results since native Chinese speakers are often confused by the mispronounced tones uttered by foreigners.

Stations are usually clean and safe, as are trains. Navigating the subway is very straightforward: station names are clearly displayed in Chinese and pinyin, and there are maps in each station. Once on board, each stop is clearly announced on a loudspeaker in Chinese and sometimes in English.

▌ BY TAXI

Taxis are plentiful, easy to spot, and by far the most comfortable way to get around Beijing, though increasing traffic means they're not always the fastest. There's a flag-fall of Y10 for the first 4 km (2½ mi), then Y2 per kilometer thereafter. After 11 PM flag-fall goes up to Y11, and there's a 20% surcharge per kilometer.

Drivers usually know the terrain well, but most don't speak English; having your destination written in Chinese is a good idea. (Keep a card with the name of your hotel on it for the return trip.) Hotel doormen can also help you tell the driver where you're going. It's a good idea to study a map and have some idea where you are, as some drivers will take you for a ride—a much longer one—if they think they can get away with it.

▌ BY TRAIN

China's enormous rail network is one of the world's busiest. Trains are usually safe and run strictly to schedule. Although there are certain intricacies to buying tickets, once you've got one, trips are generally hassle-free. Beijing is a major rail hub. Services to the rest of China leave from its four huge stations. The Trans-Siberian Railway and services to Shanghai, among others, leave from Beijing Zhan, the main station. Trains to Hong Kong and to areas in the west and south of China leave from Beijing Xi Zhan (West). Most of the Z-series trains (nonstop luxury services) come into these two stations. Lesser lines to the north and east of the country leave from Beijing Bei Zhan (North) and Beijing Dong Zhan (East). C-series and D-series

BIG TRAIN RIDES

Taking the Trans-Siberian railway is a serious undertaking. The two weekly services cover the 5,000 mi between Moscow and Beijing. The Trans-Manchurian is a Russian train that goes through northeast China, whereas the Trans-Mongolian is a Chinese train that goes through the Great Wall and crosses the Gobi Desert. Both have first-class compartments with four berths (Y1,800), or luxury two-berth compartments (Y2,200), one-way.

trains (intercity nonstop rail) go to Beijing Nan Zhan (South).

You can buy most tickets 10 days in advance; two to three days ahead is usually enough time, except around the three national holidays—Chinese New Year (two days in mid-January to February, depending on the lunar calendar of that particular year), Labor Day (May 1), and National Day (October 1). If you can, avoid traveling then—tickets sell out weeks in advance.

The cheapest rates are at the train station itself; there are special ticket offices for foreigners at both the Beijing Zhan (first floor) and Beijing Xi Zhan (second floor). You can only pay using cash. Most travel agents, including CITS, can book tickets for a small surcharge (Y20 to Y50), saving you the hassle of going to the station. You can also buy tickets through online retailers like China Train Ticket. They'll deliver the tickets to your hotel (keep in mind you often end up paying double the station rate).

Overpriced dining cars serve meals that are often inedible, so you'd do better to make use of the massive thermoses of boiled water in each compartment and take along your own noodles or instant soup, as the locals do.

Trains are always crowded, but you are guaranteed your designated seat, though not always the overhead luggage rack. Note that theft on trains is increasing;

on overnight trains, sleep with your valuables or else keep them on the inside of the bunk.

You can find out just about everything about Chinese train travel at Seat 61's fabulous Web site. China Highlights has a searchable online timetable for major train routes. The tour operator Travel China Guide has an English-language Web site that can help you figure out train schedules and fares.

Information Note that the information numbers at train stations are usually only in Chinese.

Beijing Bei Zhan (⊠ *North Station, 1 Xizhimenwai Beibinhelu, Xicheng District* ☎ *010/5186–6223*). **Beijing Nan Zhan** (⊠ *South Station, Yongdingmen, Chongwen District* ☎ *010/5183–7262*). **Beijing Xi Zhan** (⊠ *West Station, Lianhuachi Dong Lu, Haidian District* ☎ *010/5182–6253*). **Beijing Zhan** (⊠ *Main Station, Beijing Zhan Jie, Dongcheng District* ☎ *010/5101–9999*). **China Highlights** (⊕ *www.chinahighlights.com/china-trains/ index.htm*). **Seat 61** (⊕ *www.seat61.com/ China.htm*). **Travel China Guide** (⊕ *www. travelchinaguide.com/china-trains/index.htm*).

ESSENTIALS

▮ ACCOMMODATIONS

Opening a hotel seems quite the thing to do in Beijing these days. That said, it's not always easy to choose a hotel: the Chinese star system is a little unpredictable, and Web sites are often misleading. For lesser establishments, try to get recent personal recommendations: the forums on Fodors. com are a great place to start.

"Location, location, location" should be your mantra when booking a Beijing hotel, especially if you're only in town for a few days. It's a big city: there's no point schlepping halfway across it for one particular hotel when a similar option is available in a more convenient area. Consider where you'll be going (Summer Palace? Forbidden City? Great Wall?), then pick your bed. (⇨ *For dining and lodging price charts, see the opening pages of Chapters 3 and 4.*)

APARTMENT AND HOUSE RENTALS

There's an abundance of furnished short- and long-term rental properties in Beijing. Prices vary wildly. The priciest are luxury apartments and villas, usually far from the city center and best accessible by (chauffeur-driven) car. Usually described as "serviced apartments," these often include gyms and pools; rents can be over $2,000 a month. There are a lot of well-located midrange properties in the city. They're usually clean, with new furnishings; rents start at $500 a month. Finally, for longer, budget-friendly stays, there are normal local apartments. These are firmly off the tourist circuit and often cost only a third of the price of the mid-range properties. Expect mismatched furniture, fewer amenities, and—we won't lie—varying insect populations.

Property sites like Wuwoo, Move and Stay, Sublet, and Pacific Properties have hundreds of apartments all over town. The online classifieds pages in local English-language magazines such as *The Beijinger, City Weekend*, or the Craigslist Beijing page are good places to start.

ONLINE BOOKING RESOURCES

Contacts **The Beijinger** (⊕ *www.thebeijinger. com*). **City Weekend** (⊕ *www.cityweekend. com.cn*). **Craigslist Beijing** (⊕ *beijing. craigslist.com.cn*). **Move and Stay** (⊕ *www. moveandstay.com/beijing*). **Pacific Properties** (☎ *010/6581–3728* ⊕ *www.worthenpacific. com*). **Sublet.com** (⊕ *www.sublet.com*). **Wuwoo** (☎ *010/5166–7126* ⊕ *www.wuwoo. com*).

HOMESTAYS

Single travelers can arrange homestays (often in combination with language courses) through China Homestay Club. Generally these are in upper-middle-class homes that are about as expensive as a cheap hotel—prices range from $150 to $180 a week. Nine times out of 10, the family has a small child in need of daily English conversation classes. ChinaHomestay.org is a different organization that charges a single placement fee of $300 for a stay of three months or less.

Organizations **China Homestay Club** (⊕ *www.homestay.com.cn*). **ChinaHomestay. org** (⊕ *www.chinahomestay.org*).

HOSTELS

Budget accommodation options are improving in Beijing. However, the term "hostel" is still used vaguely—the only thing guaranteed is shared dorm rooms; other facilities vary and some hostels do include private rooms, so it is worth checking into. There are several clean youth hostels downtown, including three HI–affiliated properties, but flea-ridden dumps are also common, so always ask to see your room before paying. Try to pick a hostel close to a subway, and avoid properties beyond the Third Ring Road. A private room in a low-end hotel is often just as cheap as these so-called hostels; some guesthouses and hotels also have cheaper dorm beds in addition to regular rooms. Hostelworld.com is a good site to visit, especially for peer feedback on everything from service to cleanliness.

Information Hostelling International—USA (☎ *301/495–1240* ⊕ *www.hiusa.org*). **Youth Hostel Association of China** (☎ *020/8751–3733* ⊕ *www.yhachina.com*). **Hostelworld. com** (⊕ *www.hostelworld.com*).

▮ COMMUNICATIONS

INTERNET

Beijing is a very Internet-friendly place for travelers with laptop computers. Most mid- to high-end hotels have in-room Internet access—if the hotel doesn't have a server you can usually access a government-provided ISP, which only charges you for the phone call. Wi-Fi is growing exponentially. Café chains like Starbucks are good places to try.

Most hotels usually have a computer with Internet access that you can use. Internet cafés are ubiquitous; it's an unstable business and new ones open and close all the time—ask your hotel for a recommendation. Prices vary considerably. Near the northern university districts you could pay as little as Y2 to Y3 per hour; slicker downtown places could cost 10 times that.

⚠ Remember that there is strict government control of the Internet in China. There's usually no problem with Web-based mail, but you may be unable to access news and even blogging sites.

Contacts Cybercafes (⊕ *www.cybercafes. com*) lists more than 4,000 Internet cafés worldwide.

PHONES

The country code for China is 86; the city code for Beijing is 10 (omit the first "0"), and the city code for Shanghai is 21. To call China from the United States or Canada, dial the international access code (011), followed by the country code (86), the area or city code, and the eight-digit phone number.

Numbers beginning with 800 within China are toll-free. Note that a call from China to a toll-free number in the United States or Hong Kong is a full-tariff international call.

CALLING WITHIN CHINA

The Chinese phone system is cheap and efficient. You can make local and long-distance calls from your hotel or any public phone on the street. Some pay phones accept coins, but it's easier to buy an IC calling card, available at convenience stores and newsstands (⇨ *See Calling Cards, below*). Local calls are generally free from landlines, though your hotel might charge a nominal rate. Long-distance rates in China are very low. Calling from your hotel room is a viable option, as hotels can only add a 15% service charge.

Beijing's city code is 010, and Beijing phone numbers have eight digits. When calling within the city, you don't need to use "010." In general, city codes appear written with a 0 in front of them; if not, you need to add this when calling another city within China.

For directory assistance, dial 114, or 2689–0114 for help in English (though you may not get through). If you want information for other cities, dial the city code followed by 114 (note that this is considered a long-distance call). For example, if you're in Beijing and need directory assistance for a Shanghai number, dial 021–114. The operators do not speak English, so if you don't speak Chinese you're best off asking your hotel for help.

To make long-distance calls from a public phone you need an IC card (⇨ *Calling Cards, below*). To place a long-distance call, dial 0, the city code, and the eight-digit phone number.

Contacts Local directory assistance (☎ *114 in Chinese, 2689–0114 in English*). **International Directory Assistance** (☎ *100*). **Time** (☎ *117*). **Weather** (☎ *121*).

LOCAL DO'S AND TABOOS

GREETINGS

Chinese people aren't very touchy-feely with one another, even less so with strangers. Keep bear hugs and cheek kissing for your next European trip and stick to handshakes.

Always use a person's title and surname until they invite you to do otherwise.

RULES AND RULE BREAKING

By and large, the Chinese are a rule-abiding bunch. Follow their lead and avoid doing anything signs advise against.

Beijing is a crowded city, and pushing, nudging, and line jumping are commonplace. It may be hard to accept, but it has become the norm, so avoid reacting (even verbally) if you're accidentally shoved.

OUT ON THE TOWN

It's a great honor to be invited to someone's house, so explain at length if you can't go. Arrive punctually with a small gift for the hosts; remove your shoes outside if you see other guests doing so.

Tea, served in all Chinese restaurants, is a common drink at mealtimes, though many locals only accompany their food with soup.

Smoking is one of China's greatest vices. No-smoking sections in restaurants are becoming more prevalent, but people light up anywhere they think they can get away with it.

Holding hands in public is fine, but keep passionate embraces for the hotel room.

DOING BUSINESS

Time is of the essence when doing business in Beijing. Make appointments well in advance and be extremely punctual.

Chinese people have a keen sense of hierarchy in the office: the senior member should lead proceedings.

Suits are the norm in China, regardless of the outside temperature. Women should avoid plunging necklines, overly short skirts, or very high heels.

Respect silences in conversation and don't hurry things or interrupt.

When entertaining, local businesspeople may insist on paying: after a protest, accept.

Business cards are a big deal: not having one is a bad move. If possible, have yours printed in English on one side and Chinese on the other (your hotel can often arrange this). Proffer your card with both hands and receive the other person's in the same way.

Many gifts, including clocks and cutting implements, are considered unlucky in China. Food—especially presented in a showy basket—is always a good gift choice, as are imported spirits.

LANGUAGE

Learn a little of the local language. You need not strive for fluency; even just mastering a few basic words and terms is bound to make chatting with the locals more rewarding.

Everyone in Beijing speaks Putonghua ("the common language") as the national language of China is known. It's written using ideograms, or characters; in 1949 the government also introduced a phonetic writing system that uses the Roman alphabet. Known as pinyin, it's widely used to label public buildings and station names. Even if you don't speak or read Chinese, you can easily compare pinyin names with a map.

CALLING OUTSIDE CHINA

To make an international call from within China, dial 00 (the international access code within China) and then the country code, area code, and phone number. The country code for the United States is 1.

IDD (international direct dialing) service is available at all hotels, post offices, major shopping centers, and airports. By international standards prices aren't unreasonable, but it's vastly cheaper to use a long-distance calling card, known as an IP card (⇨ *Calling Cards, below),* whose rates also beat AT&T, MCI, and Sprint hands down.

CALLING CARDS

Calling cards are a key part of the Chinese phone system. There are two kinds: the IC card (integrated circuit; *àicei ka*), for local and domestic long-distance calls on pay phones; and the IP card (Internet protocol; *aipi ka*) for international calls from any phone. You can buy both at post offices, convenience stores, and street vendors.

IC cards come in values of Y20, Y50, and Y100 and can be used in any pay phone with a card slot—most Beijing pay phones have them. Local calls using them cost around Y0.30 a minute, and less on weekends and after 6 PM.

To use IP cards, you first dial a local access number. This is often free from hotels, however at public phones you need an IC card to dial the access number. You then enter a card number and PIN, and finally the phone number complete with international dial codes. When calling from a pay phone both cards' minutes are deducted at the same time, one for local access (IC card) and one for the long-distance call you placed (IP card). There are countless different card brands; China Unicom is one that's usually reliable. IP cards come with values of Y20, Y30, Y50, and Y100;however, the going rate for them is up to half that, so bargain vendors down.

CELL PHONES

If you have a multiband phone (some countries use different frequencies than what's used in the United States) and your service provider uses the world-standard GSM network (as do T-Mobile, AT&T, and Verizon), you can probably use your phone abroad. Roaming fees can be steep, however: 99¢ a minute is considered reasonable. And overseas you normally pay the toll charges for incoming calls. It's almost always cheaper to send a text message than to make a call, since text messages have a very low set fee (often less than 5¢).

If you just want to make local calls, consider buying a new SIM card (note that your provider may have to unlock your phone for you to use a different SIM card) and a prepaid service plan in the destination. You'll then have a local number and can make local calls at local rates. If your trip is extensive, you could also simply buy a new cell phone in your destination, as the initial cost will be offset over time.

■TIP➜ If you travel internationally frequently, save one of your old cell phones or buy a cheap one on the Internet; ask your cell-phone company to unlock it for you, and take it with you as a travel phone, buying a new SIM card with pay-as-you-go service in each destination.

If you have a GSM phone, pick up a local SIM card (*sim ka*) from any branch of China Mobile or China Unicom. You'll be presented with a list of possible phone numbers, with varying prices—an "unlucky" phone number (one with lots of 4s) could be as cheap as Y50, whereas an auspicious one (full of 8s) could fetch Y300 or more. You then buy prepaid cards to charge minutes onto your SIM—do this straightaway, as you need credit to receive calls. Local calls to landlines cost Y0.25 a minute, and to cell phones, Y0.60. International calls from cell phones are very expensive. Remember to bring an adapter for your phone charger. You can also buy cheap handsets from China Mobile. If you're planning to stay even a couple of days this is probably cheaper than renting a phone.

Beijing Limo rents cell phones, which they can deliver to your hotel or at the airport. Renting a handset starts at $5 a day, and you buy a prepaid package with a certain amount of call time; prices start at $50. Beijing Impression travel agency rents handsets at similar rates, and you buy a regular prepaid card for calls. You can also buy a cheap, pay-as-you-go cell phone once you arrive. Cell phone shops are plentiful, though you may need an interpreter to help you deal with the people behind the counter.

Contacts Beijing Impression (☎ 010/6400–0300 ⊕ www.beijingimpression.com). **Beijing Limo** (☎ 010/6546–1588 ⊕ www.beijinglimo.com/english). **Cellular Abroad** (☎ 800/287–5072 ⊕ www.cellularabroad.com) rents and sells GMS phones and sells SIM cards that work in many countries. **China Mobile** (☎ 10086 English-language assistance ⊕ www.chinamobile.com) is China's main mobile-service provider. **China Unicom** (☎ 10010 English-language assistance ⊕ www.chinaunicom.com.hk) is China's second-largest main mobile-phone company. **Mobal** (☎ 888/888–9162 ⊕ www.mobalrental.com) rents mobiles and sells GSM phones (starting at $49) that will operate in 140 countries. Per-call rates vary throughout the world. **Planet Fone** (☎ 888/988–4777 ⊕ www.planetfone.com) rents cell phones, but the per-minute rates are expensive.

▌CUSTOMS AND DUTIES

Except for the usual prohibitions against narcotics, explosives, plant and animal materials, firearms, and ammunition, you can bring anything into China that you plan to take away with you. Cameras, video recorders, GPS equipment, laptops, and the like should pose no problems. However, China is very sensitive about printed matter deemed seditious, such as religious, pornographic, and political items, especially articles, books, and pictures on Tibet. All the same, small amounts of English-language reading matter aren't generally a problem. Customs officials are for the most part easygoing, and visitors are rarely searched. It's not necessary to fill in customs declaration forms, but if you carry in a large amount of cash, say several thousand dollars, you should declare it upon arrival.

On leaving, you're not allowed to take out any antiquities dating to before 1795. Antiques from between 1795 and 1949 must have an official red seal attached.

U.S. Information U.S. Customs and Border Protection (⊕ www.cbp.gov).

▌EATING OUT

In China meals are a communal event, so food in a Chinese home or restaurant is always shared. Although cutlery is available in many restaurants, it won't hurt to brush up on your use of chopsticks, the utensil of choice. The standard eating procedure is to hold the bowl close to your mouth and eat the food. Noisily slurping up soup and noodles is also the norm. It's considered bad manners to point or play with your chopsticks, or to place them on top of your rice bowl when you're finished eating (place the chopsticks horizontally on the table or plate). Avoid, too, leaving your chopsticks standing up in a bowl of rice—they look like the two incense sticks burned at funerals.

If you're invited to a formal Chinese meal, be prepared for great ceremony, endless toasts and speeches, and a grand variety of elaborate dishes. Your host will be seated at the "head" of the round table, which is the seat that faces the door. Wait to be instructed where to sit. Don't start eating until the host takes the first bite, and then simply help yourself as the food comes around, but don't take the last piece on a platter. Always let the food touch your plate before bringing it up to your mouth; eating directly from the serving dish is bad form.

Beijing's most famous dish is Peking duck. The roast duck is served with thin pancakes, in which you wrap pieces of the meat, together with spring onions, vegetables, and plum sauce. Hotpot is another local trademark: you order different meats and vegetables, which you cook in a pot of stock boiling on a charcoal burner. *Baozi* (small steamed buns filled with meat or vegetables) are particularly good in Beijing—sold at stalls and in small restaurants everywhere, they make a great snack or breakfast food.

MEALS AND MEALTIMES

Food is a central part of Chinese culture, and so eating should be a major activity on any trip to Beijing. Breakfast is not a big deal in China—congee, or rice porridge (*zhou*), is the standard dish. Most mid- and upper-end hotels do big buffet spreads, whereas Beijing's blooming café chains provide lattes and croissants all over the east side of town.

Snacks are a food group in themselves. There's no shortage of steaming street stalls selling kebabs, grilled meat or chicken, bowls of noodle soup, and the ubiquitous *jiaozi* (stuffed dumplings). Pick a place where lots of locals are eating to be on the safe side.

The food in hotel restaurants is usually acceptable but overpriced. Restaurants frequented by locals always serve tastier fare at better prices. Don't shy from trying establishments without an English menu—a good phrase book and lots of pointing can usually get you what you want.

Lunch and dinner dishes are more or less interchangeable. Meat (especially pork) or poultry tends to form the base of most Beijing dishes, together with wheat products like buns, pancakes, and noodles. Beijing food is often quite oily, with liberal amounts of vinegar; its strong flavors come from garlic, soy sauce, and bean pastes. Food can often be extremely salty and loaded with MSG. If you can manage it, try to have the waitress tell the cooks

to cut back. Vegetables—especially winter cabbage and onions—and tofu play a big role in meals. As in all Chinese food, dairy products are scarce. Chinese meals usually involve a variety of dishes, which are always ordered communally in restaurants. Eat alone or order your own dishes and you're seriously limiting your food experience.

If you're craving Western food, rest assured that Beijing has plenty of American fast-food chains, as well as Western-style restaurants on the east side of town. Most higher-end restaurants have a Western menu, but you're usually safer sticking to the Chinese food.

Meals in China are served early: breakfast until 9 AM, lunch between 11 and 2, and dinner from 5 to 9. Unless otherwise noted, the restaurants listed in this guide are open daily for lunch and dinner. Restaurants and bars catering to foreigners may stay open longer hours.

PAYING

At most restaurants you ask for the bill at the end of the meal. At cheap noodle bars and street stands you pay up front. Only very upmarket restaurants accept payment by credit card. (⇨ *For guidelines on tipping see Tipping below. For dining and lodging price charts, see the opening pages of chapters 3 and 4.)*

RESERVATIONS AND DRESS

Regardless of where you are, it's a good idea to make a reservation if you can. In some places (Hong Kong, for example), it's expected. We only mention them specifically when reservations are essential (there's no other way you'll ever get a table) or when they are not accepted. For popular restaurants, book as far ahead as you can (often 30 days), and reconfirm as soon as you arrive. (Large parties should always call ahead to check the reservations policy.) We mention dress only when men are required to wear a jacket or a jacket and tie.

WINE, BEER, AND SPIRITS

Walk down any side street with outdoor restaurant seating and you'll find gaggles of men socializing around an armada of empty green beer bottles. Beijing is a beer-drinking town. Yanjing, Tsing Tao, and Snow are the local brands of choice. The bars around Sanlitun, Houhai, and Nanluguoxiang have a bigger selection of imported brews. If you are invited to a banquet or special dinner by Chinese friends or colleagues, you may be in for a long night of gluttonous eating and drinking. The spirit of choice for these occasions is *baijiu*, a noxious 56-proof rice wine that can sometimes taste of liquid blue cheese (better quality) or an old gasoline-soaked athletic sock (not so good quality). If your companions are a table of Chinese men, expect much machismo to accompany the festivities. When one of them yells "Ganbei!" you are expected to finish the entire shot. The best option for a nondrinker is to refuse any alcohol from the beginning and turn the shot glass upside down; or alternatively, if you drink, but don't think you can stomach the baijiu, have the waitress pour wine or beer into your shot glass. None of these actions are rude except backing down once you've started in on the baijiu shots.

■ ELECTRICITY

The electrical current in China is 220 volts, 50 cycles alternating current (AC), so most American appliances can't be used without a transformer. A universal adapter is especially useful in China, as wall outlets come in a bewildering variety of configurations: two- and three-pronged round plugs, as well as two-pronged flat sockets.

Consider making a small investment in a universal adapter, which has several types of plugs in one lightweight, compact unit. Most laptops and cell-phone chargers are dual voltage (i.e., they operate equally well on 110 and 220 volts), so require only an adapter. These days the same is true of small appliances such as hair dryers. Always check labels and manufacturer instructions to be sure. Don't use 110-volt outlets marked FOR SHAVERS ONLY for high-wattage appliances such as hair dryers.

Contacts Steve Kropla's Help for World Traveler's (⊕ www.kropla.com) has information on electrical and telephone plugs around the world. **Walkabout Travel Gear** (⊕ www.walkabouttravelgear.com) has a good coverage of electricity under "adapters."

■ EMERGENCIES

The best place to head in a medical emergency is the Beijing United Family Health Center, which has 24-hour emergency services. SOS is another international clinic with a good reputation; they also arrange Medivac.

Beijing has different numbers for each emergency service, though staff often don't speak English. If in doubt, call the U.S. embassy first: staff members are available 24 hours a day to help handle emergencies and facilitate communication with local agencies.

Doctors and Dentists Beijing United Family Health Center (✉ 2 Jiangtai Lu, near Lido Hotel, Chaoyang District ☎ 010/5927–7000, 010/5927–7120 for emergencies ⊕ www.unitedfamilyhospitals.com). **SOS International** (✉ Building C, BITIC Leasing Center, 1 North Road, Xing Fu San Cun, Chaoyang District ☎ 010/6462–9199 ⊕ www.internationalsos.com).

Contacts U.S. Embassy (✉ 55 Anjialou Lu, Chaoyang District ☎ 010/8531–4000

☏ *010/8531–3300* ⊕ *beijing.usembassy-china. org.cn).*

General Emergency Contacts Fire (☏ *119).* **Police** (☏ *110).* **Medical Emergency** (☏ *120).* **Traffic Accident** (☏ *122).*

Hospitals and Clinics Beijing United Family Health Center (*private* ✉ *2 Jiangtai Lu, near Lido Hotel, Chaoyang District* ☏ *010/5927–7000, 010/5927–7120 for emergencies* ⊕ *www.unitedfamilyhospitals. com).* **China Academy of Medical Science (Peking Union Hospital)** (*public* ✉ *1 Shui Fu Yuan, Dongcheng District* ☏ *010/6529–5284).* **Hong Kong International Medical Clinic** (*private* ✉ *Office Tower, 9th fl., Hong Kong Macau Center–Swissotel, 2 Chaoyangmen Bei Da Jie, Chaoyang District* ☏ *010/6553–2288* ⊕ *www.hkclinic.com).* **Sino-Japanese Friendship Hospital** (*public* ✉ *Ying Hua Dong Lu, Heping Li* ☏ *010/6422–2952).* **SOS International** (*private* ✉ *Building C, BITIC Leasing Center, 1 North Road, Xing Fu San Cun, Chaoyang District* ☏ *010/6462–9199* ⊕ *www. internationalsos.com).*

Pharmacies Beijing United Family Health Center (*private* ✉ *2 Jiangtai Lu, near Lido Hotel, Chaoyang District* ☏ *010/5927–7000, 010/5927–7120 for emergencies* ⊕ *www. unitedfamilyhospitals.com).* **International Medical Center (IMC)** (*private* ✉ *Beijing Lufthansa Center, Room 106, 50 Liangmaqiao Lu, Chaoyang District* ☏ *010/6465–1561* ⊕ *www. imcclinics.com).* **Watsons** (✉ *Holiday Inn Lido Hotel, Jichang Lu, Chaoyang District* ✉ *Full Link Plaza, 18 Chaoyangmenwai Dajie, Chaoyang District*) can also be found in most large shopping centers.

▌ HEALTH

The most common types of illnesses are caused by contaminated food and water. Especially in developing countries, drink only bottled, boiled, or purified water and drinks; don't drink from public fountains or use ice. Make sure food has been thoroughly cooked and is served to you fresh and hot; avoid vegetables and fruits that you haven't washed (in bottled or purified

water) or peeled yourself. If you have problems, mild cases of traveler's diarrhea may respond to Imodium (known generically as loperamide) or Pepto-Bismol. Be sure to drink plenty of fluids; if you can't keep fluids down, seek medical help immediately. Tap water in Beijing is safe for brushing teeth, but you're better off buying bottled water to drink.

Infectious diseases can be airborne or passed via mosquitoes and ticks and through direct or indirect physical contact with animals or people. Some, including Norwalk-like viruses that affect your digestive tract, can be passed along through contaminated food. Condoms can help prevent most sexually transmitted diseases, but they aren't absolutely reliable and their quality varies from country to country. China is notorious for fake condoms, so it might be best to bring your own from home or get them from a health clinic. Speak with your physician and/or check the CDC or World Health Organization Web sites for health alerts, particularly if you're pregnant, traveling with children, or have a chronic illness.

SPECIFIC ISSUES IN BEIJING
Pneumonia and influenza are common among travelers returning from China—talk to your doctor about inoculations before you leave. If you need to buy prescription drugs, try to go to the pharmacies of reputable private hospitals like the Beijing United Family Medical Center. Do *not* buy them in streetside pharmacies as the quality control is unreliable.

OVER-THE-COUNTER REMEDIES
Most pharmacies carry over-the-counter Western medicines and traditional Chinese medicines. By and large, you need to ask for the generic name of the drug you're looking for, not a brand name.

SHOTS AND MEDICATIONS
No immunizations are required for entry into China, but it's a good idea to be immunized against typhoid and Hepatitis A and B before traveling to Beijing; also a good idea is to get routine shots for

tetanus-diphtheria and measles. In winter, a flu vaccination is also smart.

Health Warnings **National Centers for Disease Control & Prevention** (*CDC* ☎ *877/394–8747 international travelers' health line* ⊕ *www.cdc.gov/travel*). **World Health Organization** (*WHO* ⊕ *www.who.int*).

▌ HOURS OF OPERATION

Most offices are open between 9 and 6 on weekdays; most museums keep roughly the same hours six or seven days a week. Everything in China grinds to a halt for the first two or three days of Chinese New Year (sometime in mid-January through February, depending on the lunar calendar), and opening hours are often reduced for the rest of that season.

Banks and government offices are open weekdays 9 to 5, although some close for lunch (sometime between noon and 2). Bank branches and CTS tour desks in hotels often keep longer hours and are usually open Saturday (and occasionally even Sunday) mornings. Many hotel currency-exchange desks stay open 24 hours.

Pharmacies are open daily from 8:30 or 9 AM to 6 or 7 PM. Some large pharmacies stay open until 9 PM or even later.

Shops and department stores are generally open daily 9 to 9; some stores stay open even later in summer, in popular tourist areas, or during peak tourist season.

HOLIDAYS
National holidays include New Year's Day (January 1); Spring Festival, aka Chinese New Year (mid-January/through February); Qingming Jie (a spring festival when families sweep ancestors' graves; April 5); International Labor Day (May 1); Dragon Boat Festival (late May/early June); anniversary of the founding of the Communist Party of China (July 1); anniversary of the founding of the Chinese People's Liberation Army (August 1); and National Day—founding of the People's Republic of China in 1949 (October 1); Chongyang Jie or Double Ninth Festival, aka

Mid-Autumn Festival (ninth day of ninth lunar month).

▌ MAIL

Sending international mail from China is reliable. Airmail letters to any place in the world should take five to 14 days. Express Mail Service (EMS) is available to many international destinations. Letters within Beijing arrive the next day, and mail to the rest of China takes a day or two longer. Domestic mail can be subject to search, so don't send sensitive materials, such as religious or political literature, as you might cause the recipient trouble.

Service is more reliable if you mail letters from post offices rather than mailboxes. Buy envelopes here, too, as there are standardized sizes in China. You need to glue stamps onto envelopes as they're not self-adhesive. Most post offices are open daily between 8 and 7. Your hotel can usually send letters for you, too.

You can use the Roman alphabet to write an address. Do not use red ink, which has a negative connotation. You must also include a six-digit zip code for mail within China. The Beijing municipality is assigned the zip code 100000, and each neighboring county starts with 10. For example, the code for Fangshan, to the immediate southwest of Beijing proper, is 102400.

Sending airmail postcards costs Y4.20 and letters Y5.40 to Y6.50.

Main Branches **International Post and Telecommunications Office** (✉ *Jianguomen Bei Dajie, Chaoyang District* ☎ *010/8478–0200*).

SHIPPING PACKAGES
It's easy to ship packages home from China. Take what you want to send *unpacked* to the post office—everything will be sewn up officially into satisfying linen-bound packages, a service that costs a few yuan. You have to fill in lengthy forms, and enclosing a photocopy of receipts for the goods inside isn't a bad idea, as they may be opened by customs

along the line. Large antiques stores often offer reliable shipping services that take care of customs in China. Large international couriers operating in Beijing include DHL, Federal Express, and UPS.

Express Services DHL (☎ 010/8458–0178 ⊕ www.cn.dhl.com). FedEx (☎ 010/6464–8855 ⊕ www.fedex.com). UPS (☎ 800/820–8388 ⊕ www.ups.com).

▮ MONEY

The best places to convert your dollars into yuan are at your hotel's front desk or a branch of a major bank, such as Bank of China, CITIC, or HSBC. All these operate with standardized government rates—anything cheaper is illegal, and thus risky. You need to present your passport to change money.

Although credit cards are gaining ground in China, for day-to-day transactions cash is definitely king. Getting change for big notes can be a problem, so try to stock up on 10s and 20s when you change money. ATMs are widespread, but not always reliable. Hunt around enough, though, and you're sure to find one that accepts your card. ▮TIP➜ Taxi drivers often become annoyed if you hand them a Y100 note for a Y10 ride.

▮TIP➜ Banks never have every foreign currency on hand, and it may take as long as a week to order. If you're planning to exchange funds before leaving home, don't wait until the last minute.

ATMS AND BANKS

Your own bank will probably charge a fee for using ATMs abroad; the foreign bank you use may also charge a fee. Nevertheless, you'll usually get a better rate of exchange at an ATM than you will at a currency-exchange office or even when changing money in a bank. And extracting funds as you need them is a safer option than carrying around a large amount of cash.

Out of the Chinese banks, your best bet for ATMs is the Bank of China, which accepts most foreign cards. That said, machines frequently refuse to give cash for mysterious reasons. Move on and try another. Citibank and HSBC have lots of branches in Beijing, and accept all major cards. On-screen instructions appear automatically in English.

CREDIT CARDS

Throughout this guide, the following abbreviations are used: **AE**, American Express; **D**, Discover; **DC**, Diners Club; **MC**, MasterCard; and **V**, Visa.

It's a good idea to inform your credit-card company before you travel, especially if you're going abroad and don't travel internationally very often. Otherwise, the credit-card company might put a hold on your card owing to unusual activity—not a good thing halfway through your trip. Record all your credit-card numbers—as well as the phone numbers to call if your cards are lost or stolen—in a safe place, so you're prepared should something go wrong. Both MasterCard and Visa have general numbers you can call (collect if you're abroad) if your card is lost, but you're better off calling the number of your issuing bank, since MasterCard and Visa usually just transfer you to your bank; your bank's number is usually printed on your card.

If you plan to use your credit card for cash advances, you'll need to apply for a PIN at least two weeks before your trip. Although it's usually cheaper (and safer) to use a credit card abroad for large purchases (so you can cancel payments or be reimbursed if there's a problem), note that some credit-card companies *and* the banks that issue them add substantial percentages to all foreign transactions, whether they're in a foreign currency or not. Check on these fees before leaving home, so there won't be any surprises when you get the bill.

▮TIP➜ Before you charge something, ask the merchant whether or not he or she plans to do a dynamic currency conversion (DCC). In such a transaction the credit-card processor (shop, restaurant, or hotel, not Visa or MasterCard) converts the currency and charges you in dollars. In most cases you'll pay the merchant a 3% fee for this service in addition to any credit-card company and issuing-bank foreign-transaction surcharges.

Dynamic currency conversion programs are becoming increasingly widespread. Merchants who participate in them are supposed to ask whether you want to be charged in dollars or the local currency, but they don't always do so. And even if they do offer you a choice, they may well avoid mentioning the additional surcharges. The good news is that you *do* have a choice. And if this practice really gets your goat, you can avoid it entirely thanks to American Express; with its cards, DCC simply isn't an option.

In Beijing, American Express, Master-Card, and Visa are accepted at most major hotels and a growing number of upmarket stores and restaurants. Diners Club is accepted at many hotels and some restaurants.

Reporting Lost Cards American Express
(✆ 800/992-3404 in the U.S., 336/393-1111 collect from abroad ⊕ www.americanexpress. com). **Diners Club** (✆ 800/234-6377 in the U.S., 303/799-1504 collect from abroad ⊕ www.dinersclub.com) **MasterCard** (✆ 800/622-7747 in the U.S., 636/722-7111 collect from abroad, 010/800-110-7309 in China ⊕ www.mastercard.com) **Visa** (✆ 800/847-2911 in the U.S., 410/581-9994 collect from abroad, 010/800-711-2911 in China ⊕ www.visa.com).

CURRENCY AND EXCHANGE

The Chinese currency is officially called the yuan (Y), and is also known as *renminbi* (RMB), or "People's Money." You may also hear it called *kuai*, an informal expression like "buck." After being pegged to the dollar at around Y8 for years, it was allowed to float within a small range starting in 2005. It appreciated quite a bit, especially between 2007 and the middle of 2008, then held firm again until mid-2010 when it was allowed to float again. As of this writing, the conversion was Y6.78 to $1.

Both old and new styles of bills circulate simultaneously in China, and many denominations have both coins and bills. The Bank of China issues bills in denominations of 1 (green), 5 (purple), 10 (turquoise), 20 (brown), 50 (blue-green), and 100 (red) yuan. There are Y1 coins, too. The yuan subdivides into 10-cent units called *jiao* or *mao*; these come in bills and coins of 1, 2, and 5. The smallest denomination is the *fen*, which comes in coins (and occasionally tiny notes) of 1, 2, and 5. Counterfeiting is rife in China, and even small stores inspect notes with ultraviolet lamps. Change can be a problem—don't expect much success paying for a Y3 purchase with a Y100 note, for example.

Exchange rates in China are fixed by the government daily, so it's equally good at branches of the Bank of China, at big department stores, or at your hotel's exchange desk, which has the added advantage of often being open 24 hours a day. Any lower rates are illegal, so you're exposing yourself to scams. A passport is required. Hold on to your exchange receipt, which you need to convert your extra yuan back into dollars.

▌ PACKING

Most Chinese people dress for comfort, and you can do the same. There's little risk of offending people with your dress; Westerners tend to attract attention regardless of attire. Although miniskirts are best left at home, pretty much anything else goes. Sturdy, comfortable, closed-toe walking shoes are a must. Summers are dusty and hot, so lightweight slacks, shorts, and short-sleeve shirts are great options. A light raincoat is useful in spring and fall. Come winter, thermal long underwear is a lifesaver. A long overcoat, scarf, hat, and gloves will help keep icy winds at bay. That said, in Beijing you can arrive unprepared: the city is a shopper's paradise. If you can't fit a bulky jacket in your suitcase, buy a cheap one upon arrival. Scarves, gloves, and hats are also cheap and easy to find.

Carry packets of tissues and antibacterial hand wipes with you—toilet paper isn't common in Chinese public restrooms. A small flashlight with extra batteries is also useful. Chinese pharmacies can be limited, so take adequate stocks if you're picky about lotions and potions. Beijing is quite dry, so moisturizer is a must. Choice is also limited for feminine-hygiene products, so bring along extra.

If you're planning a longer trip or will be using local guides, bring a few items from your home country as gifts, such as candy, T-shirts, and small cosmetic items like lipstick and nail polish. Be wary of giving American magazines and books, though, as these can be considered propaganda.

■TIP➔ If you're a U.S. citizen traveling abroad, consider registering online with the State Department (⊕ https://travelregistration.state.gov/ibrs/ui), so the government will know to look for you should a crisis occur in the country you're visiting.

PASSPORTS AND VISAS

All U.S. citizens, even infants, need a valid passport with a tourist visa stamped in it to enter China (except for Hong Kong, where you only need a valid passport). Getting a tourist visa (known as an "L" visa) in the United States is straightforward, but be sure to check the Chinese embassy Web site and call them to make sure you're bringing the correct documents. Visa regulations sometimes change on short notice. Standard visas are for single-entry stays of up to 30 days and are valid for 90 days from the day of issue (NOT the day of entry), so don't get your visa too far in advance. Costs range from $130 for a tourist visa issued within two to three working days to $160 for a same-day service.

Travel agents in Hong Kong can also issue visas to visit mainland China. ■TIP➔ The visa application will ask your occupation. The Chinese authorities don't look favorably upon those who work in publishing or the media. People in these professions routinely state "teacher" under "occupation."

Under no circumstances should you overstay your visa. To extend your visa, go to the Division of the Entry and Exit of Aliens of the Beijing Municipal Public Security Bureau a week before your visa expires. The office is also known as the Foreigner's Police; it's open weekdays 8 AM to noon and 1:30 PM to 4 PM. Under normal circumstances it's generally no problem to get a month's extension on a tourist visa. Bring your passport and a registration of temporary residency from your hotel. Keep in mind that you'll need to leave your passport there for five to seven days. If you're trying to extend a business visa, you'll need the above items as well as a letter from the business that originally invited you to China.

Info Visa to Asia (⊕ www.visatoasia.com/china.html) has up-to-date information on visa application to China.

In the U.S. Chinese Consulate, New York (☎ 212/244–9456 ⊕ www.nyconsulate.prchina.org). **Visa Office of Chinese Embassy, Washington** (☎ 202/326–2500 ⊕ www.china-embassy.org).

Visa Extensions Division of the Entry and Exit of Aliens, Beijing Municipal Public Security Bureau (✉ 2 Andingmen Dong Dajie, Beijing ☎ 010/8401–5300).

■ RESTROOMS

Public restrooms abound in Beijing—the street, parks, restaurants, department stores, and major tourist attractions are all likely locations. Most charge a small fee (usually less than Y1), and seldom provide Western-style facilities or private booths. Instead, expect squat toilets, open troughs, and rusty spigots; WC signs at intersections point the way to these facilities. Toilet paper or tissues and antibacterial hand wipes are good things to have in your day pack. The restrooms in the newest shopping plazas, fast-food outlets, and deluxe restaurants catering to foreigners are generally on a par with American restrooms.

Find a Loo The Bathroom Diaries (⊕ www. thebathroomdiaries.com) is flush with unsanitized info on restrooms the world over—each one located, reviewed, and rated.

▌ SAFETY

There is little violent crime against tourists in China, partly because the penalties are severe for those who are caught—China's yearly death-sentence tolls run into the thousands. Single women can move about Beijing without too much hassle. Handbag snatching and pickpocketing do occur in markets and on crowded buses or trains—keep an eye open and your money safe and you should have no problems. Use the lockbox in your hotel room to store any valuables. You should always carry either your passport or a photocopy of the information page and the visa page of your passport with you for identification purposes.

Beijing is full of people looking to make a quick buck. The most common scam involves people persuading you to go with them for a tea ceremony, which is often so pleasant that you don't smell a rat until several hundred dollars appear on your credit-card bill. "Art students" who pressure you into buying work is another common scam. The same rules that apply to hostess bars worldwide are also true in Beijing. Avoiding such scams is as easy as refusing *all* unsolicited services—be it from taxi or pedicab drivers, tour guides, or potential "friends."

Beijing traffic is as manic as it looks, and survival of the fittest (or the biggest) is the main rule. Crossing streets can be an extreme sport. Drivers rarely give pedestrians the right-of-way and don't even look for pedestrians when making a right turn on a red light. Cyclists have less power but are just as aggressive.

Beijing's severely polluted air can bring on, or aggravate, respiratory problems. If you're a sufferer, take the cue from locals, who wear surgical masks, or a scarf or bandana as protection.

■ **TIP**➔ Distribute your cash, credit cards, IDs, and other valuables between a deep front pocket, an inside jacket or vest pocket, and a hidden money pouch. Don't reach for the money pouch once you're in public.

Safety Transportation Security Administration (*TSA*; ⊕ www.tsa.gov).

▌ TAXES

There is no sales tax in China. Hotels charge a 5% tax; bigger, joint-venture hotels also add a 10% to 15% service fee. Some restaurants charge a 10% service fee.

▌ TIME

Beijing is 8 hours ahead of London, 13 hours ahead of New York, 14 hours ahead of Chicago, and 16 hours ahead of Los Angeles. There's no daylight saving time, so subtract an hour in summer.

Time Zones Timeanddate.com (⊕ www. timeanddate.com/worldclock) can help you figure out the correct time anywhere in the world.

▌ TIPPING

Tipping is a tricky issue in China. It's officially forbidden by the government, and locals simply don't do it. In general, follow their lead without qualms. Nevertheless, the practice is beginning to catch on, especially among tour guides, who often expect Y10 a day. You don't need to tip in restaurants or in taxis—many drivers insist on handing over your change, however small.

▍TOURS

SPECIAL-INTEREST TOURS

BIKING

The Adventure Center has two cycling packages to China, one of which follows the route of the Great Wall. You can hire bikes from them, or take your own. Bike China Adventures organizes trips of varying length and difficulty all over China.

Contacts Adventure Center (☎ 800/228-8747 ⊕ www.adventurecenter.com). **Bike China Adventures** (☎ 800/818-1778 ⊕ www.bikechina.com).

CULTURE

Local guides are often creative when it comes to showing you history and culture, so having an expert with you can make a big difference. Learning is the focus of Smithsonian Journeys' small-group tours, which are led by university professors. China experts also lead National Geographic's trips, but all that knowledge doesn't come cheap. Wild China is a local company with unusual trips: one of their cultural trips explores China's little-known Jewish history. The China Culture Center is a wonderful resource for tours, classes, lectures, and other events in Beijing.

Contacts Smithsonian Journeys (☎ 877/338-8687 ⊕ www.smithsonianjourneys.org). **National Geographic Expeditions** (☎ 888/797-4686 ⊕ www.nationalgeographicexpeditions.com). **Wild China** (☎ 010/6465-6602 ⊕ www.wildchina.com).

China Culture Center (☎ 010/6432-9341 ⊕ www.chinaculturecenter.org).

CULINARY

Intrepid Travel is an Australian company offering a China Gourmet Traveler tour with market visits, cooking demonstrations, and plenty of good eats. Imperial Tours Culinary Tour combines sightseeing with cooking lectures and demonstrations, and lots of five-star dining.

Contacts Imperial Tours (☎ 888/888-1970 ⊕ www.imperialtours.net). **Intrepid Travel** (☎ 613/9473-2673 ⊕ www.intrepidtravel.com).

HIKING

The Adventure Center's Walking the Great Wall is an eight-day hiking tour along the wall itself.

Contacts The Adventure Center (☎ 800/228-8747 ⊕ www.adventurecenter.com).

▍VISITOR INFORMATION

For general information, including advice on tours, insurance, and safety, call, or visit China National Tourist Office's Web site, as well as the Web site run by the Beijing Tourism Administration (BTA). ▍**TIP→** The BTA maintains a 24-hour hotline for tourist inquiries and complaints, with operators fluent in English. BTA also runs Beijing Tourist Information Centers, whose staff can help you with free maps and directions in Beijing.

The two best-known Chinese travel agencies are China International Travel Service (CITS) and China Travel Service (CTS), both under the same government ministry. Although they have some tourist information, they are businesses, so don't expect endless resources if you're not booking through them.

China National Tourist Offices United States (☎ 888/760-8218 New York, 800/670-2228 Los Angeles ⊕ www.cnto.org).

Beijing Tourist Information Beijing Tourism Administration (☎ 010/6513-0828 BTA ⊕ english.visitbeijing.com.cn). **China International Travel Service** (☎ 010/6522-2991 CITS in Beijing ⊕ www.cits.com.cn ☎ 626/568-8993 U.S. ⊕ www.citsusa.com). **China Travel Service** (☎ 010/6462-2288 CTS Beijing Head Office, 800/899-8618 CTS New York ⊕ www.ctsho.com).

ONLINE TRAVEL TOOLS

For a general overview of traveling in China, try the China National Tourism Office's Web site. The state-run travel agency, China Travel Services, is another helpful starting place.

All About Beijing Beijing Expat (⊕ *beijing. asiaxpat.com*) has pages and pages of advice and listings from foreigners living in Beijing.

Beijing International (⊕ *www.ebeijing.gov. cn*), if slightly dry, is the comprehensive government guide to the city.

Beijing Tourism Administration (⊕ *english. visitbeijing.com.cn*) offers well-organized information on sights and activities in Beijing, as well as hotel and restaurant information.

China Digital Times (⊕ *www.chinadigitaltimes. net*) is an excellent Berkeley-run site tracking China-related news and culture, though you won't be able to access it from inside China.

Chinese Government Portal (⊕ *english.gov.cn*).

China National Tourism Office (⊕ *www.cnto. org*).

China Travel Services (⊕ *www. chinatravelservice.com*).

Business China Business Weekly (⊕ *www. chinadaily.com.cn*) is a weekly magazine from *China Daily* newspaper. **Chinese Government Business Site** (⊕ *english.gov.cn/business. htm*) offers news, links, and information on business-related legal issues from the Chinese government.

Culture and Entertainment Beijing This Month (⊕ *www.btmbeijing.com*) is the online version of a free monthly magazine with useful information for tourists. **Beijing Weekend** (⊕ *www.chinadaily.com.cn*) is a weekly supplement from *China Daily* newspaper, with shopping, dining, and entertainment reviews. **Chinese Culture** (⊕ *www.chinaculture.org*) has a detailed, searchable database with information on Chinese art, literature, film, and history. **China Vista** (⊕ *www.chinavista. com/experience*) presents incredibly detailed information on all aspects of Chinese arts and culture. **The Beijinger** (⊕ *www.thebeijinger. com*) has a weekly e-mail newsletter about what's going on in the city. Their classifieds section is excellent, too.

INDEX

PHOTO CREDITS

1, Boaz Rottem / age fotostock. 2-3, TAO IMAGES / age fotostock. 5, lu linsheng/iStockphoto. **Chapter 1: Experience Beijing.** 8-9, SuperStock/age fotostock. 10, Brian Jeffery Beggerly/Flickr. 11 (left), Fan Ping/Shutterstock. 11 (right), Wikimedia Commons. 12 (left), Ivan Walsh/Flickr. 12 (top center), claudio zaccherini/Shutterstock. 12 (bottom right), Jonathan Larsen/Shutterstock. 12 (top right), Ivan Walsh/Flickr. 13 (top left), zhang bo/iStockphoto. 13 (bottom left), fotohunter/Shutterstock. 13 (right), claudio zaccherini/Shutterstock. 14, China National Tourist Office. 15 (left), Honza Soukup/Flickr. 15 (right), claudio zaccherini/Shutterstock. 16, Holly Peabody, Fodors.com member. 17 (left), yxm2008/Shutterstock. 17 (right), bbobo, Fodors.com member. 19 (left), Eastimages/Shutterstock. 19 (right), gary718/Shutterstock. 20, Artifan/Shutterstock. 21 (left), Hotel G Beijing. 21 (right), DK.samco/Shutterstock. 22, Johann 'Jo' Guzman, Fodors.com member. 23, Steve Slawsky. 24, Gretchen Winters, Fodors.com member. 25 (left), Frans Schalekamp, Fodors.com member. 25 (right), huang shengchun/iStockphoto. 28, Stefano Tronci/Shutterstock. 29, qingqing/Shutterstock. 30 (left), Kowloonese/Wikimedia Commons. 30 (top right), Daniel Shichman & Yael Tauger/Wikimedia Commons. 30 (bottom right), wikipedia.org. 31 (left), Hung Chung Chih/Shutterstock. 31 (right), rodho/Shutterstock. 32 (left), Chinneeb/Wikimedia Commons. 32 (top right), B_cool/Wikimedia Commons. 32 (bottom right), Imperial Painter/Wikimedia Commons. 33 (left), Wikimedia Commons. 33 (top right), Joe Brandt/iStockphoto. 33 (bottom right), 34 (all), and 35 (top left), Wikimedia Commons. 35 (bottom left), ImagineChina. 35 (right), tomislav domes/Flickr. **Chapter 2: Exploring.** 37, TAO IMAGES / age fotostock. 38, fotohunter/Shutterstock. 41, TAO IMAGES / age fotostock. 42, Luis Castañeda / age fotostock. 46, lu linsheng/iStockphoto. 47 (top), TAO IMAGES / age fotostock. 47 (bottom), Bob Balestri/iStockphoto. 48, Lance Lee | AsiaPhoto.com/iStockphoto. 49 (left), Jiping Lai/iStockphoto. 49 (top right), May Wong/Flickr. 49 (right, 2nd from top), William Perry/iStockphoto. 49 (right, 3rd from top), bing liu/iStockphoto. 49 (bottom right), William Perry/iStockphoto. 50 (top), Helena Lovincic/iStockphoto. 50 (bottom left and right), Wikipedia. 51 (top), rehoboth foto/Shutterstock. 51 (bottom left and right), Wikipedia. 52, Alexander Savin/Flickr. 53, claudio zaccherini/Shutterstock. 55, shalunishka/Shutterstock. 56, TAO IMAGES / age fotostock. 59, P. Narayan / age fotostock. 60, claudio zaccherini/Shutterstock. 61, Jose Fuste Raga / age fotostock. 63, claudio zaccherini/Shutterstock. 64, TAO IMAGES / age fotostock. 67, Ivan Walsh/Flickr. 69, claudio zaccherini/Shutterstock. 71, JTB Photo / age fotostock. 74, Lim Yong Hian/Shutterstock. 77, sanglei slei/iStockphoto. 79, William Ju/Shutterstock. 81, FRILET Patrick / age fotostock. 82, Sylvain Grandadam / age fotostock. 83 and 85, Daderot/Wikimedia Commons. 87, TAO IMAGES / age fotostock. 90, View Stock / age fotostock. **Chapter 3: Where to Eat.** 95, TAO IMAGES / age fotostock. 96, Frans Schalekamp, Fodors.com member. 105, FOTOSEARCH RM / age fotostock. 106 (bottom), FotoosVanRobin/Wikimedia Commons. 106 (top), Chubykin Arkady/Shutterstock. 107 (left), ImagineChina. 107 (top right), hywit dimyadi/iStockphoto. 107 (bottom right), Maria Ly/Flickr. 108 (bottom), Hannamariah/Shutterstock. 108 (top), zkruger/iStockphoto. 109 (top left), Ritesh Man Tamrakar/Wikimedia Commons. 109 (center left), Rjanag/Wikimedia Commons. 109 (bottom left), Craig Lovell / Eagle Visions Photography / Alamy. 109 (right), Cephas Picture Library / Alamy. 110 (top left), Eneri LLC/iStockphoto. 110 (bottom left), Man Haan Chung/iStockphoto. 110 (top right), Holger Gogolin/iStockphoto. 110 (bottom right), Eneri LLC/iStockphoto. 115, Fumio Okada / age fotostock. 118, beggs/Flickr. 123, patrick frilet / age fotostock. 126, Thomas Roetting / age fotostock. **Chapter 4: Where to Stay.** 133, The Ritz-Carlton Beijing , Financial Street. 134, Hotel G Beijing. 142 (top), Red Capital Residence. 142 (bottom left), Hotel G Beijing. 142 (bottom right), Epoque Hotels. 155 (top), Hyatt Hotels. 155 (bottom), Starwood Hotels and Resorts. **Chapter 5: Shopping.** 163, Oote Boe / age fotostock. 164, firepile/Flickr, 167, Renaud Visage / age fotostock. 173, TAO IMAGES / age fotostock. 176, Christian Kober / age fotostock. 179, TAO IMAGES / age fotostock. **Chapter 6: Arts and Nightlife.** 183, Peter Adams / age fotostock. 184, PhotoTalk/iStockphoto. 189, Werner Bachmeier / age fotostock. 194, TAO IMAGES / age fotostock. 196-97, Sylvain Grandadam / age fotostock. 199, J.D.Heaton / age fotostock. **Chapter 7: Best Side Trips.** 205, Sylvain Grandadam / age fotostock. 206, dspiel, Fodors.com member. 207 (top left), chenyingphoto/Flickr. 207 (top right), Richardelainechambers/Wikimedia Commons. 207 (bottom), Lukas Kurtz/Wikimedia Commons. 208, Hung Chung Chih/Shutterstock. 212, John W. Warden/age fotostock. 213, Wikipedia. 214-15, Liu Jianmin/age fotostock. 218, Alan Crawford/iStockphoto. 219, Eugenia Kim/iStockphoto. 220, Jarno Gonzalez/iStockphoto. 221, Chris Ronneseth/iStockphoto. 225, SuperStock/age fotostock. 226, JTB Photo / age fotostock.

NOTES

NOTES

NOTES